ALASTAIR SAWDAY'S
SPECIAL PLACES TO STAY

BRITISH
HOTELS
INNS AND
OTHER
PLACES

The unusual guide that goes for beauty,

a dash of fun, great food

— and a touch of originality.

EDITED BY STEPHEN TATE

Design: Caroline King

Maps & Mapping: Bartholomew Mapping, a division of HarperCollins,
                   Glasgow

Printing: Canale, Italy

UK Distribution: Portfolio, Greenford, Middlesex

US Distribution: The Globe Pequot Press, Guilford, Connecticut

Published in October 2002

Alastair Sawday Publishing Co. Ltd
The Home Farm Stables, Barrow Gurney, Bristol BS48 3RW
Tel: +44 (0)1275 464891 Fax: +44 (0)1275 464887
E-mail: info@specialplacestostay.com Web: www.specialplacestostay.com

The Globe Pequot Press
P. O. Box 480, Guilford, Connecticut 06437, USA
Tel: +1 203 458 4500 Fax: +1 203 458 4601
E-mail: info@globe-pequot.com Web: www.globe-pequot.com

Fourth edition

ISBN 1-901970-29-9 in the UK
ISBN 0-7627-2461-7 in the US

Printed in Italy

ALASTAIR SAWDAY'S
SPECIAL PLACES TO STAY

BRITISH
HOTELS
INNS AND
OTHER
PLACES

The
Globe
Pequot
Press

Guilford
Connecticut, USA

Alastair Sawday Publishing
Bristol, UK

CONTENTS

Acknowledgements • A word from Alastair Sawday
Introduction • General map • Maps

england

CONTENTS

channel islands

CONTENTS

wales

CONTENTS

scotland

See the back of the book for:

- Calendar of events • Meaning of place names •
- What is Alastair Sawday Publishing? •
- www.specialplacestostay.com •
- Alastair Sawday Special Places to Stay series •
- Little Earth Book • Report form • Quick reference indices •
- Index by property name • Index by place name •
- Exchange rates • Explanation of symbols •

ACKNOWLEDGEMENTS

This is a tough book to produce – though aren't they all! Whereas the owners of B&Bs tend to reply to phone calls and letters, hotel owners often don't. They are busier, perhaps, and certainly more importuned by publishers and an assorted band of sales people. However, Stephen Tate persevered and found a warm reception from those who identified with our aims. He has travelled the width and length of the UK in his search – a deeply discriminating one – for the special places that make up this selection of hotels, inns and other places. He can spot a pretender at a hundred paces; only the authentic and the genuine have been chosen. And he has a fine literary touch, benefitting an ex-journalist who reads voraciously. I give him credit for an opus that has been more magnum than expected.

Behind Stephen has been an effective support team: Sarah Bolton, Rachel Coe, Tom Dalton, Laura Kinch and Danielle Williams. Then there was Bridget Bishop in Accounts and many others who will, I hope, forgive me for the 'thank you' of being listed below.

Alastair Sawday

Series Editor:	Alastair Sawday
Editor:	Stephen Tate
Editorial Director:	Annie Shillito
Production Manager:	Julia Richardson
Web Producer:	Russell Wilkinson
Production Assistants:	Rachel Coe, Tom Dalton, Paul Groom
Editorial Assistants:	Jo Boissevain, Laura Kinch
Administration:	Sarah Bolton, Danielle Williams
Accounts:	Bridget Bishop
Photo of Alastair Sawday:	Fiona Duby
Country photos:	Michael Busselle
Inspections:	Tom Bell, Sorrel Everton, Rosie Ferguson, Sue Gray, Joanne MacInnes

A special thank you, too, to other inspectors who saw just one or two houses for us – often at short notice.

And from Stephen: "Thank you to Grace who kept me smiling."

Photo of Orchards Restaurant at Wrexon Farmhouse courtesy of Limited Edition magazine, Taunton

A WORD FROM
ALASTAIR SAWDAY

The bookshops and tourist offices are awash with books on hotels... so why this one too?

Well — where to start? Many of those books simply don't tell you what you need to know. And few, if any, of them are written and researched with the 'values' to which we are wedded. In other words, we think we are different and, beyond all things, we can be trusted. Perhaps we can be compared to your friendly local butcher whom you can trust to sell you sausages made of meat, and beef from that good and genial farmer down the road. You get superb meat at a decent price — and you know where the money is going. (There don't seem to be many of them left.)

A word about our new cover design: we hope that it is fresher and more contemporary than those lovely water-colours – which we are sad to lose. They have always set us apart but we feel that our style is now well-entrenched and respected and we are free to branch out with a new design. Fingers crossed that the change pleases many and seduces even more.

We are devoted to the search for genuine characters, authentic places, beautiful places and places doing their own, modern thing, but with flair rather than pomposity. And we tell the truth about them all. Once you have learned to rely on us, and to read between our lines, you will not be let down.

A recent article in the Sunday Times described the author's despondent early return from a "holiday from hell" and how her "salvation" was being able to use 'our' French hotels on the way back. She trusted our choices and it worked. Thus it is in Britain, too. Turn these pages and you will see a wonderfully, richly differing collection of places chosen because they are special — that's all.

Laurie Lee wrote a line about returning home to "the pale domesticated kiss of Kent". It catches that warm glow we have when returning home (rather to Kent than to Heathrow). Britain is, somehow, domesticated — and that is partly why we love her. Nearly every square inch has been explored, over and over again. We are rooted to this place and it is heart-warming to experience the individual ways in which the owners of these hotels share their sense of belonging.

If you have ever spent a night in a grim hotel it will not have been in vain if it has driven you to buy this book.

Alastair Sawday

INTRODUCTION

Here is the very best of British, inspected and selected for Sawday readers. Be it grand, groovy or gastronomic, this fabulous collection of places is testimony to a rejuvenated industry. It's not so much cheerio chintz, as hello design, and welcome to food that tastes better than it ever did.

British 'hospitality' has never been in better shape. There's been a definite sea change in the past few years; expectations have grown and people expect a warm welcome, good food and comfortable, stylish rooms – traditionally an elusive quarry here. Britain is just emerging from a long shadow cast by the aloof, the stuffy and the obsequious, partly because good people are bringing fresh ideas and experience from other walks of life.

Not that it's all been rosy. Until hospitality is recognised as a profession in Britain, as it is elsewhere, owners will struggle to find staff who take pride in their work. Several in this book have given up trying to recruit locally, and have looked abroad.

The foot and mouth crisis in 2001 proved to be a double-edged sword for us. We lost one special place, which went under when the countryside was closed. Most survive, but with a new emphasis on sourcing fresh food locally, much of it organic, which has pumped life into the rural economy. We hope you enjoy this book and the company and good cheer it will provide.

The fee We charge a fee to be included in this guide, a fee that goes towards the high inspection and production costs. No one bribes their way in. Each place is chosen because we like it and we keep editorial control over what we write.

How we choose our Special Places? We choose people who enjoy individuality, flair and good food. Good value is important too. We visit every property and evaluate each place on its merits. We are unashamedly subjective and like people who do their own thing, though idiosyncrasy is no excuse for poor standards.

What to expect Many readers tell us they've come to trust what we say, which is gratifying! We hope the book is fun to read as well. There's no brochure-speak, no tired cliché, and there are no league tables. If it's in, it's special and the write-up should tell you if it's your sort of special.

Our information is as up-to-date as possible but things can change. Check our web site at www.specialplacestostay.com for news.

INTRODUCTION

One way of deciding when and where to go is by looking at the list of annual events at the back of the book.

England

Why not try somewhere new like the Suffolk coast, or the North Yorkshire Moors – one of the loveliest parts of the country. We have new places in Manchester, Brighton, Cambridge and Exeter, too.

Channel Islands

These islands are the last remnants of the medieval Dukedom of Normandy. You still find folk who speak the old Norman-French dialect on Guernsey. Sark and Herm are tiny, and exquisite.

Wales

This book puts the whole of this rich and varied country within reach. From Snowdonia National Park and the wide beaches of Anglesey in the north, via the captivating beauty of the Brecon Beacons and the Black Mountains near the English border, to Pembrokeshire's coastline of rocky headland and sandy bay. For the first time, we have also included a place in vibrant Cardiff.

Scotland

This is Britain's last real wilderness. The Highlands' highest peaks are white-capped all year, and mirror-like lochs are fringed with fir and purple-capped silver birch. The east has long, mind-clearing sandy beaches and towering cliffs. The Outer Hebrides have a barren beauty, as does Orkney, which has even fewer trees. The Isle of Mull is one of the most magical places in the British Isles. We've also found the best place to stay in Edinburgh.

About half the places in the book are hotels, 60 are inns and 34 are restaurants with rooms. The remainder are what we refer to as 'Other Places' and defy an obvious pigeonhole. They include a castle, a lighthouse, a vineyard, and even an eco-friendly adventure centre.

Hotels, Inns and Other Places

Hotels

Hotels range from the small and intimate to the grand and gracious. Most hotels are small and owner-run so don't automatically expect room service, or porters to take your luggage to your room.

INTRODUCTION

Inns

Inns vary enormously. Some are almost hotels, others are
known as gastro pubs where food is a real focus, and there are
also the traditional ale houses that mix local brio, style and
exceptional food under the same roof.

Restaurants with rooms

These wonderful owner-run places are springing up all over the
country. Most are run by passionate foodies. It is often a way of
life and their efforts have done much to raise the standard of
restaurant food in this country.

**How to use
this book**

Map

Each property is mapped by postcode and flagged with its entry
number on maps at the front of the book. Our maps are only
rough guides. You will get lost if you try navigating with them.
We recommend the Ordnance Survey road map of Britain
which is clear and easy to use.

Bedrooms and bathrooms

Brochures often refer to many different types of rooms and
beds, from the ill-named standard, to superior, master, four-
poster, junior suite, suite, through to executive, or even
penthouse suite. In this book, to keep things simple, we use
only the following:

Double One bed big enough to be shared by two people.
Beds range in size from standard (135cm wide), through
queen/king (150cm wide) to super-king-size (180cm wide).

Single Single bed widths vary too. 90cm wide is standard.

Twins two separate single beds.

Twin/Double Also known as 'zip and link', these are
two single beds that can be joined together to make a wide
double bed.

Family/Triple These rooms may have a mixture of beds. Some
places come up with ingenious arrangements to accommodate
you. Check the possibilities.

Four-poster Usually the best room, with a four-poster bed.

Suite There are junior suites and suites proper. A junior suite is
usually a big room with a sofa or armchairs in which to relax. A
suite usually has its own sitting room. 'Suite' means big and
luxurious, generally with a price to match.

INTRODUCTION

Penthouse Big enough to be an apartment.

Miscellany Some places may have cottages, cabins or huts, which can be let by the night, or for self-catering. We alert you to the oddities; ask for more details.

Bathrooms

Assume all bedrooms are en suite, either with bath or shower. If not, we let you know if a bedroom has either a private bathroom, or a shared bathroom. For simplicity we refer to 'bath'. This doesn't necessarily mean it doesn't have a shower.

Prices

The first room price quoted on each entry is the price for two people sharing, with full breakfast included. If breakfast is not included, or there's only a continental breakfast, we say so and give the price.

If a price range is given then the lowest price is usually for the least expensive double room in low season and the highest for the most expensive room in high season.

It's worth asking, or checking websites, to see if there are any deals available. It's amazing what a little digging can unearth, especially if you're flexible about when you stay.

Singles

Prices for singles are given after the price for two people sharing. If the hotel doesn't have a single room, but quotes a single price, it refers to single use of a double or a twin room. Most owners charge extra for single occupancy because the room could earn them more and requires the same amount of work to clean. Note, however, that most of these places are far friendlier to singles then less 'special' hotels.

Half-board / Dinner, Bed & Breakfast

The price quoted is per person per night and includes a three-course meal. If the number of nights is mentioned without brackets (such as 'Half-board, 2 nights, £100 p.p.') the price quoted is for the full stay.

Meals

Most places serve breakfast from 8am to 10am. We mention in the write-up those that let you lie in longer. Breakfast in bed seems to be making something of a comeback, which we also mention where we can. Always check the night before.

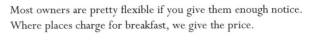

INTRODUCTION

Most owners are pretty flexible if you give them enough notice. Where places charge for breakfast, we give the price.

Breakfast is usually a feast that sets you up for the day. A continental breakfast may include fruit juices, yogurt, fruit compotes, cereals, home-made muesli, pancakes, cold meats, cheeses, toast, marmalade, jams and tea or coffee. A full breakfast is the full cholesterol-boosting Monty to which we all seem so drawn when on holiday. Ingredients are usually local, sometimes organic.

A lunch price refers to two courses, a dinner price to three, unless stated otherwise. Some places have set menus at a fixed price. Where menus are à la carte we give an average price for either two courses for lunch, or three courses for dinner. Prices do not include wine.

Closed

When given in months, this means for the whole of both months named; 'Closed: November-March' means closed from 1 November to 31 March. However, many places will consider opening for large groups. It all depends on whether they think it's worth turning the heating on or not!

Symbols ## Children

Our symbol shows you which places welcome children of all ages – although it doesn't necessarily mean there are 'facilities' for them. We mention in italics at the end of the description those that only accept children over a certain age. In many places, babysitting can be arranged with advance notice, while some may also provide children's suppers. Many hotels prefer not to allow children in the restaurant after a certain time in the evening.

Pets

Where pets are welcome, owners nevertheless expect you to control them. Please be considerate. Our symbol means that pets are allowed in some bedrooms. That does not mean they are also allowed in the sitting room, dining room or swimming pool. Always let the hotel know beforehand, or Fido may have to sleep in the car. There may be a pet supplement to pay.

Payment

MasterCard and Visa are generally welcome; American Express is sometimes accepted, Diners Club hardly ever. Debit cards, such as Switch, are widely accepted. A few places don't accept credit cards. Those entries are marked with a symbol to say they only accept cash or cheques.

Smoking

Most bedrooms and nearly all dining rooms and restaurants are non-smoking. Some places are entirely non-smoking and this is mentioned in the text. Inns are less likely to have smoking restrictions, but their restaurants usually do.

Leisure

The relevant symbol says where there is a swimming pool or tennis court. Many places have croquet lawns, many others provide free or discounted membership to local leisure centres. Sauna and massage treatment may also be available in-house. There are often lots of activities, such as fishing and horse-riding, that can be arranged for you locally.

Practical matters

Booking

Most hotels require a deposit by cheque or credit card to secure a room. You are likely to lose part, or all of it, if you cancel. Check the exact terms when you book.

Many places only accept a minimum two-night stay at weekends. A handful will insist on a three-night stay over a Bank Holiday weekend.

Arrivals and departure

Generally your bedroom should be ready by mid-afternoon and you will be expected to vacate it on the day you leave by about 11am. Many places are happy for you to linger but not in your room!

Tipping

Tipping is appreciated but not obligatory.

Hotel telephones

Ask for the price per minute before making a call as charges can be huge.

Problems, problems...

You are paying to be looked after, in different ways in different places. But if the chicken isn't chicken, you are entitled to complain. Speak to a member of staff straightaway, or ask to speak to the owner or the manager. If you get nowhere, please let us know.

INTRODUCTION

At the back of the book is a quick reference guide to help direct you to the places that suit you, be they restaurants with rooms, places that cook organic or home-grown food, or places with rooms under £40 per person per night.

Our web site www.specialplacestostay.com has online pages for all the places featured here and many from our other books. For more details see the back of the book.

We try to reduce our impact on the environment by:

* planting trees. We are officially Carbon Neutral®. The emissions directly related to paper production, printing and distribution of this book have been 'neutralised' through the planting of indigenous woodlands with Future Forests.

* re-using paper, recycling stationery, tins, bottles, etc.

* encouraging staff use of bicycles (they're loaned free) and encouraging car sharing.

* celebrating the use of organic, home-grown, and locally-produced food.

* publishing books that support, in however small a way, the rural economy and small-scale businesses.

* running an Environmental Benefit Trust to stimulate business interest in the environment.

* We publish The Little Earth Book (www.littleearth.co.uk), a collection of essays on environmental issues. We also have a new title in production called The Little Food Book, another hard-hitting analysis – this time of the food industry.

We make no claims to pure objectivity in judging our special places to stay. They are here because we like them. Our opinions and tastes are ours alone; we hope you share them.

We want to hear whether your stay was wonderful or whether there were any problems – passing on praise is as important to us as clearing up a complaint. Please fill out the report form at the back of the book, or e-mail us at the address below. We would also like to hear of any treasured find for this or any other edition in the series. We will send you a free book if your recommendation leads to its inclusion.

Chocks away!

Stephen
britishhotels@sawdays.co.uk

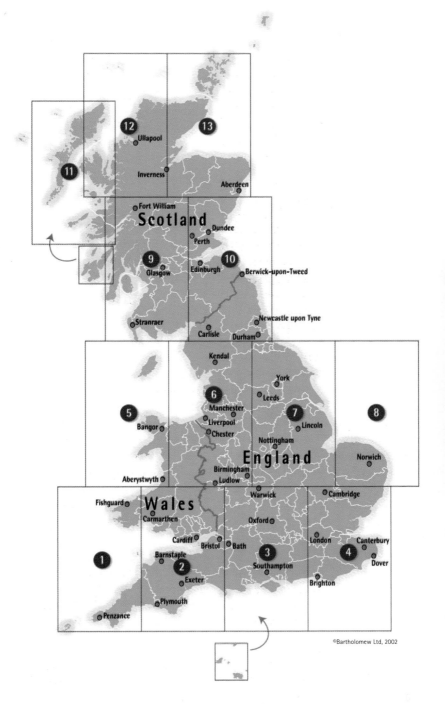

A guide to our map numbers

©Bartholomew Ltd, 2002

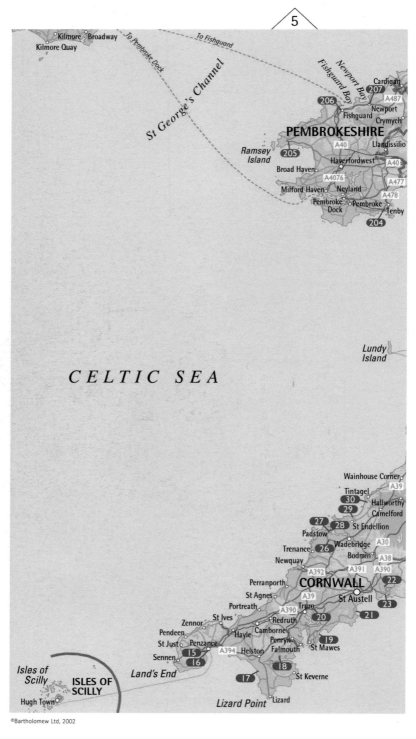

Kilmore Broadway
Kilmore Quay
To Pembroke Dock
To Fishguard
St George's Channel
Newport Bay
Fishguard Bay
Cardigan
207
A487
206
Newport
Fishguard Crymych
PEMBROKESHIRE
Llandissilio
Ramsey
Island
205
A40
Haverfordwest
A40
Broad Haven
A4076
A477
Milford Haven Neyland
A478
Pembroke Pembroke
Dock Tenby
204

Lundy
Island

CELTIC SEA

Wainhouse Corner
Tintagel
A39
30
Hallworthy
29
Camelford
27
St Endellion
28
Padstow
Trenance 26 Wadebridge A30
Newquay Bodmin A38
A392 A391 A390
Perranporth CORNWALL 22
St Agnes St Austell
Portreath A39 Truro 23
St Ives A390 20
Zennor Redruth
Pendeen Camborne 21
St Just Penzance Hayle Penryn 19
Sennen Helston Falmouth St Mawes
15 A394
16 18
Isles of 17 St Keverne
Scilly **ISLES OF**
SCILLY Land's End
Hugh Town Lizard Point Lizard

©Bartholomew Ltd, 2002

Map 1

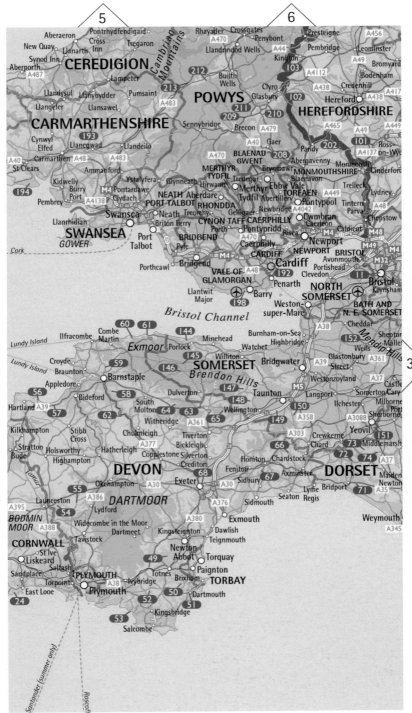

Map 2

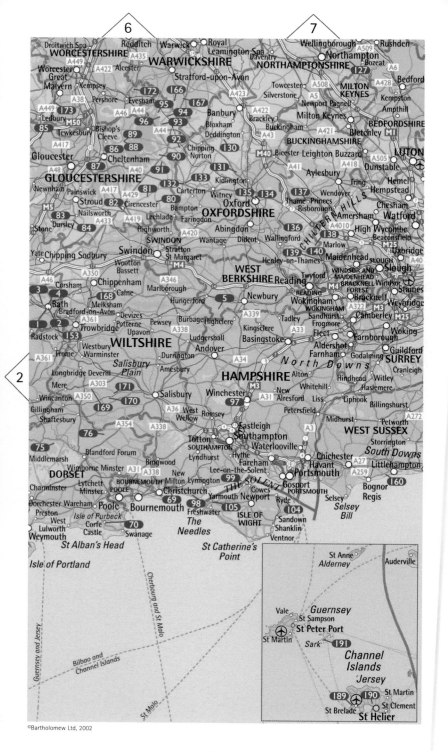

Map 3

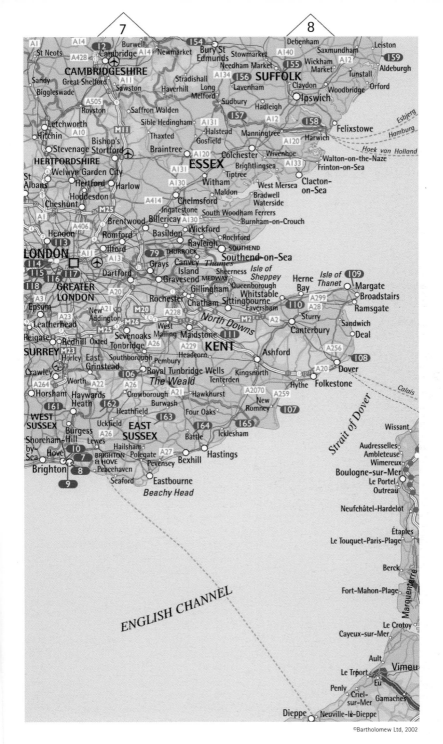

Map 4

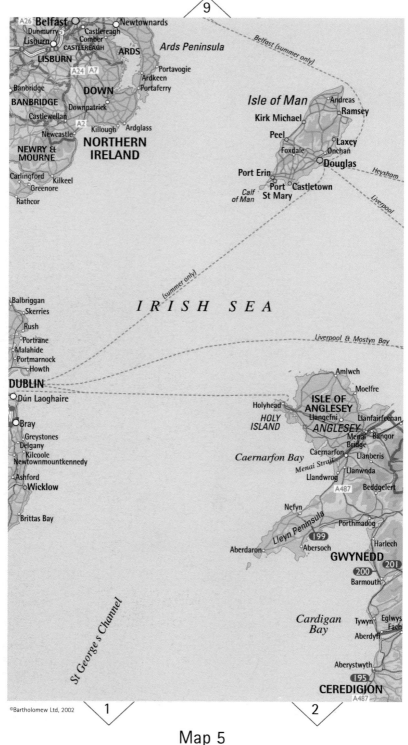

Belfast
A26
Dunmurry · Castlereagh · Newtownards
Lisburn · Comber
CASTLEREAGH · ARDS
LISBURN
A24 A7
Portavogie
Banbridge · Ardkeen
DOWN · Portaferry
BANBRIDGE
Castlewellan · Downpatrick
A2 · Killough · Ardglass
Newcastle
NEWRY &
MOURNE · NORTHERN
IRELAND
Carlingford · Kilkeel
Greenore
Rathcor

Ards Peninsula

Belfast (summer only)

Isle of Man
Andreas
Kirk Michael · Ramsey
Peel · Laxey
Foxdale · Onchan
Douglas
Port Erin · *Heysham*
Calf · Port · Castletown
of Man · St Mary
Liverpool

I R I S H   S E A

(summer only)

Liverpool & Mostyn Bay

Balbriggan
Skerries
Rush
Portrane
Malahide
Portmarnock
Howth
DUBLIN
Dún Laoghaire

Bray
Greystones
Delgany
Kilcoole
Newtownmountkennedy
Ashford
Wicklow

Brittas Bay

Amlwch
Moelfre
ISLE OF
ANGLESEY
Holyhead · Llangefni · Llanfairfechan
HOLY · *ANGLESEY*
ISLAND · Menai · Bangor
Bridge
Caernarfon Bay · Caernarfon · Llanberis
Menai Strait · Llanwnda
Llandwrog
A487 · Beddgelert

Nefyn
Lleyn Peninsula · Porthmadog
199
Aberdaron · Abersoch · Harlech
GWYNEDD
201
200
Barmouth

St George's Channel

Cardigan · Tywyn · Eglwys
Bay · Fach
Aberdyfi

Aberystwyth
195
CEREDIGION
A487

©Bartholomew Ltd, 2002

1

2

Map 5

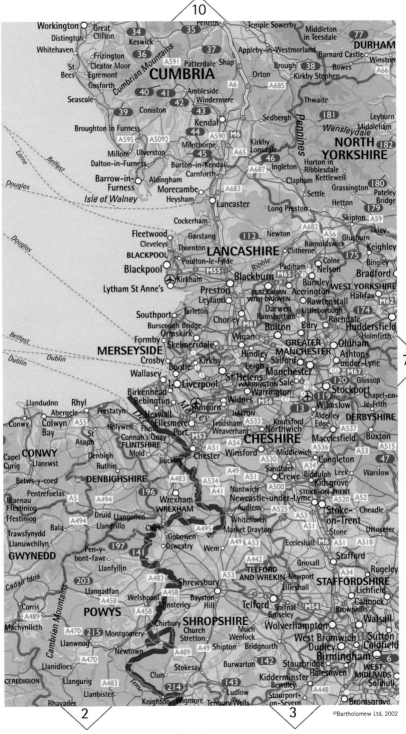

Map 6

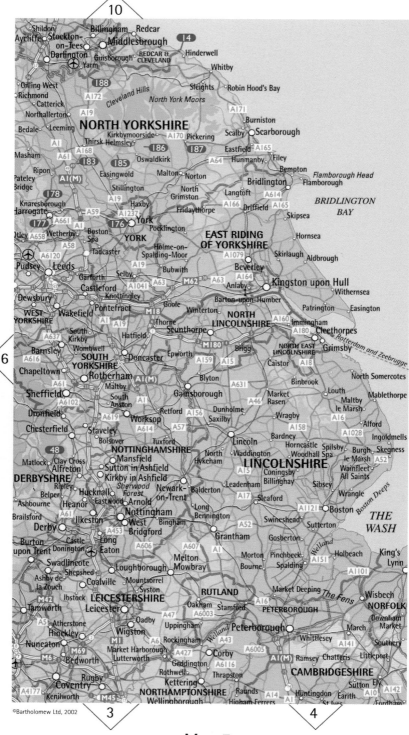

©Bartholomew Ltd, 2002

Map 7

4

Map 8

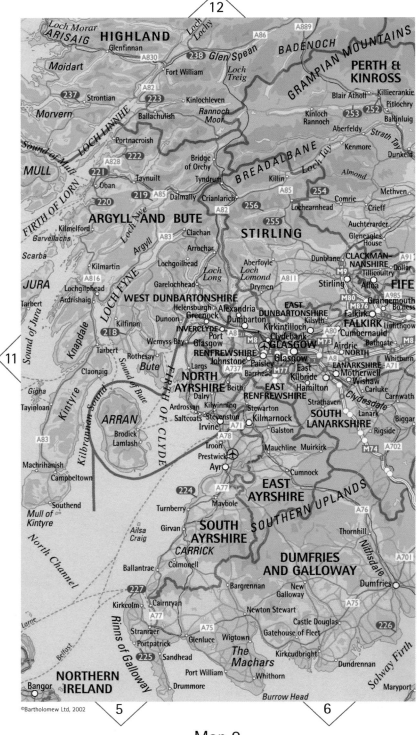

©Bartholomew Ltd, 2002

Map 9

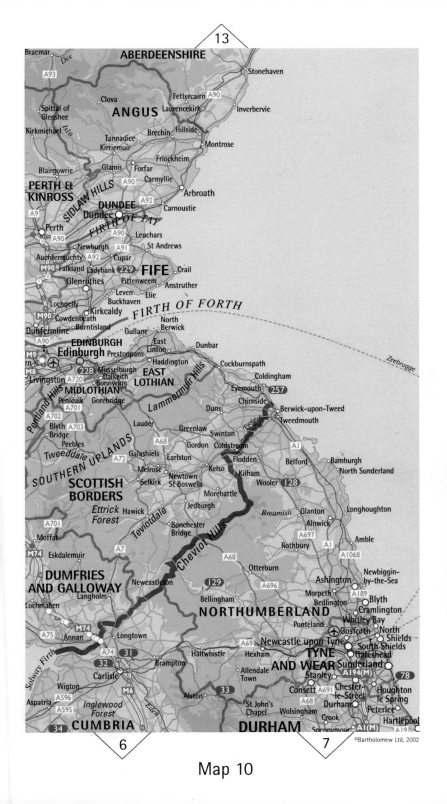

Map 10

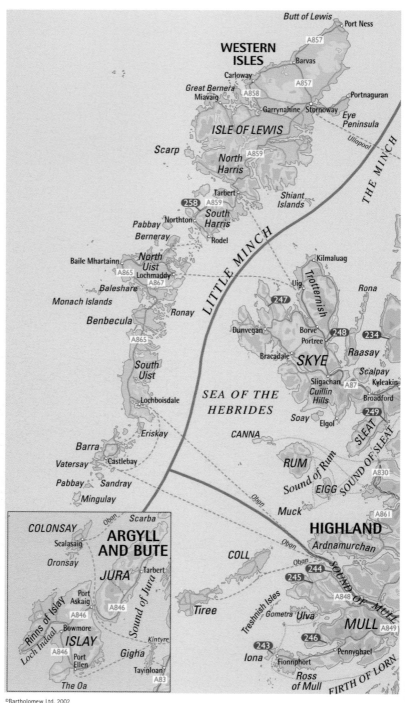

WESTERN ISLES

Butt of Lewis
Port Ness
A857
Barvas
Carloway
A857
Great Bernera
Miavaig
A858
Portnaguran
Garrynahine Stornoway
ISLE OF LEWIS
Eye Peninsula
Scarp
Ullapool
North Harris
A859
THE MINCH
Tarbert
Shiant Islands
258 A859
South Harris
Pabbay Northton
Bernera
Rodel
Baile Mhartainn
North Uist
Kilmaluag
A865 Lochmaddy
Uig
Trotternish
Rona
A867
Baleshare
247
Monach Islands
Benbecula
Ronay
Dunvegan
Borve
Portree
248
234
A865
Bracadale
SKYE
Raasay
South Uist
Scalpay
Sligachan
A87
Kyleakin
Lochboisdale
Cuillin Hills
Broadford
SEA OF THE HEBRIDES
Soay Elgol
249
Eriskay
CANNA
SLEAT
Barra
RUM
Vatersay Castlebay
SOUND OF SLEAT
Pabbay Sandray
Sound of Rum
A830
Mingulay
EIGG
Oban
Muck
A861

LITTLE MINCH

HIGHLAND
Ardnamurchan
Oban
Scarba
COLONSAY
ARGYLL AND BUTE
Scalasaig
COLL
Oban
Oronsay
JURA
Tarbert
244
Treshnish Isles
245
Port Askaig
Sound of Jura
A848
SOUND OF MULL
Rinns of Islay
A846
Tiree
Gometra Ulva
MULL
A849
Bowmore
ISLAY
Kintyre
243
246
Pennyghael
Loch Indaal
A846 Port Ellen
Gigha
Iona Fionnphort
Tayinloan
Ross of Mull
FIRTH OF LORN
The Oa
A83

Map 11

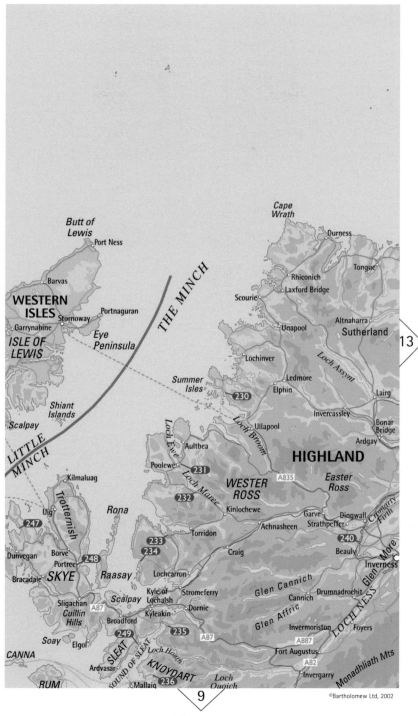

13 >

< 9

Map 12

©Bartholomew Ltd, 2002

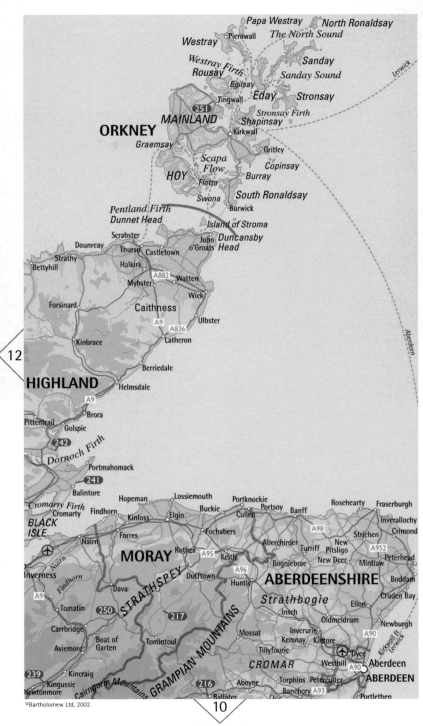

Papa Westray
North Ronaldsay
The North Sound
Westray
Pierowall
Westray Firth
Rousay
Sanday
Sanday Sound
Egilsay
Tingwall
Eday
Stronsay
Stronsay Firth
MAINLAND
Shapinsay
ORKNEY
Kirkwall
Graemsay
Gritley
Scapa
Copinsay
Flow
Burray
HOY
Flotta
Swona
South Ronaldsay
Burwick
Pentland Firth
Dunnet Head
Island of Stroma
Scrabster
John Duncansby
Dounreay
Thurso Castletown
o'Groats Head
Strathy
Halkirk
Bettyhill
Mybster
Watten
Forsinard
Wick
Caithness
A9
Ulbster
A836
Kinbrace
Latheron
HIGHLAND
Berriedale
Helmsdale
A9
Brora
Pittentrail
Golspie
Dornoch Firth
Portmahomack
Balintore
Hopeman Lossiemouth Portknockie Rosehearty Fraserburgh
Cromarty Firth Findhorn Buckie Portsoy Banff
Cromarty Kinloss Elgin Cullen Inverallochy
BLACK Nairn Forres Fochabers A98 Strichen Crimond
ISLE Aberchirder Turriff New Pitsligo A952
MORAY Rothes A95 Keith New Deer Mintlaw Peterhead
Inverness Dufftown Bogniebrae Boddam
A9 Dava Huntly ABERDEENSHIRE
Tomatin STRATHSPEY Strathbogie Cruden Bay
Carrbridge 250 Insch Oldmeldrum Ellon Newburgh
Boat of 217 Mossat Inverurie A90
Aviemore Garten Tomintoul Kemnay Kintore
239 Kincraig Tillyfourie Westhill Dyce
Newtonmore Kingussie CROMAR Peterculter Aberdeen
Cairngorm Mountains GRAMPIAN MOUNTAINS 216 Torphins ABERDEEN
Aboyne Banchory A93
Ballater Dee Portlethen

©Bartholomew Ltd, 2002

12

10

Map 13

Photography by Michael Busselle

ENGLAND

"I don't even butter my bread;
I consider that cooking."
KATHERINE CEBRIAN

Dorian House

One Upper Oldfield Park, Bath, Bath & N. E. Somerset BA2 3JX

A cellist with a love of interior design is rare enough, but to find one running a hotel amid the beautiful surroundings of Bath is exceptional. Tim is the London Symphony Orchestra's principal cellist and was once taught by the late and great Jacqueline du Pré: "She played with abandon – she was herself," he says of his tutor. Be yourself in the cosy, spoiling luxury of this converted Victorian house; it feels more home than hotel. Tim and Kathryn have restored everything inside – the original tiled hallway is lovely. Sit with afternoon tea in deep sofas in the lounge, or enjoy one of six types of champagne in comfortable bedrooms all named after cellists; no surprise that the most exquisite – and the most secluded – is du Pré; a huge four-poster bed is reached up a flight of stairs. Every room is decorated with beautiful fabrics and Egyptian linen; those on the first floor are more traditional, those on the second more contemporary, with Scandinavian pine and sloping ceilings. Tim's art collection is everywhere; one gallery in Portugal pays him to perform in paintings. Relaxation assured, maybe some music, too.

rooms	11: 3 doubles, 2 twin/doubles, 1 single, 2 family, 3 four-posters.
price	£65-£140; singles £47-£59.
meals	Restaurants in Bath.
closed	Christmas.
directions	From Bath centre, follow signs to Shepton Mallet to sausage-shaped r'bout, then A37 up hill, 1st right. House 3rd on left, signed.

Kathryn & Tim Hugh

tel	01225 426336
fax	01225 444699
e-mail	info@dorianhouse.co.uk
web	www.dorianhouse.co.uk

Paradise House

Holloway, Bath, Bath & N. E. Somerset BA2 4PX

The magical 180-degree panorama from the garden of Paradise is a dazzling advertisement for Bath. The view draws you out as soon as you enter the house – the Royal Crescent and the Abbey are floodlit at night and in summer, hot air balloons float by low enough for you to hear the roar of the burners. Wonderful. Most of the rooms make full use of the view; the best have bay windows. All have a soft, luxurious country feel, with drapes, wicker chairs and good bathrooms. There are also two garden rooms in an extension that planners took six years to approve – it's a remarkable achievement in keeping with the original Bath stone house and David is justly proud. The whole place seems to use glass in all the right places; the sitting room has lovely stone-arched French windows that draw in the light. Two doors up on Holloway – the old Roman road into this ancient city – is the old Monastery owned by a music teacher; sit outside with afternoon tea and hear the sound of piano music drift gently across the garden. Further away, the occasional peal of bells. *Seven minutes' walk from the centre.*

rooms	11: 4 doubles, 4 twins, 1 family, 2 four-poster.
price	£75–£155; singles £55–£95.
meals	Restaurants in Bath.
closed	Christmas.
directions	From train station take one-way system to Churchill Bridge. Take A367 exit from r'bout up hill. After 0.75 miles left at Andrews estate agents. Left down hill into cul-de-sac. On left.

David & Annie Lanz

tel	01225 317723
fax	01225 482005
e-mail	info@paradise-house.co.uk
web	www.paradise-house.co.uk

map 3   entry 2

Apsley House

141 Newbridge Hill, Bath, Bath & N. E. Somerset BA1 3PT

Apsley House takes its name from the Duke of Wellington's main London residence which had the mighty address 'No. 1, London'. The Iron Duke is thought to have lived here, though if he did, the tempo was probably a little stiffer than it is now. Claire and Nicholas are relatively new to the hotel industry but are industrious by nature – desert exploration became a fond past-time during a long stint in the Middle East. It took them two years to find Apsley but they instantly knew this was the place. They've sensibly left things much as they were. The house is full of great furniture, tallboy porter chairs, gilt mirrors and rich Colefax & Fowler fabrics. Take a drink from the bar, then collapse into one of the sofas in the drawing room and look out through a huge, arched window to the garden. The dining room shares the same, warm elegance, separated by antique screens, with fresh flowers on all the tables and nice touches like jugs of iced water at breakfast. Most of the pretty bedrooms are huge and have good bathrooms. Morning papers are dropped off at your door, your clothes can be laundered, and there's a car park – precious indeed in this city. *Children over five welcome.*

rooms	9: 3 doubles, 5 twin/doubles, 1 four-poster.
price	£75–£140; singles £60–£85.
meals	Restaurants in Bath.
closed	Christmas.
directions	A4 west into Bath. Keep right at 1st mini-r'bout. On for about 2 miles, then follow 'Bristol A4' signs. Pass Total garage on right. At next lights, branch right. On left after 1 mile.

Claire & Nicholas Potts

tel	01225 336966
fax	01225 425462
e-mail	info@apsley-house.co.uk
web	www.apsley-house.co.uk

The Queensberry Hotel & Olive Tree Restaurant

Russel Street, Bath, Bath & N. E. Somerset BA1 2QF

The Queensberry is an old favourite, grand but totally unpretentious and immensely enjoyable. It is rare to find a hotel of this size and elegance still in private hands, rarer still to find the owners so actively deployed. Stephen is 'everywhere' and even though he no longer cooks in the famous basement restaurant, his Dauphinoise potatoes remain, rightly, legendary. The bedrooms are magnificent – contemporary and dramatic, with bold, inspirational colours and fabrics. If you feel like spoiling yourself, have breakfast brought up to you – croissants, orange juice, fresh coffee, warm milk and a newspaper. Then pad around in wonderful white bathrobes feeling a million dollars. The bath runs in seconds, the shower imitates a monsoon. At night, pop down to supper and when you get back, your bed will have been turned

down, your towels refreshed. As for the home-made fudge after supper... just wonderful. All this in a John Wood house in the centre of Bath, a minute's walk from the Assembly Rooms.

rooms	29: 28 twin/doubles, 1 four-poster.
price	£120-£225; singles from £90.
meals	Continental breakfast included; full English £9.50. Lunch £13.50. Dinner £26.
closed	Christmas.
directions	Into Bath on A4 London Rd to Paragon, then 1st right into Lansdown, 2nd left into Bennett St and 1st right into Russel St.

Stephen & Penny Ross

tel	01225 447928
fax	01225 446065
e-mail	enquiries@bathqueensberry.com
web	www.bathqueensberry.com

map 3   entry 4

Crown & Garter

Great Common, Inkpen, Hungerford, Berkshire RG17 9QR

The Crown & Garter lies in a lush paradise just south of the M4 motorway. Quiet lanes dip through fields and woodland, past cottages draped in honeysuckle – England rarely feels this dreamy. Candida and Peter left catering careers in London to resuscitate this 16th-century inn. The charming bedrooms in a new build around a pretty garden are the best surprise of all. Candida has resourcefully blended voile and Bennison fabrics with painted floorboards, recycled furniture and handmade cushions to create colourful, eclectic rooms – none are the same. The bar is full of odd curios, testament to Candida's maxim that "if your partner's short on chat, there should be lots to look at"; the wonderful throne-like chair by the front door is actually part wine box, part trapdoor but is often mistaken for an antique. Bistro-style food includes home-made pasta and paté, and the ales are all local. Peter loves cycling and will suggest routes. There are also plenty of super walks across Inkpen Common and a pretty beer garden under an old oak tree. Hard to imagine London's so close.

rooms	10: 7 doubles, 3 twins.
price	£65; singles £45.
meals	Bar lunch from £6. Dinner from £10.
closed	Inn closed for food & drink Monday & Tuesday lunchtime.
directions	From M4, junc. 13, A34 Basingstoke; left on A4 for Hungerford. After 2 miles, left for Kintbury & Inkpen. In Kintbury, left opp. corner shop, marked Inkpen Rd. Inn on left after 2 miles.

Candida Leaver & Peter Starling

tel	01488 668325
fax	01488 669072
e-mail	peter@crowngarter.freeserve.co.uk
web	www.crownandgarter.com

Hotel du Vin & Bistro

Church Road, Birmingham B3 2NR

Hotel du Vin micro-chain's fourth venture has converted the disused Birmingham & West Midlands' eye hospital into a palace of art, style and fun on five floors. They've kept the original double staircase, the granite pillars and an oddly-shaped Victorian lift designed to take stretchers but the rest bears the new residents' unmistakable signature: the Parisian-style courtyard, full of bronze statues and palm trees, the cosy cellar bar, with squidgy sofas and funky lobster art, and the Bubble Lounge, done in the style of Venice's Café Florin – it stocks 60 kinds of champagne. As you'd expect, the restaurant is emphatically French: the waiters' uniforms, the Lautrec posters and small tables set comfortably apart transport you to Paris. Minimalist bedrooms please the eye, with Henderson & Redfearn furniture, natural fabrics, huge beds – the biggest measures eight feet square – and bathrooms with roll-top Edwardian baths and "monsoon-like" showers. Pamper yourself silly in the health and fitness suite, then relax with a long cocktail. Birmingham is a city on the up and worth re-discovering.

rooms	66: 55 twin/doubles, 11 suites.
price	From £110; suites from £185.
meals	Breakfast £9.50-£13.50. Lunch & dinner £16-£30.
closed	Never.
directions	M6, junc. 6, A38(M) Aston Expressway into city centre. Over flyover, left up slip road, signed Snowhill Station, 2nd exit at r'bout, then 1st left, 3rd right and 1st right into Church Rd.

Michael Warren

tel	0121 236 0559
fax	0121 236 0889
e-mail	info@birmingham.hotelduvin.com
web	www.hotelduvin.com

map 6   entry 6

Paskins Town House

18/19 Charlotte Street, Brighton BN2 1AG

Others will soon follow in the steps of Paskins – it has resolutely cast aside ordinariness in favour of its own values. It is neither grand nor chic, fancy nor smart, just easy-going and genuinely 'green' in outlook. Spread across two handsome townhouses, the hotel is just yards from the beach. Inside, paint is used to mask some dilapidation and the colour schemes can be a little overwhelming. Some of the rooms are lovely, with the odd four-poster; all are colourful, with old prints, cabaret posters and modern art on the walls, and all are impeccably clean and snug. It is fun, too. The Art Deco breakfast room is a joy to behold, as is breakfast – some say it's worth travelling to Brighton for: organic tomatoes sprinkled with basil, oak-smoked bacon and many varieties of sausage. Vegetarians are treated royally, too – they claim to serve the best veggie food on the south coast. All the food is organic where available, from local farms if possible. On top of all that, the coffee is Fair Trade, the smellies are free of the taint of animal testing and you're so close to the centre of things – let your excellent room guide point the way. Terrific value.

rooms	19: 6 doubles, 2 twin/doubles, 7 singles, 1 triple, 3 four-posters.
price	£60–£105; singles £30–£40.
meals	Sandwiches £3.60. Restaurants in Brighton.
closed	Never.
directions	M23/A23 to Brighton. Left at seafront r'bout opp. pier. Hotel 13th street on left.

Roger Marlow

tel	01273 601203
fax	01273 621973
e-mail	welcome@paskins.co.uk
web	www.paskins.co.uk

Blanch House
17 Atlingworth Street, Brighton BN2 1PL

Dr Who used a phone box and Mr Benn a shop; Chris and Amanda do the same in a Georgian townhouse, transporting your imagination into the realms of luxurious fantasy. Travel back to the days of 70s glam rock chic and the decadent Edwardian house party, or go back even further to the Renaissance. Exotic countries lie behind other doors: stay in an Indian palace, or a Moroccan kasbah. Another two are devoted to roses and champagne. All are lavishly decorated with authentic detail, and no expense has been spared; all come with handmade chocs, CD player, TV and video. The restaurant looks like something out of a 70s sci-fi film, with white moulded chairs, lots of white décor and light flooding through big windows. The menu is ambitious: try salmon cured with jasmine tea, black-leg crab cake, baked fig with a balsamic

strawberry turnover. The house may once have been a church, judging by the two-storey arched window. Owners and staff alike are approachable and friendly, and more than happy to point you in the direction of Brighton's groovier side. Be manicured, pedicured, styled or massaged – all can be done in-house. Cheeky chic and great fun.

rooms	12: 9 doubles, 3 suites.
price	From £110; singles from £80; suites from £220.
meals	Dinner, à la carte, from £17.
closed	Christmas.
directions	M23/A23 to Brighton. Left at seafront r'bout opp. pier along Marine Parade to traffic lights, then left, 1st right and 1st right again. Hotel on left.

Chris & Amanda Blanch

tel	01273 603504
e-mail	info@blanchhouse.co.uk
web	www.blanchhouse.co.uk

map 4   entry 8

Hotel du Vin & Bistro

Ship Street, Brighton BN1 1AD

Those clever folk at Hotel du Vin have done it again — this time with a seaside twist yards from Brighton promenade. Their fifth hotel venture sees more of what we've come to expect from these stylish innovators: funky, ever so luxurious and oozing with class. It's not without a sense of humour either — they've kept a plaque on the front of the building that says 1695, placed there by the Victorian builder responsible for its mock-Tudor façade. Beyond is a vibrant 21st-century hotel, tailored to the original building and its location in the city's Old Lanes. A whacky wrought iron gate leads to a Mediterranean-style courtyard with a vine-covered pergola, a bar with a vaulted ceiling, carved staircases, big, squashy sofas to kick back in. Large Cape Cod style bedrooms will leave you lost for words; some have balconies, others look onto Ship Street through big, arched, stained-glass windows; all are adoringly done with handmade beds, leather armchairs, woollen carpets, Egyptian linen, embracing towels, and the best bubble-baths known to man! Walk to galleries, cafés and the new Dome Theatre. A snooze in a deckchair is compulsory.

rooms	37: 31 doubles, 3 twins, 3 suites.
price	From £115; suites from £185.
meals	Continental breakfast £9.50, full English £13.50. Lunch & dinner £22–£30.
closed	Never.
directions	M23/A23 to Brighton. Right at seafront r'bout opp. pier, 4th right into Middle St then bear right into Ship St. Hotel on right.

Nigel Buchanan

tel	01273 718588
fax	01273 718599
e-mail	info@brighton.hotelduvin.com
web	www.hotelduvin.com

Claremont House Hotel

13 Second Avenue, Hove BN3 2LL

A prep school during the early part of the last century, this handsome Victorian villa is being gently renovated by its new owners. They're not aiming for opulence, although original 19th-century chandeliers, fireplaces and cornices survive in many rooms and the jazzy black and white entrance steps are worthy of a film set. What Russell and Michael are passionate about is making guests feel genuinely welcome and cared for in their home. They're also seriously keen on food – no special diet is too much trouble. Fresh, local and seasonal food is cooked here daily and that includes the puddings. You can eat out on the back lawn shaded by mature trees and if you need to get an early start, a breakfast tray is no problem. Flowers – outside and in – smell gorgeous. The whole place feels hugely cared for. High-ceilinged bedrooms have good beds and linen, pristine bathrooms, good showers and little extras. Hove is a classically good spot for all sorts at any time of year with nearby castles, seaside, South Downs and, of course, there's opera at Glyndebourne and the Brighton Festival.

rooms	12: 6 doubles, 5 singles, 1 four-poster.
price	£75–£120; singles £45–£65.
meals	Dinner £16.50; book in advance.
closed	Never.
directions	M23/A23 to Brighton. At seafront r'bout opp. pier, right on A259 Kings Rd/Kingsway for 1.5 miles, then right into Second Ave. Hotel near top of road on right.

Russell Brewerton & Michael Reed

tel	01273 735161
fax	01273 735161
e-mail	claremonthove@aol.com
web	www.claremonthousehotel.co.uk

map 4   entry 10

Hotel du Vin & Bistro

The Sugar House, Narrow Lewins Mead, Bristol BS1 2NU

Robin Hutson and his team get better and better as they cover the country with their reinvention of the grand townhouse hotel, turning 'grand' to 'casual' in the process, to the joy of all. This, their third venture and first in a big city, will win awards, as have the previous two, but it's the inherent good value that's most notable – if they can do such luxury for these prices, then others must look to their laurels. There's lots of space, stone walls, floorboards, rugs, squishy sofas and sandblasted beams. A sprinkling of tables and chairs around a fountain in the courtyard adds further style, as does the fire that shoots up a 100-foot chimney in the glass-fronted lobby, a remnant of the building's warehouse past. Up the steel staircase, spectacular bedrooms have a minimalist Manhattan-loft feel – low-slung furniture, handmade beds, off-white walls, hessian and big bathrooms, with walk-through showers, and baths. But always at the heart of a Hotel du Vin beats the bistro, French to the core, full of life and a great place to be. You can also play billiards or walk into the *humidor* and buy a Havana.

rooms	40: 25 doubles, 5 twins, 10 suites.
price	From £120; suites from £175.
meals	Breakfast £9.50-£13.50. Lunch & dinner £25-35.
closed	Never.
directions	M32 into Bristol, right at lights, follow city centre. Left at big r'bout onto inner ring road. 500 yards on, double back at traffic lights. Hotel on left down small side road after 100 yds.

Lesley Skelt

tel	0117 925 5577
fax	0117 925 1199
e-mail	info@bristol.hotelduvin.com
web	www.hotelduvin.com

Hotel Felix

Whitehouse Lane, Huntingdon Road, Cambridge, Cambridgeshire CB3 0LX

It's been a long time coming but Cambridge has finally got the hotel it deserves. Hotel Felix is funky and up to date, a sophisticated country house with a modern twist and just a mile from the charming parts of this historic city. Finding the right site was always going to be difficult as the university colleges own most of the old buildings, but owners Vivien and Jeremy Cassel knew what they were up against having successfully opened The Grange in York. They've centred the hotel around a Victorian villa in several acres of parkland; home, it's said, to the black squirrel! Two new bedroom wings have been added at right angles to the original building to create a courtyard with statue and plants – that leads to a grand entrance hall. Vivien's bedrooms are luxurious: huge beds, plump cushions, silk fabrics, stone floors in bathrooms with gleaming chrome, and hi-tech TVs that supply films on demand. Food in the Graffiti restaurant draws on the simple, flavoursome approach of Mediterranean and Italian cooking, and there is lots of light, airy space in which to sit and relax. Contemporary style without the attitude. *Opens November 2002.*

rooms	52 twin/doubles.
price	£155-£210; singles £125.
meals	Continental breakfast included; full English £8. Bar meals from £4.95. Lunch about £16. Dinner about £28.
closed	Never.
directions	A1 north, then A1307/A14 turn-off onto Huntingdon Rd into Cambridge. Hotel on left.

Shara Ross

tel	01223 277977
fax	01223 277973
e-mail	info@grangehotel.co.uk
web	www.hotelfelix.co.uk

map 4   entry 12

Belle Epoque Brasserie

60 King Street, Knutsford, Cheshire WA16 6DT

Walking round this extravagant 1901 building gives you the sense that it was destined to become something far more indulgent than a temperance hall. The audacity of architect Richard Harding Watt's untethered imagination is a delight: the beamed Arts and Crafts style of a function room upstairs, the wooden-floored private dining room where Georgie Fame and Stephane Grappelli played in the Seventies, and the two massive stone columns in the courtyard hauled by horse and cart from Manchester infirmary; two of the original cartwheels are still propped against the wall. The Mooneys arrived 25 years ago, injecting lots of pazazz and lavish Art Nouveau style. What you see is original: the alabaster clocks, the two blackamoors and the statue of a goddess, arms held skywards. Today, David and Matthew run it with just the same energy as did their parents, Keith and Nerys, who still pop in. They've added a stylish bar and gorgeous, contemporary bedrooms, but pride of place is still the restaurant – an alcove guarded by two Doric columns is special, as is the food.

rooms	6 doubles.
price	£80-£85; singles £50.
meals	Continental breakfast included; full English £4.95. Bar lunches £4-£7. Dinner, à la carte, £25-£30.
closed	Christmas & Bank Holidays. Restaurant closed Monday, Saturday lunch & Sunday evening.
directions	M6, junc. 19, Knutsford. Enter town, right at r'bout; left at 2nd lights, for Macclesfield. Down hill, 1st left into King St. Halfway up on left.

David & Matthew Mooney

tel	01565 633060
fax	01565 634150
e-mail	info@thebelleepoque.com
web	www.thebelleepoque.com

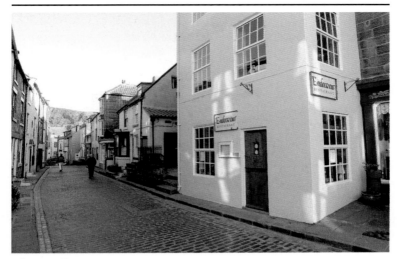

The Endeavour

1 High Street, Staithes, Cleveland TS13 5BH

Like Captain James Cook before them, Charlotte and Brian have embarked on their own big adventure in this forgotten gem on the north-east coast. Themselves explorers of psychology and film-making, they've squeezed a super little fish restaurant with rooms into four storeys of an old terraced house. Elegantly-laid tables occupy two floors, and look onto a narrow street of pretty Victorian shop fronts. Bedrooms above are equally comfortable, simply done and great value; from the top floor, look over rooftops to a huge slab of terracotta cliff that dwarfs all. Staithes is still a working village, much as it would have been when Cook served his sailor's apprenticeship here in the early 19th century. Some of the best seafood in Britain is landed locally, most of it at Whitby: hake, crab, lobster, cod, turbot, mullet and wild salmon. Oysters from further afield make an occasional appearance, too. Both cook, and Charlotte bakes exotic bread – a big bag of frozen rolls left by the previous owner was being ceremoniously dumped when our inspector arrived. Walk to Cook's museum, or the tiny harbour – we're assured the locals are friendly! A hidden treasure.

rooms	3 doubles.
price	£55–£65; singles £45.
meals	Dinner, à la carte, about £25. Lunch for groups of 4+ by arrangement.
closed	1st 2 weeks in December. Restaurant closed Sunday & Monday.
directions	From Whitby, A174 for about 8 miles, then right, signed Staithes. Head right down into old village. Restaurant on right about 100 yds before quayside.

Charlotte Willoughby & Brian Kay

tel	01947 840825
e-mail	theendeavour@ntlworld.com
web	www.endeavour-restaurant.co.uk

map 7   entry 14

The Summer House Restaurant with Rooms

Cornwall Terrace, Penzance, Cornwall TR18 4HL

After trawling through the hotels of Britain to find ones to include in this book, we consider the Summer House a glittering catch: stylish, imaginative, bustling, informal, and so, so colourful. Sunshine yellows and strong Tuscan shades bring a dreamy sense of the Mediterranean to the bustling industry of Penzance. Linda and Ciro, English and Italian respectively, run the place with energy and warmth. Food is a celebration here – *le patron mange ici*; dishes are fresh, simple and cooked with flair. Linda describes it as "a gentle meander through Provence and Italy", with fish bought daily from nearby Newlyn market. Clusters of shells decorate tables in the restaurant, local artists' work hangs on the walls. Outside, a walled garden of terracotta pots and swishing palm trees is a magical setting for dinner at night – *al fresco* breakfasts in good weather are just as good. Unwind on squashy sofas in a drawing room with Gothic carvings and exotic houseplants, and talk away to other guests – most do. Bedrooms combine beautiful 'collectables' and family pieces with resourceful dabs of peppermint, or lemon stripe; some look over the garden. Fairy-tale luxury.

rooms	5: 3 doubles, 2 twin/doubles.
price	£65–£85; singles from £60.
meals	Dinner £22.50. Packed lunch from £7.50.
closed	January & February. Restaurant closed Sunday.
directions	With sea on left, drive along harbourside, past open-air pool, then immediate right after Queens Hotel. House 30 yds up on left.

Linda & Ciro Zaino

tel	01736 363744
fax	01736 360959
e-mail	summerhouse@dial.pipex.com
web	www.summerhouse-cornwall.com

Penzance Arts Club

Chapel House, Penzance, Cornwall TR18 4AQ

Amusing, quirky and original... the Arts Club has brought a little fun to old Penzance. Belinda has created an easy-going but vital cultural centre. Fall into bed after a combination of poetry and jazz in the bar – or an intimate meal in the downstairs restaurant. The bar is a riot of paintings, ever-changing as most are for sale. There are fireplaces at either end and comfortable sofas hug an ancient wooden floor that fills with people as the laid-back party atmosphere warms up – invariably it does! Presiding over all in his unassuming way is Dave the barman, ready to pour a pint; the local organic beer is superb. Upstairs, attractive and colourful bedrooms are as charmingly flamboyant as the bar is raffish. The house was the Portuguese Embassy in the town's more prosperous days – a little garden and balcony off the bar look over the harbour. Not luxurious but good value and one of the most individual places in this book. A must for the open-minded and for those who dream of waking up to the sound of seagulls.

rooms	7: 2 doubles; 1 double, with private bath; 1 double, 3 family, all with shower, sharing wc.
price	£60–£100; singles £30–£45.
meals	Lunch & dinner £15–£20.
closed	Restaurant closed Sunday, plus Monday in winter.
directions	Drive along harbourside with sea on left. Opp. the docks, right into Quay St (by Dolphin pub). Up hill; house on right opp. St Mary's Church.

Belinda Rushworth–Lund

tel	01736 363761
fax	01736 363761
e-mail	reception@penzanceartsclub.co.uk
web	www.penzanceartsclub.co.uk

map 1   entry 16

Halzephron

Gunwalloe, Helston, Cornwall TR12 7QB

An opera singer running an old smuggler's inn on the remote Lizard Peninsula – incomparable. Angela is carrying on a tradition started by her late husband, Harry – the bottom-worn armchair in the bar is a fond memento. She runs the whole show with charm, passion and cheery ebullience and has a few words for everyone. The inn has been taking in travellers – and smugglers, judging by the shaft behind the bar that connects to an underground passage – for 500 years. It reopened in 1958 as the Halzephron, old Cornish for 'cliffs of hell', a phrase that seafarers past and present use to describe the beautiful but treacherous coastline. The inn has two cosy rooms, with deep-sprung beds, patchwork quilts, the odd heirloom, fresh fruit and cafetière coffee. Downstairs, Angela has created some marvellous eating areas – the mock sea cove, with marine-blue wood panelling and a necklace of tiny lights, is delightful. The food is among the best in these parts – freshly cooked, carefully presented, with a supporting cast of 10 local cheeses. Walk to Gunwalloe's 13th-century church or explore the unspoilt fishing villages of Cadgwith, Coverack and Mullion.

rooms	2 doubles.
price	£72; singles £40.
meals	Lunch £10–£15. Packed lunch £12. Dinner £25.
closed	Christmas Day.
directions	From Helston, A3083, signed The Lizard, past Culdrose air base, then right, signed Gunwalloe, for 2 miles. Inn on left after houses.

Angela Davy Thomas

tel	01326 240406
fax	01326 241442
e-mail	halzephroninn@bandbcornwall.net
web	www.halzephron.co.uk

Trengilly Wartha Inn

Nancenoy, Constantine, Falmouth, Cornwall TR11 5RP

It's hard to believe the River Helford is navigable up to this point, simply because it's hard to navigate a car down the narrow, steep lanes to this deeply rural hideaway. It's worth the effort. Trengilly started life as a simple crofter's house before a small bar was added to supplement a previous owner's meagre farming income. The pub has grown organically ever since, winning lots of awards along the way, from 'Pub of the Year' to 'Best Dining Pub in Cornwall'. Expect honourable ales, comfy wooden settles and good meals; *all* the locals come here. Wine is important, too; Nigel knows his grapes, learning much from female wine writers — they're considered better at telling good from bad! Those wanting a less boisterous atmosphere can eat in a restaurant of conservative pastel colours and families can use a no-smoking conservatory. A small, cosy sitting room away from the buzz of the bar has an open fire and lots of books. Country cottage style bedrooms are nicely done: those above the bar have more character than ones in an annexe; all bar one have valley views. In summer, the six-acre garden fills with a happy throng. Arrive by horse... locals do.

rooms	8: 5 doubles, 1 twin, 2 family.
price	£68–£95; singles £48.
meals	Bar meals £4–£15. Dinner, 2 courses, £21.50; 3 courses, £27.
closed	No meals on Christmas Day. Restaurant closed New Year's Eve.
directions	Approaching Falmouth on A39, follow signs to Constantine for about 7 miles. Approaching village, inn signed left, then right.

Michael & Helen Maguire,
Nigel & Isabel Logan

tel	01326 340332
fax	01326 340332
e-mail	trengilly@compuserve.com
web	www.trengilly.co.uk

map 1   entry 18

Driftwood Hotel

Rosevine, Portscatho, Cornwall TR2 5EW

Perfectly positioned and full of curiously vibrant design, Driftwood is a welcome change from the formula beach hotel. It's said the original owner of this 1930s beach villa wandered all over the Roseland Peninsula for the right spot and chose here. The view is wonderful: the sun rises over Nare Head, Portscatho village peeks from a small inlet, and boats criss-cross the bay. Fiona and Paul are relaxed hosts who make the place feel more like a home. The refreshing Cape Cod style is clean but not clinical, full of texture, natural colours and lots of light; all puts you at ease. The restaurant is an expanse of white and wooden floor, with simply-laid tables and driftwood 'fish' on the wall. Food is fresh and often from the sea; their chef has cooked in the best London restaurants. There's a bar with comfy window seats and a lounge with handsome driftwood lamps, luxurious sofas and a log fire. Bedrooms are simply done with neutral fabrics and sand-coloured furniture. A cabin near the hotel sleeps four – views are superb. Sit outside on the decked balcony for breakfast and candlelit dinners, or take a hamper to the private beach – you may see a rare hairy snail.

rooms	11: 7 doubles, 3 twins, 1 cabin.
price	£130–£160.
meals	Dinner £32.
closed	January.
directions	From St Austell, A390 west, left on B3287, signed St Mawes, then left at Tregony on A3078 for about 4 miles. Signed left down lane.

Paul & Fiona Robinson

tel	01872 580644
fax	01872 580801
e-mail	info@driftwoodhotel.co.uk
web	www.driftwoodhotel.co.uk

Manor Cottage

Tresillian, Truro, Cornwall TR2 4BN

Don't let the slightly shabby exterior of this engagingly unpretentious restaurant with rooms put you off – locals break out in nostalgic smiles at the mere mention of the place, their memory jogged by some sublime dish that Carlton once whisked up for them. This is a small, very relaxed operation and everything you come across is the work of either Carlton or Gillian; they painted the yellow walls, polished the wooden floors, hung the big mirror, arranged the flowers and planted the plumbago and passionflower that wander on the stone walls in the conservatory where you eat. Carlton cooks from Thursday to Saturday – the restaurant is closed for the rest of the week, presumably to let him indulge his other talents. He even put in the bathrooms: they're excellent, some with hand-painted tiles. Bedrooms are small but, for their price, superb and full of pretty things. You might have a Heal's of London bed, a hint of Art Deco or scented candles. Wonderful old farm quilts hang on the banister, so grab one and roast away till morning. A little noise from the road, but it's worth it.

rooms	5: 2 doubles; 1 double with private shower; 1 twin, 1 single sharing shower.
price	£55–£75; singles £28–£45.
meals	Dinner £29.95.
closed	Christmas. Restaurant closed Sunday-Wednesday.
directions	From Truro east A390, for about 3 miles. House on left when entering village, signed.

Carlton Moyle & Gillian Jackson

tel	01872 520212
e-mail	man.cott@cwcom.net
web	www.manorcottage.com

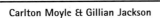

map 1   entry 20

Trevalsa Court Hotel

School Hill Road, Mevagissey, Cornwall PL26 6TH

Trevalsa is a classic example of how the fortunes of a hotel can fluctuate wildly — in this case, for the better. When we first visited, the hotel was in a shambolic state — nobody seemed to want to run it with the affection it deserved. But with Matthew, the new manager, at the helm, it feels like a different place, full of stylish good taste and youthful energy. Candles and roses add atmosphere and colour to the bar, restaurant and sitting room downstairs, and small but significant changes have made all the difference to what were mediocre bedrooms: Farrow & Ball paints, autumnal fabrics, painted wooden blinds, the odd rattan chair, dimmer switches — and binoculars; the gorgeous view of sea and coast was one thing that didn't need altering. It's also the story of a unified Germany working together in the unlikely setting of deepest Cornwall — Matthew is from East Germany and Klaus the owner, who may cook for you, is from West. There's also a garden terrace, a private beach and lots of walks. The healthy European-style buffet breakfast makes a welcome change, too.

rooms	14: 8 doubles, 2 twins, 2 singles, 2 suites.
price	£90-£120; singles £50-£60. Suite £150.
meals	Light meals on request.
closed	December-February.
directions	From St Austell, B3273, signed Mevagissey, for about 5.5 miles past beach caravan park, then left at top of hill. Over mini-r'bout. Hotel on left, signed.

Klaus Wagner & Matthew Mainka

tel	01726 842468
e-mail	stay@cornwall-hotel.net
web	www.cornwall-hotel.net

Cormorant on the River

Golant, Nr. Fowey, Cornwall PL23 1LL

Golant is well-hidden from Cornwall's tourist trail and the Cormorant is well-hidden from Golant. You drive along the quay, then climb a short, steep hill. The reward is a breathtaking view of the Fowey estuary (pronounced 'Foy'), flowing through a wooded landscape. Boats tug on their moorings and birds glide lazily over the water – this is a very English paradise. The view is so good the architect made sure it leapt into every room; 10 of the 11 bedrooms have French windows. They're fabulous to wake up in, and not bad to sleep in either, with comfy beds, pastel colours and spotless bathrooms. From the entrance, steps lead to a huge light-filled sitting room with log fire, colourful pictures and a big map of the estuary to help plan adventures – walks start from the door. There's a small bar with a good smattering of whiskies and a pretty dining room themed on the legend of Tristam, Yseult and jilted King Mark (the love story was made into an opera by Wagner; a nearby 13th-century church once belonged in the king's domain). In summer, have tea under parasols on the terraced lawn and watch the boats zip by. A marvellous spot.

rooms	11 twin/doubles.
price	£90–£150; singles from £65 (winter only).
meals	Dinner, 4 courses, from £20.
closed	Never.
directions	A390 west towards St Austell, then B3269 to Fowey. After 4 miles, left to Golant. Continue into village, along quay, hotel signed right, up very steep hill.

Carrie & Colin King

tel	01726 833426
e-mail	relax@cormoranthotels.co.uk
web	www.cormoranthotels.co.uk

map 1   entry 22

The Old Quay House Hotel

28 Fore Street, Fowey, Cornwall PL23 1AQ

As work in progress, The Old Quay House has everything going for it – a gorgeous waterside location and charming owners determined to make their new lifestyle work. Jane and Roy almost bought a beach hotel but the sale collapsed at the last hair-pulling minute. It was a blessing in disguise as these ex-Londoners have found what they really wanted. Fowey is an enchanting place bustling with local life and passing sailors. Their chef Henry, an ex-submariner, was a blessing, too. He walked in off the street one day and has been cooking brilliantly ever since: try his sauté potatoes with rosemary for breakfast. The hotel was built in 1889 for ex-mariners who needed somewhere to live – women lived opposite in what was the temperance house! The place was in a dreadful state when they took it over but every nook and cranny is being revived. The bedrooms are nicely done in a light, contemporary style; six have angled patios with estuary views. Downstairs, you can look right through the building past the swish bar and restaurant to the decked sun terrace. Come and take it all in – you may see a giant Cornish pastie. *Opens March 2003.*

rooms	12 twin/doubles.
price	£110; singles £75.
meals	Lunch about £14. Dinner about £22.
closed	Never.
directions	Entering Fowey, follow one-way system past church. Hotel on right where road is at narrowest point, opp. Old House of Foye.

Jane & Roy Carson

tel	01726 833302
e-mail	oldquayhouse@hotmail.com

Talland Bay Hotel

Talland, Nr. Looe, Cornwall PL13 2JB

Decidedly old-fashioned, with decidedly old-fashioned ideas about looking after people. If you want to be by yourself you may curl up with a book at the end of the garden, or just lie by the pool and listen to the seagulls. A peaceful place, with two acres of subtropical gardens and a beautifully mown lawn ending in a ha-ha and a 150-foot drop down to the bay, with long views out to sea. The air is clear and fresh, and the sea view through pine trees has a Mediterranean feel, reflected in the style and flavour of the hotel's food. The house is surprisingly ancient, mentioned in the Domesday book and once owned by the famous Trelawney family. French windows open from the sitting room, dining room (both part-panelled), bar and library onto a paved terrace and a heated swimming pool. There's a little upstairs sitting area, too. The bedrooms are traditional-luxurious, Laura Ashley in parts, impeccable and bathed in light. The traditions go as far as croquet and a Cornish clotted cream tea, as well as lots of fresh fish and seafood from Looe, including lobster, crab and scallops.

rooms	22: 20 twin/doubles, 2 singles.
price	£90–£160; singles £45–£80.
meals	Light lunch £4–£12. Packed lunch from £5. Dinner £27.50.
closed	10 January–mid-February.
directions	From Looe, A387 for Polperro. Ignore 1st sign to Talland. After 2 miles, left at x-roads; follow signs.

George & Mary Granville

tel	01503 272667
fax	01503 272940
e-mail	george@brook-farm.demon.co.uk
web	www.tallandbayhotel.co.uk

map 2   entry 24

The Hotel L'Arret

Bleak Hill, B4574, Ventongimps, Cornwall NO CCTV

A touch of pretension about the name of this hotel, we admit, but it is — under the circumstances — forgivable. While most hotels can trumpet their virtues — or 'facilities' — this one has had a hard time on the PR front and we are delighted to be able to put the record straight. We do like, as you know, to select hotels because they are unusual and 'different', run by equally unusual and interesting people. (See our Introduction.) Well this place, for all its transparency, fits most of our definitions of 'special'. It is in the most gloriously, bleakly, remote piece of countryside, far from any crowd let alone a madding one. It is exquisitely served by public transport so you can dispense altogether with your car. It is quiet, entirely lacking in unnecessary frills, architecturally forward-looking and, best of all, flooded with natural light. Lastly, who can resist the welcome? Is there another hotel — anywhere in the world — that provides a welcome fanfare for every guest? You will, we hope, understand our reluctance to enter into a detailed description of the interior. *Viewing possible — Isle of Unst (sic).*

rooms	Space for 2 seated and 4 standing (sofa-bed unextended).
price	£60: £40 one-way.
meals	On wheels, but not all of them stop here.
closed	All statutory holidays.
directions	From A303 to Bodmin, follow the Number 161 bus until you spot the stop. Don't blink. Parking prohibited.

The Driver

tel	0100 000010
e-mail	stop@thestop.ok
web	www.wheredoyouwanttogotodaythen?

Molesworth Manor

Little Petherick, Nr. Padstow, Cornwall PL27 7QT

Art, wine and rugby make a refreshing combination at this friendly, down-to-earth old rectory. Geoff and Jessica have given up the treadmill of London to bring up their small child in the country, buying this family hotel from her parents; apart from the odd hankering for a curry, and Geoff's beloved London Irish, they haven't looked back, adding their own touches slowly. Both love trawling local galleries and auctions for art and interesting antiques. Geoff is also a modest wine buff with a good cellar; the local Camel Valley vintage isn't bad. The huge drawing room draws the morning sun; the music room with log fire blazing suits the evening. A carved staircase – no insert is the same – leads to bedrooms that vary in style and size: two at the front are grand; ones in the eaves are bright and beamed. Three in a converted barn across the courtyard are fabulous. The rectory garden is as you'd expect – mature, well-tended and peaceful; a wooden bridge used to cross the road to more land but it came down in the 60s to let double decker buses pass. Breakfast in the gorgeous tropical-style conservatory – the freshly-made muffins are superb. You'll eat well in Padstow, too.

rooms	13: 9 doubles; 1 double, 1 twin, 1 family, all with private shower; 1 single, with private bath.
price	£47–£74. Group rates for whole house.
meals	Restaurants in Padstow.
closed	November–January. Open off-season by arrangement.
directions	From Wadebridge, A389 towards Padstow for 4 miles. Road dips into Little Petherick, then climbs again. House up hill on right, signed.

Geoff French & Jessica Clarke

tel	01841 540292
e-mail	molesworthmanor@aol.com
web	www.molesworthmanor.co.uk

map 1   entry 26

Tregea Hotel

16-18 High Street, Padstow, Cornwall PL28 8BB

Few places have as much going for them as Padstow: pretty quayside, superb fish restaurants, good beaches nearby, and in the midst of the old town, Tregea Hotel. Humorous, hands-on and genuinely welcoming, owners like Tim and Amanda make this book a joy to produce. Tim had just whisked Amanda off for a surprise 40th birthday treat in Marrakesh thanks to loyal staff happy to take up the slack. "They are lovely, caring people," said Jane, their right-hand woman, who stood outside the hotel waving to help guide in our disorientated inspector. Rooms have a fresh cosmopolitan feel and guests assume London influences, but Tim is Devonian through and through, and Amanda's roots blend Lancashire with Africa. Her flair for interior design befits the setting: sea-chalet blues, sandy-coloured fabrics and cute bathroom fittings with tongue-in-cheek seaside themes. Bedrooms have town or estuary views. Downstairs hang amusing Sasha Harding prints of seaside life. There's a big sitting area with a bar and a roomy dining room: try the daily fish special for breakfast, caught locally... and if you can guess Tim's previous occupation, you win a bottle of champagne!

rooms	8: 6 doubles, 2 twin/doubles.
price	£72–£92.
meals	Restaurants in Padstow.
closed	Christmas & New Year.
directions	From Wadebridge, A389 west to Padstow. Past turning to town centre & docks, then right after fire station, signed Prideaux Place. 2nd left into Tregirls Lane, then immediate right into High Street. Hotel 200 yds on left.

Tim & Amanda Perring

tel	01841 532455
fax	01841 532542
e-mail	tim@tregea.co.uk
web	www.tregea.co.uk

Number 6

Middle Street, Padstow, Cornwall PL28 8AP

If you dream of the Mediterranean, but don't want to leave the country, pack your bags and head to beatific Number 6. It's the sort of place you'd hope to stumble upon in the back street of an unspoilt fishing village in the south of France. Brenda and Paul came to live by the sea, to fulfil the dream, and their place is perfect: small, informal and beautifully decorated. Not a place to come looking for spa baths and room service; it's more about style without pretension, and superb fish landed by local trawlermen, laid on your plate the same day. Eat in the light, fresh, almost Bauhaus-style restaurant with its checkerboard floor, white-painted brickwork, wooden blinds and plants, or outside in a tiny courtyard full of pots and passionflower. The restaurant is well known and extremely popular locally so book early if you

do want to dine *al fresco*. Upstairs, the three bedrooms vary in size but not charm: Edwardian beds, the best linen, piles of pillows, coir matting, maybe a stainless steel propeller fan, and wonderful bathrooms that bring the beach to you. All bang in the middle of Padstow. Marvellous.

rooms	3 doubles.
price	£75-£90.
meals	Lunch & dinner, 2 courses, £22; 3 courses, £25.50.
closed	Occasionally in winter.
directions	From Wadebridge, A389 west into Padstow. Drop bags off at door; parking five minutes' walk away.

Brenda & Paul Harvey

tel	01841 532093
fax	01841 532093
web	www.number6inpadstow.co.uk

map 1   entry 28

The Port Gaverne Hotel

Port Gaverne, Nr. Port Isaac, Cornwall PL29 3SQ

Having successfully created the relaxed country house splendour of Polsue Manor on the south coast of Cornwall, Graham and Annabelle have turned their attention to overhauling a seaside hotel on the north coast. It's an exciting challenge and very much work in progress but we're confident they have the flair and eye for detail to turn Port Gaverne into a stylish little enclave. The hotel is an old 17th-century inn set back from a rocky, funnel-shaped cove near the pretty fishing village of Port Isaac — it's safe to swim. Bedrooms in the oldest part of the building have lots of beamed character, while those in the modern wing have received the Sylvester treatment; some have access to a small balcony. Down in the warren-like bar, snug cubby-holes are an ideal place to recuperate with a pint after a hike along the coast, or a stroll up an inland valley — both walks start outside. A wonderful stained-glass sailing rigger leads to the formal restaurant. The food has come on in leaps and bounds since they took over, cooked fresh in a modern English style. Come for the sea and quiet relaxation. *Reopens February 2003.*

rooms	15: 8 doubles, 2 twins, 4 family, 1 triple.
price	£70–£90; singles £45–£55.
meals	Bar meals from £4.50. Dinner £20.
closed	January–mid-February.
directions	From Wadebridge, B3314, then B3267 to Port Isaac. There, follow road right to Port Gaverne. Inn up lane from cove on left.

Graham & Annabelle Sylvester

tel	01208 880244
fax	01208 880151

The Mill House Inn

Trebarwith, Nr. Tintagel, Cornwall PL34 0HD

It's no surprise the folk behind the Mill House Inn work in the movie business. Imagine the brief: import the atmosphere of a stylish London bistro into an old mill house next to the rolling surf of the north Cornish coast, then add chic, affordable rooms. Such a cracking idea, it's a wonder no-one thought of it before. Arrive down a steep winding lane to a pretty woodland setting, ticking along at its own contented pace. All you need is within walking distance — a glorious sandy beach to suit sunbather or surfer, and coastal trails that lead to Tintagel, official home of the Arthurian legends. Inside, a dark and cosy bar has easy-going panache, with old floorboards, gnarled wooden tables and blissed-out tunes. The dining room over the old mill stream is light and elegant: sea blues, crisp white linen and chapel chairs create a tongue-in-cheek formality. Try old Cornish dishes with a modern take. There's a snug living room for guests, with lots of old movies and CDs, and state-of-the-art equipment to play them on. A funky oasis for the chintz-weary.

rooms	9: 7 doubles, 1 single, 1 family.
price	£70–£90; singles £45.
meals	Bar meals from £3.95.
	Dinner, à la carte, about £20.
closed	Never.
directions	From Tintagel, B3263 south, following signs to Trebarwith Strand. Inn at bottom of steep hill.

Nigel Peters, John Beach &
John Bamford

tel	01840 770200
fax	01840 770647
e-mail	management@themillhouseinn.co.uk
web	www.themillhouseinn.co.uk

map 1   entry 30

Crosby Lodge

High Crosby, Carlisle, Cumbria CA6 4QZ

Restful, grandly comfortable and blissfully detached from the outside world, Crosby Lodge is almost like walking into a gentleman's club – only it welcomes all. Come to elope – Gretna is close – or just to escape. Patricia is everywhere, always impeccably dressed, never seeming to stop, but never seeming to hurry. She used to be a banker – the considerate kind, what else! – and this original 'country house hotel' remains a laid-back family affair in every sense. Michael and Patricia came here 30-odd years ago. Today, their son, James, has joined them in the kitchen, and their daughter, Pippa, owns a wine company that... you guessed, supplies their wine. There could be grandchildren around as well – not that you'd mind. Inside is warm and cosy, with opens fires, the odd *chaise longue*, oak furniture and lots of rugs. Bedrooms are fun. Pat won't have "square corners", so you get arches and alcoves instead. They're big and bright, with good fabrics, and maybe arrow slits, or a lovely gnarled half-tester. Outside, you might find the local blacksmith, or an artist sketching a gorgeous pastoral view. Hadrian's Wall is only 10 miles away.

rooms	11: 5 twin/doubles, 2 doubles, 1 single, 3 family.
price	£120-£160; singles £82-£85.
meals	Lunch from £5. Dinner, 4 courses, £30; à la carte, £13-£30.
closed	Christmas-mid-January.
directions	M6, junc. 44, A689 east for 3.5 miles, then right to Low Crosby. Through village. House on right.

Michael & Patricia Sedgwick

tel	01228 573618
fax	01228 573428
e-mail	enquiries@crosbylodge.co.uk
web	www.crosbylodge.co.uk

Number Thirty One

31 Howard Place, Carlisle, Cumbria CA1 1HR

Anything seems possible here – totally unconventional, yet totally comfortable, a splash of flamboyancy in an old Victorian house. Philip sparkles in the kitchen – and cooks in the Floyd manner, glass in hand, though it never contains more than fizzy spring water. He has his own smoker for salmon and trout caught the same day. He bakes the bread, makes the muesli, stuffs the sausage and boils his own marmalade. You could drink an 'infusion' of wild blackberry and nettle, or perhaps mango indico. He and Judith are experienced hoteliers, doing it their own, very modern way. No. 31 was recently voted top townhouse of the year. In the hall, a gilt-framed mirror, Greek architectural prints and a newspaper rack for a leisurely read over breakfast. The three bedrooms are individually done: the Green room has a Japanese theme, the Blue room is the largest and the Yellow room at the front can see the north Pennines, one of the best but least visited places in the country to go fell walking. A splendid oasis in ancient, tree-lined Carlisle where more than just a meal awaits. *This is a no smoking house.*

rooms	3: 2 doubles, 1 double/twin.
price	£85–£100; singles £60.
meals	Dinner £20; Packed lunch £7.50.
closed	November–March.
directions	From M6, junc. 43, A69 Warwick Rd towards city centre. Right after 5th set of traffic lights into Howard Place. House at far end on left.

Philip & Judith Parker

tel	01228 597080
fax	01228 597080
e-mail	bestpep@aol.com
web	www.number31.freeservers.com

map 10 entry 32

Lovelady Shield

Nenthead Road, Nr. Alston, Cumbria CA9 3LF

From the front door of Lovelady, walk straight into an area of the High Pennines that is remote and utterly unspoilt. The River Nent runs through the garden and at the bridge, four footpaths meet. The house, hidden away down a long and suitably bumpy drive, was rebuilt in 1832. The cellars date from 1690, the foundations from the 14th century when a convent stood here. No noise, save for antiphonal sheep in the fields and a burbling river that you can hear if you sleep with your window open. Peter and Marie have been here five years and run the place with a hint of eccentricity and a lot of good-natured charm. A small rag-rolled bar and pretty sitting rooms give a low-key, country-house feel. Long windows in all rooms bring the views inside and French windows open up in summer for Pimms on the lawn. The food is wonderful; you eat in the very pretty dining room surrounded by gilt mirrors, sash windows and fresh flowers. Upstairs, dark hallways lead through old pine doors to bright bedrooms with window seats, maybe a sofa, good furniture and Scrabble; most have gorgeous views.

rooms	10: 7 doubles, 2 twins, 1 four-poster.
price	Half-board £60–£110 p.p.
meals	Dinner, 4 courses, included; non-residents £32.50. Lunch by arrangement.
closed	Never.
directions	From Alston, A689 west for 2 miles. House on left at junction of B6294, signed.

Peter & Marie Haynes

tel	01434 381203
fax	01434 381515
e-mail	enquiries@lovelady.co.uk
web	www.lovelady.co.uk

The Pheasant

Bassenthwaite Lake, Nr. Cockermouth, Cumbria CA13 9YE

The snug at The Pheasant is wonderful, a treasured relic of times past as a busy coaching inn. A barman guards 40 malts at a low-slung wooden bar and walls shine from a combination of 300 years of tobacco smoke and polish. The inn has since turned into a hotel, and drinks are now usually served in sitting rooms of understated elegance: gilt mirrors, sprays of garden flowers, trim carpets, fresh, yellow walls and fine furniture – all immaculate, yet immediately relaxing. The bedrooms have been beautifully remodelled, too, revealing the odd hidden beam; mellow lighting has been added, warm colours put on the walls and a rug or two thrown in for good measure. Most are in the main part of the inn; three are in a nearby garden lodge... and though pristine throughout, you'll still come across Housekeeping armed with feather dusters! There's a kennel for visiting dogs, Skiddaw to be scaled and Bassenthwaite Lake to be paddled. A perfect place to take your time. *Children over 8 welcome.*

rooms	13: 10 twin/doubles, 1 single, 2 suites.
price	£110–£160; singles £65–£80. Half-board (min. 2 nights) from £71 p.p.
meals	Light lunch from £5. Dinner, à la carte, about £24.95.
closed	Christmas Day.
directions	From Keswick, A66 north-west for 7 miles. Hotel on left, signed.

Matthew Wylie

tel	017687 76234
fax	017687 76002
e-mail	pheasant@easynet.co.uk
web	www.the-pheasant.co.uk

map 6   entry 34

The Mill Hotel

Mungrisdale, Nr. Penrith, Cumbria CA11 0XR

A small, eclectic bolt hole, this 1651 mill house on the northern border of the lakes has a stream racing past that is fed by fells that rise behind. Richard and Eleanor belong to that band of innkeepers who do their own thing instinctively and immaculately – this is the antithesis of a big, impersonal hotel. Richard comes out to greet you at the car, to help with the bags, to show you up to your room, and finally, invites you down for drinks "whenever you're ready". Downstairs you'll find a tiny library and a homely sitting room with rocking chair, ancient stone fireplace, wood carvings and piles of reference books on every subject under the sun. All the while, Eleanor has been cooking up five courses of heaven for your supper, all home-made and organic where possible, from the olive bread to the watercress soup; breakfasts, too, are first class. Bedrooms range in size, but not style. The old mill, wrapped in clematis montana, has its own sitting room where you can fall asleep to the sound of the river. In the main house, beams, bowls of fruit, African art, fresh flowers and good linen induce perfect slumber.

rooms	9: 4 doubles, 3 twins; 1 double, 1 twin, sharing bath.
price	Half-board £59-£79 p.p.
meals	Dinner, 5 courses, included.
closed	November-February.
directions	M6, junc. 40 (Penrith), A66 west for Keswick for 7 miles, then right, for Mungrisdale. Hotel next door to Mill Inn.

Richard & Eleanor Quinlan

tel	01768 779659
fax	01768 779155
e-mail	themill@quinlan.evesham.net
web	www.themillhotel.com

Swinside Lodge

Grange Road, Keswick, Cumbria CA12 5UE

A short stroll takes you to the edge of Derwentwater – the Queen of the Lakes. Immediately behind, fells rise and spirits soar. At Swinside – a small-scale model of English country-house elegance – reception rooms are crisp and fresh, with fine period furniture offset by pastel blues and yellows. In the bold dining room, deep reds combine with oil-burning lamps... formal, yet very relaxed. There are lots of books in the sitting rooms, maps for walkers, bowls of fruit, fresh flowers and no clutter. Every tiny detail has been well thought out, not least in the bedrooms where flair and forethought have pulled off a maestro's touch – the rooms have been furnished with cream furniture to make them feel bigger than they are, and it works a treat. The bedrooms are all good and two are huge. You'll find drapes, more crisp materials and uplifting views – you can watch the weather change. Food is honest and delicious; perhaps try asparagus and herb risotto, celery and apple soup, lamb, or warm chocolate mousse. *Children over 10 welcome.*

rooms	7: 5 doubles, 2 twins.
price	Half-board £67–£95 p.p.
meals	Dinner, 4 courses, included; non-residents £28. Booking essential.
closed	Never.
directions	M6, junc. 40. A66 west past Keswick, over r'bout, then 2nd left, for Portiscale & Grange. Follow signs to Grange for 2 miles. House signed on right.

Kevin & Susan Kniveton

tel	017687 72948
fax	017687 72948
e-mail	info@swinsidelodge-hotel.co.uk
web	www.swinsidelodge-hotel.co.uk

map 6   entry 36

The Old Church Hotel

Watermillock, Penrith, Cumbria CA11 0JN

Like the beautiful fir-cone wallpaper that's hung on the walls for almost two decades, the philosophy of this quiet, unpretentious hotel on the shores of Lake Ullswater is "why change what works". It's the sort of place you search high and low for. The drive winds down through fields, past a 1,500-year-old yew tree, to lawns that hug the water's edge. The house is on a tiny peninsular, bounded on three sides by lake – once inside, the view just follows you around. Take a long drink to the gorgeous living room and watch the wind turn up the volume in front of your eyes, choreographing yachts moored off the shore. A church used to stand on the site and a calm spirituality remains. Kevin could have been a good vicar but he chose the hotel game instead: it's the easy rapport, the dry humour and a knack for looking after people – no "patronising condescension" here. Bedrooms are nicely done in a conservative style and smell of luxury – most have a lake view. A snug bar, with games, books and maps for walkers, provides quiet diversions. The food doesn't pretend either – steaks are still the most popular request. Why change?

rooms	10: 9 doubles, 1 twin.
price	£130–£180; singles £65–£85. Half-board £75–£100 p.p.
meals	Dinner £29.50. Packed lunch £7.
closed	November–March.
directions	M6, junc. 40, A66 west towards Ullswater for 0.5 miles, then left onto A592. Hotel on left by lake, just after Watermillock. Entrance down private drive, signed.

Kevin Whitemore

tel	017684 86204
fax	017684 86368
e-mail	info@oldchurch.co.uk
web	www.oldchurch.co.uk

Augill Castle

Brough, Kirkby Stephen, Cumbria CA17 4DE

In our fair quest to find places for you to stay, fate led us to a castle in the garden of Eden... well, almost. Augill Castle is an early Victorian folly in Cumbria's beautiful Eden Valley. It was completed in 1841 for John Bagot Pearson, the eldest of two brothers; he was determined to build a bigger and better house overlooking the family pile at Park House after a sibling row. The result is wonderfully over the top, with turrets, arched fairy-tale windows, a castellated tower and monstrously large rooms – how green with envy his brother must have been! Simon and Wendy rescued the building after years of neglect in 1997 and lavishly decorated the whole caboodle; there's no stinting on anything here, be it fabric, colour, food, or welcome. The bedrooms ooze baronial style: four-posters, roll-top baths, swagged curtains, maybe a turret wardrobe. Downstairs, relax in the elegant library bar, and banquet around a huge table in the grand dining room beneath a panelled ceiling of light and dark blue. The Bennetts also know a thing or two about food, having owned a part share in a Mayfair restaurant. Explore Eden on foot, or bag a bargain antique in Barnard Castle.

rooms	10: 4 doubles, 3 twin/doubles, 3 four-posters.
price	£100-£200; singles £50-£100.
meals	Dinner Friday & Saturday, or by arrangement, £25.
closed	Christmas & New Year.
directions	M6, junc. 38, A685 through Kirkby Stephen, then right 2 miles out of town, signed to hotel. On left.

Simon & Wendy Bennett

tel	01768 341937
fax	01768 341936
e-mail	enquiries@augillcastle.co.uk
web	www.augillcastle.co.uk

map 6   entry 38

The King George IV Inn

Eskdale, Holmrook, Cumbria CA19 1TS

Amid the lush, green folds of Eskdale lies this earthy inn, feeding and sheltering folk drawn to this magnificent landscape. Home to peregrine falcons and soaring crags, waterfalls and jewel-like tarns, the valley has inspired folk since prehistoric times. AW Wainwright, author of many beautifully illustrated walking guides to Britain, thought it the loveliest valley in the Lakes. Approach via Hardknott Pass, England's highest road crossing – awe-inspiring. The George IV is at the lower end, run for many years with hearty good cheer by Jacqui and Harry. The gnarled bar, with cosy cubby holes and dried hops nailed to seasoned beams, comes alive in the evening; two wonderful stools shaped like tractor seats are for local farmers! The menu is unfussy, and all is local. There's also a small gift bazaar. Bedrooms are in a lacey, cottage style, with good bathrooms; one has a four-poster. Walk to the lost 'City of Barnscar', a Bronze Age settlement of 400 huts. Elsewhere, churches, stone circles, a Japanese garden... and La'al Ratty, England's first narrow gauge railway, will take you to the sea and the timeless beauty of Ravenglass. *Self-catering flat also available.*

rooms	3: 2 doubles, 1 twin.
price	£50; singles £28.
meals	Bar meals from £8.50. Packed lunch £5.
closed	Christmas Day.
directions	From Ambleside, A593 for Coniston, past Skelwith Bridge, then right, for Little Langdale. Follow single-track road over Hardknott Pass and into Eskdale valley. Inn on left at road junction.

Jacqui & Harry Shepherd

tel	01946 723262
fax	01946 723334
e-mail	kinggeorgeiv@eskdale83.fsnet.co.uk
web	www.kinggeorge-iv.co.uk

Old Dungeon Ghyll

Great Langdale, Ambleside, Cumbria LA22 9JY

This is an old favourite of hardy mountaineers and it comes as no surprise to learn that Tenzing and Hillary stayed here. The hotel is at the head of the valley, surrounded by spectacular peaks, heaven for hikers and climbers, a place to escape to. The scenery is breathtaking, and this is a solid and genuine base from where to plan your ascent. Eclectic bedrooms are decorated with the odd brass bed, patchwork quilts, floral wallpaper and patterned carpets. All are blissfully free of phones and TVs – you wouldn't want them here, not when there's so much going on downstairs. In winter, a fire crackles in the sitting room, all the food is home-cooked – fresh bread, teacakes and flapjacks every day – and there's a small snug resident's bar. Best of all is the famous hiker's bar – hotel wedding parties always seem to end up here. Guitars and fiddles appear – do they carry them over the mountain? – *ceilidhs* break out and laughter fills the rafters – all overseen by Neil, Jane and great staff. Come to walk and to leave the city far behind.

rooms	14: 4 doubles, 4 twin/doubles, 1 twin, 2 family, 3 singles, all sharing 4 baths & 1 shower.
price	£73–£82; singles from £36.50; single occ. from £35.
meals	Bar meals from £6. Packed lunch £3.95. Dinner £18.50.
closed	Christmas.
directions	From Ambleside, A593 for Coniston, right on B5343. Hotel on right after 5 miles, signed, past Great Langdale campsite.

Neil & Jane Walmsley

tel	015394 37272
fax	015394 37272
e-mail	neil.odg@lineone.net
web	www.odg.co.uk

map 6　entry 40

White Moss House

Rydal Water, Grasmere, Cumbria LA22 9SE

This is the epicentre of Wordsworth country; walk north a mile to his home at Dove Cottage or west to his somewhat more salubrious house at Rydal Mount. The paths are old and you can follow his footsteps up fell and through wood. He knew White Moss, too – he bought it for his son and came here to escape. The Dixons have lived here for 23 years and they have kept the feel of a home: flowers everywhere, a woodburning stove, pretty floral fabrics and lots of comfy sofas and chairs. There's a small bar in an old linen cupboard, and after-dinner coffee in the sitting room brings out the house-party feel. Upstairs, bedrooms range in size, but not comfort. All are different and have good views: maybe a glazed pine-panelled bay window, an old wooden bed, a sprinkling of books and magazines, and a bathroom, with Radox to soothe fell-fallen feet. Further up the hill, the cottage is in a quiet, beautiful spot with the best view of all right out across Rydal Water; ideal for longer stays. Then there's also the small matter of food, all cooked by Peter – five courses of famed indulgence await. *Children over 5 welcome.*

rooms	5: 2 doubles, 3 twin/doubles. Also 1 cottage for 4.
price	Half-board £65–£95 p.p.
meals	Dinner, 5 courses, included; non-residents £30.
closed	December-mid-February. Restaurant closed Sunday night.
directions	From Ambleside, north on A591. House signed on right at far end of Rydal Water.

Susan & Peter Dixon

tel	015394 35295
fax	015394 35516
e-mail	sue@whitemoss.com
web	www.whitemoss.com

The Samling

Ambleside Road, Windermere, Cumbria LA23 1LR

Possibly the best hotel in Britain? It's hard not to reach this conclusion after you've been to The Samling. The brochure for once is telling the truth: "it's like no other place you've stayed" – especially in the Lakes, which has been gasping for an alternative to chintz and rhododendrum for years. There's not a swirly-whirly carpet in sight, just lots of good taste in 67 acres overlooking Lake Windermere – Wordsworth came here to pay his rent. The Maxfields are great patrons of the arts so you'll find beautiful paintings inside and sculptures to contemplate on garden wanderings. Nothing's showy or grand, it's about relaxing in style – hotel policy encourages breakfast in bed! Designer Amanda Rosar did the interiors. Start with the snug, autumnal sitting room of checked sofas, fresh lilies, a bowl of apricots and a big, open fire, then go from there. Fabulous bedrooms named after the Cumbrian counting system are full of texture, colour and surprises: furry glam rock cushions, stucco walls of orange ochre, slate floors, candles in every bathroom and most have lake views; suites in the converted "bothy" are superb... so are the food and the service. Worth every penny.

rooms	10: 7 doubles, 1 twin/double, 2 suites.
price	£145-£225; singles from £130; suite £340. Half-board from £99 p.p.
meals	Full English breakfast included. Dinner, à la carte, £40; menu gourmand, 8 courses, £60.
closed	Never.
directions	From Windermere, A59 towards Ambleside for 3 miles. Hotel on right up steep drive, signed.

Tom Maxfield

tel	01593 431922
fax	01593 430400
e-mail	info@thesamling.com
web	www.thesamling.com

map 6   entry 42

Miller Howe Hotel & Restaurant

Rayrigg Road, Bowness-on-Windermere, Cumbria LA23 1EY

Looking over Lake Windermere to majestic peaks in the distance, Miller Howe can justly claim to have one of the best views in England. A cottage containing three luxurious suites uses it to amazing effect: huge windows on three walls suck in fell, lake, hill and mountain. The cottage can be used individually, or by groups wanting extra privacy; you can enjoy the best of both worlds as the hotel is just a short walk through a fragrant herb garden. Charles, a former national newspaper editor, has taken the hotel "up a notch" since he arrived in 1997, improving an already enviable reputation for good food and service; staff are trained to be "brilliant today; better tomorrow". He's hands-on, too, welcoming guests with a friendly arm round the shoulder. Gail does the design side. Handsome rooms use the best of everything: Beaumont & Fletcher wallpaper, handmade fabrics, the odd Chesterfield. In the evening, you'll be served the view with your meal in a dining room of wrought iron verdigris, gilded ceilings and honey limestone tiles; menus point out landmarks. Perfect whatever the weather.

rooms	15: 7 twin/doubles, 5 doubles, 3 suites.
price	Half-board: £75-£135 p.p.; suite £135-£175 p.p.
meals	Light lunch from £7. Picnic £14. Tea £4.50-£9.99. Dinner, 5 courses, included; non-residents £39.50.
closed	6-18 January.
directions	From Kendal, A591 to Windermere; left at mini-r'bout onto A592 for Bowness; 0.25 miles on right.

Charles & Gail Garside

tel	015394 42536
fax	015394 45664
e-mail	lakeview@millerhowe.com
web	www.millerhowe.com

The Old Vicarage

Church Road, Witherslack, Cumbria LA11 6RS

Thank goodness for the Browns and the Reeves — these four effervescent souls did the unthinkable, leaving cosy jobs 'down south' to run a hotel in a quiet part of the Lakes... and they've never looked back. They arrived about 20 years ago, first swapping their suits for overalls — the house needed a lot of work — then aprons. They've been indulging their passion for food ever since. Locals all recommend you eat here; even TV cameras paid a visit to see what the fuss was about. Today, the baton has been passed to the next generation with James — Jill and Roger's son —now in the kitchen. Add to this, rooms of simple, stylish luxury, and you have guests as happy as the owners. Rooms in the main house look out over the garden and are closer to the fun; those in Orchard House are bigger and utterly secluded — stroll through damson trees and past the tennis court on your way up. Maps and routes for walkers, high teas and chairs for children, and Yewbarrow Fell — 'The Noddle' — just behind; a ten-minute walk to the top brings spectacular views. Quite simply, heaven-sent and down-to-earth.

rooms	12: 6 doubles, 4 twins, 1 family, 1 four-poster.
price	£100–£150; singles from £65. Half-board £65–£100 p.p.
meals	Dinner from £25. Sunday lunch £15.50. Packed lunch by arrangement.
closed	Never.
directions	M6, junc. 36, then A590 for Barrow. After 6 miles, right for Witherslack. In village, left after phone box. House on left just before church.

	Jill & Roger Brown, Irene & Stanley Reeve
tel	015395 52381
fax	015395 52373
e-mail	hotel@oldvicarage.com
web	www.oldvicarage.com

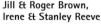

map 6   entry 44

Aynsome Manor Hotel

Cartmel, Nr. Grange-over-Sands, Cumbria LA11 6HH

Stand at the front door of Aynsome and look across ancient meadows to Cartmel Priory, still magnificent after 800 years and still the heart of a small, thriving community; the view is almost medieval. Strike out across the fields to the village – a walk of about three-quarters of a mile – and discover its gentle secrets. The house, too, echoes with history: it was home to the descendants of the Earl of Pembroke; in 1930, it gave up a long-held secret when a suit of chain armour dating back to 1335 was found behind a wall in an attic bedroom. The panelled dining room has a remarkable tongue-and-ball ceiling, the hall a melodious grandfather clock, a wood and coal fire and carved oak panels – the gift of an 1839 storm. A cantilevered spiral staircase with a cupola-domed window leads up to the first-floor sitting room where newspapers hang from poles and a welcoming fire burns in a marble Adams-style fireplace. Bedrooms vary in size; all are simple and comfortable, some with gently sloping floors. Race-goers will love the National Hunt racecourse – the annual August Bank Holiday meet is one of the oldest in Britain. *No under fives in the restaurant.*

rooms	12: 5 doubles, 4 twins, 2 family, 1 four-poster.
price	£72–£90; singles from £42. Half-board £51–£72 p.p.
meals	Dinner, 4 courses, £22.
closed	January.
directions	M6 junc. 36; A590 for Barrow; at top of Lindale Hill, follow signs left to Cartmel. Hotel on right 3 miles from A590.

Christopher & Andrea Varley

tel	01539 536653
fax	01539 536016
e-mail	info@aynsomemanorhotel.co.uk
web	www.aynsomemanorhotel.co.uk

Hipping Hall

Cowan Bridge, Kirkby Lonsdale, Cumbria LA6 2JJ

One of Lancashire's best kept secrets, Hipping Hall is the surviving remnant of a 15th-century hamlet. The only other clues are an old stone wash-house, a stream and spring-fed pond, and an ancient well that's now part of a flagstoned conservatory. The Skeltons have kept the feel much as it always was: informal, stylish and relaxed, adding a treasure trove of antiques, paintings, prints and numerous teddy bears and dolls for good measure. Jean's father used to be an antique dealer but she prefers to consider her passion a hobby; you'll find a tiny curio shop in one of the cellars. Groups can dine in true house-party style in the Great Hall – once the hamlet's town hall – with old oak floors, rugs, candles and beams. Smaller groups eat in the old morning room now converted into an intimate dining room. Richard grows organic vegetables for the table – beans, spinach and carrots – and home-made truffles round off your meal. Bedrooms are warm and homely, stacked with books, and bathrooms are spotless. Wander in three acres of garden, or majestic countryside – a path leads over Leck Fell to Barbondale. Ingleton waterfalls are also close. *Pets welcome in cottage suites.*

rooms	6: 3 doubles, 1 twin, 2 cottage suites.
price	From £96; singles from £75.
meals	Lunch £12.95. Dinner £29.
closed	23 December-9 January; Monday & Tuesday September-February. Groups all year by arrangement.
directions	M6, junc. 36, then A65 east. House on left, 2.5 miles after Kirkby Lonsdale.

Richard, Jean & Tamara Skelton

tel	01524 271187
fax	01524 272452
e-mail	hipping-hall@kirkby-lonsdale.com
web	www.dedicate.co.uk/hipping-hall

map 6　entry 46

Biggin Hall

Biggin-by-Hartington, Buxton, Derbyshire SK17 0DH

Biggin Hall, a 17th-century Grade II*-listed farmhouse, lies knee-deep in lovely countryside. A path from the house leads out past the geese hut and stables to fields, hills, woods, rivers and waterfalls. Not far away is the 1831 Cromford and High Peak Railway, one of the first in the world – now the preserve of cyclists and walkers. James, gently-spoken and humorous, knows his patch of England well and will guide you to its many secrets. He came here 26 years ago and started his labour of love, the restoration of Biggin Hall, keeping its fine old character – stone-flagged floors, old beams, the original fireplace, mullioned windows and leaded lights – while adding contemporary comforts. The bedrooms in the old house have bags of character and there's also a pretty dining room for good, wholesome, home-cooked English food. The view through its big window is a seamless transition from garden to paddock, then country beyond. Not surprising that guests go away gleamingly happy. *Children over 11 welcome. Pets by arrangement.*

rooms	20: 16 twin/doubles, 1 single, 3 suites.
price	£84–£104; singles £55; suite £104–£124. In annexe £60–£90.
meals	Continental breakfast included; full English £3.80. Dinner, 4 courses, £15.50. Tea & packed lunch.
closed	Never.
directions	From Ashbourne, A515 for Buxton, then left, signed to Biggin. Entrance on right in village just after Waterloo pub.

James Moffett

tel	01298 84451
fax	01298 84681
e-mail	enquiries@bigginhall.co.uk
web	www.bigginhall.co.uk

Riber Hall

Matlock, Derbyshire DE4 5JU

Alex is wonderfully 'old school', very much his own man, and has run this 14th-century Elizabethan manor house for 30 years with one foot firmly in the past. Fires gently smoulder all year in the sitting room and dining room, giving the grandeur of Riber a warm intimacy. Bedrooms are great fun; most have antique four-posters, timber-framed walls, beams, mullioned windows, thick fabrics, good furniture. All have spoiling touches that pamper you rotten: beds turned down discreetly, super bathrooms with Royal Spa toiletries, umbrellas, fresh fruit and home-made shortbread. There's a secret conservatory full of colour and scent, and a walled orchard garden with long views for those seeking pure tranquillity – look out for the grafted 180-year-old weeping copper beech that lets you walk under its stunning canopy. The food has won many awards and the cellar is stocked with some of the best wine in Britain. Alex is a gentle, engaging host, who speaks with passion about Spain, wine and the 37 species of bird that live in the garden. Chatsworth House is close by. Darley Dale, one of the best views in Derbyshire, is even closer... five minutes on foot. *Children over 10 welcome.*

rooms	14: 3 doubles, 2 twins, 9 four-posters.
price	£136–£182; singles £101–£116.
meals	Continental breakfast included; full English £8. Lunch from £13. Dinner, 2 courses, £29.75; 3 courses £35.75.
closed	Never.
directions	From Matlock, A615 to Tansley, turn at Royal Oak into Alders Lane. Wind up hill for 1 mile to hotel.

	Alex Biggin
tel	01629 582795
fax	01629 580475
e-mail	info@riber-hall.co.uk
web	www.riber-hall.co.uk

map 7   entry 48

Kingston House

Staverton, Nr. Totnes, Devon TQ9 6AR

It's hard to know where to begin describing this stupendous house – the history in one bathroom alone would fill a small book. "It's like visiting a National Trust home where you can get into bed," offers Elizabeth, your gentle and erudite host. Set in a flawless Devon valley, Kingston is one of the finest surviving examples of early 18th-century architecture left in England. Arrive down a long country lane that rises and falls, increasing your expectations; at the brow of the last hill, the house comes into view, utterly majestic, demanding your attention – as do the Great Danes that come to greet you. Completed in 1735 for a wealthy wool merchant, many original features remain, including the 24 chimneys. The craftsman who carved the marble hallway would later work on the White House in Washington DC; the marquetry staircase is the best example in Europe; and the magnificent bed in the Green Room has stood there since it was put up in 1830. There's a thunder-box loo, an Angel tester bed, a painted china closet, ancient wall paintings... you get the idea. The cooking is historic, too – devilled kidneys, syllabub and proper trifle. A genuine one-off and so welcoming.

rooms	3 doubles.
price	£130–£150; singles £85–£95.
meals	Dinner £32.50; 4 courses, £34.50.
closed	Christmas & New Year.
directions	From A38, A384 to Staverton; at Sea Trout Inn, left fork for Kingston; halfway up hill right fork; at top of hill, straight ahead at x-roads. Road goes up, then down to house; right to front of house.

Michael & Elizabeth Corfield

tel	01803 762235
fax	01803 762444
e-mail	info@kingston-estate.co.uk
web	www.kingston-estate.co.uk

Fingals

Dittisham, Dartmouth, Devon TQ6 0JA

Where else can one find this magic? Richard miraculously combines a rare *laissez-faire* management style with a passionate commitment to doing things well. He is ever-present without intruding, fun without being challenging, spontaneous without being demanding. This is his place, his style, his gesture of defiance to the rest of the hotel world. He does things his way, and most people love it. And he is backed by Sheila, whose kindness and perennial good nature are a constant source of wonder. The food is good, the meals around the big table memorable, the comfort indisputable. You may find children and dogs wandering freely, happy adults – certainly – and Sheila's ducks being marshalled home in the evening. The indoor pool beckons, and sauna and jacuzzi, ping-pong and croquet for all, perhaps tennis on the lawn and cosy conversation in the bar. But don't be misled, you can do peace and quiet here, too. Perfect for the open-hearted.

rooms	10: 8 doubles, 1 twin, 1 family. Also self-catering barn for 4.
price	£70-£125.
meals	Dinner £27.50.
closed	2 January-26 March.
directions	From Totnes, A381 south up hill, then left for Cornworthy & Ashprington. Right at x-roads, for Cornworthy, then right at ruined gatehouse, for Dittisham. Down steep hill, over bridge, hotel signed on right.

Richard Johnston

tel	01803 722398
fax	01803 722401
e-mail	richard@fingals.co.uk
web	www.fingals.co.uk

map 2　　entry 50

Barrington House

Mount Boone, Dartmouth, Devon TQ6 9HZ

General Eisenhower billeted here prior to the Normandy landings and one can only assume he left this lovely spot feeling rested and ready for the arduous task ahead. The south-facing garden overlooks the Dart estuary and has magnificent views across to Kingswear and out to sea past the castle. The house was originally built for a member of the Peake-Frean family, whose biscuit empire brought us the famous 'Nice' biscuit. More recently, Simon and Lizzie have created a fabulous place to stay in the colonial style. Smart, uncluttered rooms are a delightful mix of kilim rugs, wall hangings, grey slate, polished pine floors, huge modern sofas and a welcoming open fire; the dining room opens out onto the garden for afternoon tea, or lazy contemplation after breakfast. Big bedrooms have radiant yellow walls that absorb the light, and swish bathrooms full of luxurious extras; all have sea views. The Baldwins are a relaxed young couple full of good advice; the gentle river trip to Totnes sounds divine. *Self-catering penthouse sleeps six.*

rooms	3: 2 doubles, 1 twin.
price	£80-£95; singles from £50. Self-catering £350-£825 p.w.
meals	Packed lunch £5.50. Restaurants in Dartmouth.
closed	Never.
directions	Entering Dartmouth on A3122, turn right opp. top gate to Royal Naval College into Townstal Rd, then 1st left into Mount Boone. 3rd house on left, signed.

	Lizzie Baldwin
tel	01803 835545
fax	01803 835545
e-mail	enq@barrington-house.com
web	www.barrington-house.com

Hazelwood House

Loddiswell, Nr. Kingsbridge, Devon TQ7 4EB

Set amid 67 acres of woodland, meadows and orchards in an untamed river valley, Hazelwood House is no ordinary hotel. It is a place of exceptional peace and natural beauty, created more as a relaxed, unpretentious country house. It might not be for everyone, but those who like it, love it. Come through the front door, pass rows of books and paintings, and enter a world to revive the spirit. Chances are Daisy the dog will be there to roll over and greet you. Lectures and courses and evenings of music from classical to jazz play a big part – they have a knack of attracting the best – and all is carried off with a relaxed and friendly approach. Anabel and Gillian came here 12 years ago and the place has evolved ever since. They are involved with 'Through the Heart to Peace', a peace initiative started in 1993. The atmosphere outweighs any decorative shortfalls, the food is delicious and fully organic and they produce their own spring water. Cream tea on the veranda is wonderful, or roam past ancient rhododendrons and huge camellias to fields of wild flowers and grazing sheep. *Self-catering cottages also available.*

rooms	15: 1 twin, 1 twin/double; 8 twin/doubles, 2 singles, 3 family, sharing 4 bathrooms.
price	£50–£95; singles £35.25.
meals	Lunch from £8. Packed lunch £5–£8. Dinner £15–£18.
closed	Never.
directions	From Exeter, A38 south then A3121 south. Left onto B3196 south. At California Cross, 1st left after petrol station. After 0.75 miles, left for Hazelwood. Gates on right.

Janie Bowman, Gillian Kean & Anabel Watson

tel	01548 821232
fax	01548 821318

map 2   entry 52

The Henley

Folly Hill, Bigbury-on-Sea, Devon TQ7 4AR

The view from this Edwardian summer house is truly uplifting, a head-clearing vision of sand, sea and lush headland. The garden falls away gently, disappearing over a shallow cliff to an inviting expanse of golden sand and white surf – nothing jars the eye and a footpath leads the way down. The hotel entrance creates the second good impression: bold red walls lead to two sitting areas and a conservatory, all decorated with homely elegance. A dining room of Lloyd Loom chairs, pot plants, seagrass and candles sucks in the view to maximum effect; every table has its own special portion. Martyn cooks fresh, unpretentious food: one reviewer said the view and the food combined were enough to make him feel content with the world. Bedrooms are small and adequate; all have the view. Reach Burgh Island by a narrow causeway at low tide; by sea tractor at high tide. The beach is popular with surfers and sun-seekers. A friendly, informal retreat.

rooms	6 doubles.
price	£78-£88; singles £49-£54.
meals	Dinner £22.
closed	November-March.
directions	From A38, A3121 to Modbury, then B3392 to Bigbury-on-Sea. Hotel on left as road slopes down to sea.

Martyn Scarterfield & Petra Lampe

tel	01548 810240
fax	01548 810240
e-mail	enquiries@thehenleyhotel.co.uk
web	www.thehenleyhotel.co.uk

The Arundell Arms

Lifton, Devon PL16 0AA

A tiny interest in fishing would not go amiss – though the people here are so kind, they welcome anyone. Anne has been at the helm for 40 years – an MBE for services to tourism is richly deserved – while chef Philip Burgess has been here for half that time. This is a *very* settled hotel, with Mrs VB, as staff call her fondly, quietly presiding over all: during a superb lunch with our inspector – St Enodoc asparagus, scallops and home-made chocs – she asked after an 80th birthday party, ensuring their day was memorable. Over the years, the hotel has resuscitated buildings at the heart of the village: the old police station and magistrates court is a pub, the old school a conference centre. Pride of place is the funnel-roofed cock-fighting pit, one of only two left in England and now the rod room where novice and hardy fisherfolk alike begin salmon and trout fishing courses; spy otter and kingfisher on 20 miles of their own water on the Tamar and five tributaries. No surprise it's the best fishing hotel in England – Anne's late husband wrote about fly-fishing for *The Times*; Ambrosia rice started life just down the road, too.

rooms	27: 8 doubles, 11 twins, 7 singles, 1 suite.
price	£93–£120; singles from £46.50. Half-board from £73 p.p.
meals	Bar meals £4–£15. Dinner £31; à la carte, about £37.
closed	Christmas.
directions	A30 south-west from Exeter, past Okehampton. Lifton is 0.5 miles off A30, 3 miles east of Launceston and signed. Hotel in centre of village.

Anne Voss-Bark

tel	01566 784666
fax	01566 784494
e-mail	reservations@arundellarms.com
web	www.arundellarms.com

 map 2   entry 54

Lewtrenchard Manor

Lewdown, Nr. Okehampton, Devon EX20 4PN

A thrilling, historical pastiche set in a Tudor mansion, outstanding in every way, only Edwardian radiators belie the fact you're not in 16th-century England. Entering the hall, your senses just explode with the magnificence of it all... you almost expect to be set upon by hounds. Nothing so ill is in store, however. Sue and James are the perfect counterbalance to the formality of their home, ever so charming and willing to explain the house's rich past. Most of what you see was put together in the late 1800s by the Reverend Sabine Baring-Gould, author of *Onward Christian Soldiers*. He was an avid collector of ornamental wooden friezes – the ones in the dining room are extraordinary – but he left no record of where they came from. One fabulous room follows another until you reach the 1602 gallery, with the salvaged, honeycombed, plaster-moulded ceiling, grand piano and 1725 Bible – one of the most beautiful rooms you will see through this book. Bedrooms are exemplary, too, and tremendous value for money; one has Queen Henrietta Maria's four-poster. The gardens are outstanding, as is sixth-century St Petroc's church next door. Unmissable.

rooms	9: 2 doubles, 4 twin/king, 2 four-posters, 1 suite.
price	£130–£195; singles from £100.
meals	Lunch £10–£15. Sunday lunch £19.50. Dinner £35; booking essential.
closed	Never.
directions	From Exeter, exit A30 for A386. At T-junc., right, then 1st left, for Lewdown. After 6 miles, left for Lewtrenchard. House signed left after 0.75 miles.

Sue & James Murray

tel	01566 783256
fax	01566 783332
e-mail	s&j@lewtrenchard.co.uk
web	www.lewtrenchard.co.uk

The Red Lion Hotel

The Quay, Clovelly, Bideford, Devon EX39 5TF

Clovelly has been spared time's march, partly because of its position – and partly because it is a tenanted estate. It is completely car-free. The houses perch like seagulls' nests on ledges cut into the cliff and many still have original cob walls of red earth and straw. A steep cobbled path snakes down to a small harbour. The Red Lion is right on the quayside, looking out across the Atlantic – you'll hear the sound of the sea from every room. It's an eccentric place, but pleasantly so, with laid-back staff and a friendly manager – Michael cuts a striking figure in this seafaring enclave, dressed impeccably in a suit whatever the weather. Smart bedrooms are up-to-date, thanks to a recent makeover; all have sea or harbour views. Wonderful seafood is delivered straight from the fishing boat to the kitchen. Travel out to Lundy Island, a wildlife sanctuary, or walk along Hobby Drive, a beautiful coastal walk laid out in the early 1800s. The late Christine Hamlyn, anointed 'Queen of Clovelly', restored many of the cottages and is still loved by villagers. There's nowhere quite like it. *The New Inn, in the village, has eight en suite rooms.*

rooms	11: 7 doubles, 2 twins, 2 family.
price	£85–£104; singles from £42.50. Half-board (min. 2 nights) £110–£144.50 p.p.
meals	Bar lunch from £3.25. Dinner £25.
closed	Never.
directions	From Bideford, A39 for Bude for 12 miles, right at r'bout, for Clovelly. Left fork before Visitor Centre, left at white rails down steep hill.

	John Rous
tel	01237 431237
fax	01237 431044
e-mail	redlion@clovelly.co.uk
web	www.clovelly.co.uk

map 2   entry 56

The Hoops Country Inn & Hotel

Horns Cross, Bideford, Devon EX39 5DL

Blissfully out of kilter with the outside world, entering Hoops Inn is like stepping into a timewarp. It's changed little in 800 years – there are just fewer smugglers rubbing shoulders with the local gentry at the bar these days. The lack of road signs to say you've arrived in this tiny hamlet – Hoops comes from 'hoopspink', the Devon word for bullfinch – adds to the splendid sense of disorientation. The signs were taken down to confuse an enemy invasion during the Second World War and never put back. The bar has a mellow tick-tock atmosphere, with lots of irregular beams, uneven floors, snug corners, low-hung doorways and blazing fires in winter; newspapers are there to browse over a pint. Above the bar, baroque-style bedrooms are magnificent; the four-poster beds were made from one massive oak bed that originally slept up to 20 people (sic). Pass a pretty courtyard – lovely for afternoon tea – to bedrooms in an old coachhouse. They're smaller but have the same luxurious period feel. Fresh fish, an ample vegetarian menu and the friendliest welcome makes this special indeed.

rooms	12: 4 doubles, 2 twin/doubles, 1 family, 1 twin, 3 four-posters, 1 suite.
price	£80–£140; singles £53–£85.
meals	Bar lunch from £8.50. Dinner £12–£18.
closed	Christmas Day.
directions	From Bideford, A39 towards Bude (North Devon coastal road) for 6 miles. Just past Horns Cross, road dips. Inn on right.

Gay Marriott

tel	01237 451222
fax	01237 451247
e-mail	sales@hoopsinn.co.uk
web	www.hoopsinn.co.uk

Halmpstone Manor

Bishop's Tawton, Barnstaple, Devon EX32 0EA

Charles and Jane are preserving a long tradition of excellent farmhouse hospitality at Halmpstone that's gently at odds with the rough and tumble of the 21st century. In 1630, John Westcote described his stay here as "delightful" and the handsome Queen Anne manor you see today was completed in 1701, after fire destroyed much of the original house of 22 rooms in 1633. Its proportions remain delightful. Fresh flowers adorn every room, pink walls cheer, family photos beam from silver frames, china figures stand on parade... all is very traditional. Bedrooms in pink and peach are immaculate, with floral coronets, draped four-posters, a decanter of sherry, fresh fruit and more flowers. Afternoon tea is included, as are the newspapers. Dine by candlelight in the lovely panelled dining room. Jane's cooking has won heaps of awards: try Clovelly scallops, local lamb, and maybe a selection of north Devon cheeses. Charles was born here and has run the farm for much of his life. Both are 'hands-on' and welcoming. Halmpstone means 'Holy Boundary Stone' and the building faces south to Dartmoor. Walk in the pretty garden, or stray further.

rooms	5: 3 twin/doubles, 2 four-posters.
price	£100–£140; singles £70.
meals	Dinner, 5 courses, £25.
closed	Christmas & New Year, & February.
directions	From Barnstaple, south on A377. Left opposite petrol station, after Bishop's Tawton, signed Cobbaton and Chittlehampton. After 2 miles, turn right. House on left after 200 yds.

Jane & Charles Stanbury

tel	01271 830321
fax	01271 830826
e–mail	charles@halmpstonemanor.co.uk
web	www.halmpstonemanor.co.uk

map 2   entry 58

Broomhill Art Hotel & Sculpture Gardens

Muddiford, Devon EX31 4EX

This is real devotion to art in a raw, relaxed and unpretentious setting. Rinus bought his first piece at the age of 17 and hasn't been able to stop since – he's now a young-looking 40-something. He and Aniet had a gallery in Holland, but after falling in love with Devon, decided to ship the contents over here. Now you'll find 150 pieces of contemporary sculpture in their wild garden, eight international exhibitions a year in the hotel, live jazz the first Friday of each month, a ceramics shop and a programme of events that includes be-bop, lectures and poetry... if it comes along, they put it on. Every piece of art is original, including some in the bedrooms, and the range is wide – classical, abstract, conceptual. As you'd expect, there are no airs and graces (leave your pearls at home), the atmosphere is completely informal, the food generous, and the wine flows. Bedrooms are simple, warm and comfortable; you might find the odd wobbly shower head, but in the midst of all this inspirational art, it pales into insignificance. A unique experience.

rooms	5: 4 twin/doubles, 1 four-poster.
price	£55-£65; singles £35-£45.
meals	Lunch from £5. Dinner, 2 courses, £16.
closed	20 December-mid-January. Restaurant closed Sunday & Monday evening.
directions	From Barnstable, A39 north towards Lynton, then left onto B3230, following brown signs to Sculpture Gardens and hotel.

Rinus & Aniet Van de Sande

tel	01271 850262
fax	01271 850575
e-mail	info@broomhillart.co.uk
web	www.broomhillart.co.uk

The Old Rectory Hotel

Martinhoe, Exmoor National Park, Devon EX31 4QT

As you quietly succumb to the wonderful sense of spiritual calm here, it's hard to conceive that one field away the land skids to a halt and spectacular cliffs drop 800 feet. The Exmoor plateau meets the sea abruptly at the village of Martinhoe – 'hoe' is Saxon for high ground – creating a breathtaking view as you approach. This lovely understated hotel stands next to an 11th-century church in three acres of mature garden. Loved and nurtured by clergy past, the garden now occupies the affection of Christopher and Enid: birdsong, waterfalls, scented azaleas and the bizarre gunnera only hint at its allure. This is a gentle retreat, dedicated to food and marvellous hospitality. Enid has been cooking since she was a child and makes most things mouth-wateringly well... even the water from a nearby bore hole tastes good; so good, guests take it away by the litre. Traditional bedrooms have Laura Ashley wallpaper and the odd Waring & Gillow antique; one has a balcony. Downstairs, curl up in comfy sofas by an open fire, or drift off in the conservatory; grapes from the 200-year-old vine above your head fill fruit bowls in season. *2 self-catering cottages, sleep 4-6.*

rooms	8: 4 doubles, 2 twins, 2 twin/doubles.
price	£104; singles £67. Half-board plus afternoon tea £79 p.p.
meals	Dinner, 5 courses, £28.50.
closed	November–February.
directions	A39 towards Lynton, by-passing Parracombe, then left after about 3 miles, signed Martinhoe. Across common, left into village, entrance 1st on right by church.

Christopher & Enid Richmond

tel	01598 763368
fax	01598 763567
e-mail	reception@oldrectoryhotel.co.uk
web	www.oldrectoryhotel.co.uk

map 2   entry 60

The Rising Sun Hotel

Harbourside, Lynmouth, Devon EX35 6EG

A head-ducking, boat-bobbing place with an entirely unexpected level of luxury. As the tide rises, so do the boats in the tiny harbour just across the road, creating a sensation of mobility as you idle in bed under Jane Churchill fabric. The Rising Sun strides modestly through much of the village, absorbing a string of ancient houses, with low beams made from reclaimed timber, twisting spaces, thoughtfully padded doorways for taller folk and probably the narrowest staircase in the world. A local shipwright tenderly carved the panels in the snug dining room, where the atmosphere is as delicious as the food. Design and fabric freaks can drop names to each other: Gaston y Daniela, Monkwell, Colefax & Fowler, Farrow & Ball, Telenzo – all applied with verve and superb effect. It's not pretentious, just honest good taste in small but perfect rooms. Throw open the doors of a balconied lounge and enjoy afternoon tea, with the sun streaming in and a gentle sea breeze on your face. Make time to explore this interesting little village. Walkers can head straight up the valley into good hill country.

rooms	16: 12 doubles, 1 twin, 2 singles, 1 cottage suite.
price	£94–£146; singles £66. Half-board £74.50–£102.50 p.p.
meals	Dinner about £27.50.
closed	Never.
directions	From A39 into town centre, follow sign to harbour. Hotel overlooks harbour at the end on the left.

David Yoxall & Steve Lundy

tel	01598 753223
fax	01598 753480
e-mail	risingsunlynmouth@easynet.co.uk
web	www.risingsunlynmouth.co.uk

Northcote Manor

Burrington, Umberleigh, Devon EX37 9LZ

As it was for the monks who came here to spend their last days in the 15th century, Northcote remains a haven from the bedlam of life. The setting is magical, reached by a long driveway that climbs lazily through woodland. The hotel is surrounded by 20 acres of lawn and garden and dreamy views that stretch across the soft, yielding countryside of the Taw River Valley. All is deliriously peaceful; beautiful specimen trees, sweet birdsong and the faint smell of wood smoke on the breeze. The older half of the building was completed in 1716, the rest was added in the Victorian era – you enter by the later part through a studded oak door to an open hallway with lilies, newspapers and an open fire which welcomes all year. Stairs lead to bedrooms in matching fabrics; no surprises but all is smart. Karen manages with genuine care, while husband Chris stars in the kitchen. The formal dining room is in the oldest part, down carpeted steps; hand-painted murals on the wall bathe one corner in a warm, pinky glow – they depict times past, present and future here. We can but look forward to the advent of flying monks shown in one; in the meantime, let your spirits soar.

rooms	11: 4 doubles, 1 twin/double, 1 twin, 1 four-poster, 4 suites.
price	£132-£220; singles from £80. Half-board (min. 2 nights) from £75 p.p.
meals	Dinner £35.
closed	Never.
directions	M5, junc. 27, A361 to South Molton. Fork left onto B3227, then right on A377 for Barnstaple. Entrance 6 miles on left, signed (ignore signs to Burrington village).

David & Marian Boddy

tel	01769 560501
fax	01769 560770
e-mail	rest@northcotemanor.co.uk
web	www.northcotemanor.co.uk

map 2   entry 62

Bark House Hotel

Oakfordbridge, Nr. Bampton, Devon EX16 9HZ

Alastair left the family business to become a hotelier, trained at all the best places, then searched high and low for the right place to call his own. He found it in a wooded valley scored by the River Exe and taught himself to cook, winning plaudits almost immediately. The day we visited, he was orchestrating an overhaul of the garden; nothing, it seems, is beyond his grasp. The house is quietly stylish, not grand, but soothing – look in vain for signs of bad taste – with cosily low ceilings, a basket of logs by the fire, newspapers and magazines on tables, and rooms that suck in the daylight. In the evening, flickering candles, fresh flowers and fine linen transform the restaurant ready for Alastair's excellent cooking. Upstairs, bedrooms are simple, spotless and perfectly comfortable, with flowers from the garden and the odd piece of oak furniture; one room has a beautiful, curved, bay window. The service is superb: morning tea is brought to your room and breakfast is a feast of yogurt with flaked almonds, fresh juice, fruit and porridge. There's Mike, too, handy-man, porter and waiter – it's that sort of place.

rooms	5: 2 doubles, 2 twin/doubles; 1 double, with private bath.
price	£79–£110; singles £45–£55. Half-board from £66 p.p.
meals	Dinner £26.50.
closed	Monday & Tuesday.
directions	From Tiverton, A396 north towards Minehead. Hotel on right, 1 mile north of junction with B3227.

Alastair Kameen & Justine Hill

tel 01398 351236

The Masons Arms Inn

Knowstone, South Molton, Devon EX36 4RY

Knowstone is a funny old place with a folksy old pub, a friendly old landlord and a fabulous "one-bedroomed hotel" up the road – perhaps it's the 65 inches of rain that fall each year? Arrive through fern, or twisting lane, to this thatched 13th-century inn, wood piled up outside, windows a warm orange glow, welcoming you in. The dimly lit, flagstoned bar, with inglenook and elaborately-cast fireplace, congregates with locals in the evening – leather straps attached to ancient ceiling beams give valuable support as the night wears on. Down some worn, stone steps, the atmosphere changes to one of a smart pub restaurant, with a jumble of old, wooden tables and chairs lit by candles – the food is superb. Tables spill into a new extension with uninterrupted views of Exmoor starting its windswept ascent a few fields away. Behind the bar, Paul watches over all, smartly turned out in a bow tie, a mix of *bon viveur* and parental landlord. This showman has been buying and selling pubs for years – he claims this is the last! You stay in a fully-equipped cottage a short stroll away: bath in bedroom, fire in hearth, and breakfast in the fridge – what else do you need?

rooms	1 cottage, sleeps 2.
price	£60; singles £35.
meals	Breakfast in fridge to cook yourself. Lunch £4.50–£10. Dinner, à la carte, about £20.
closed	Kitchen closed over Christmas.
directions	M5, junc. 27. A361 past Tiverton for Barnstaple. After about 20 miles, pub signed right. Follow signs to village. Pub opp. church. Cottage 100 yds away.

Paul & Jo Stretton-Downes

tel	01398 341231
e-mail	masonsarmsinn@aol.com
web	www.masonsarmsinn.com

map 2   entry 64

Huntsham Court

Huntsham, Nr. Bampton, Devon EX16 7NA

Two pianos in your bedroom and a fireplace primed for combustion – such may be your lot if you draw the short straw. The whole place has a rare aura of originality. As you enter you may wonder at the lack of staff to greet you, but they are there somewhere – solicitous, informal and competent. You are likely to find music filling the great hall, a fire roaring in the hearth, perhaps the clacking of billiard balls in the distance. Or, if you are late, the dinner party will be in full swing around the long, damask-adorned table: it seats 30 and you eat traditionally (four courses, more often than not) and well. Later still and there may be games in the drawing room. But I don't want to give the impression of formality; far from it. This is one of the most easy-going and unpretentious hotels in the country, one that combines good taste, irony (viz. the 50s furniture and odds and ends), all in a surprisingly grandiose setting. It may be a touch faded in places, definitely not deluxe in others, but the mood is priceless. A great place for a private party.

rooms	14: 11 twin/doubles, 3 family.
price	£130–£150.
meals	Dinner £38.
closed	Never.
directions	M5, junc. 27, to Sampford Peverell. Sharp right on bridge to Uplowman, then straight on for 4 miles to Huntsham.

Mogens & Andrea Bolwig

tel	01398 361365
fax	01398 361456
e-mail	andrea@huntshamcourt.co.uk
web	www.huntshamcourt.co.uk

Kings Arms

Stockland, Nr. Honiton, Devon EX14 9BS

Stay for a week and you'll almost be a fully-fledged local, a member of the skittles team, an expert in line-dancing and probably a tambourine player for the folk club. You'll also be a stone or two heavier with seemingly endless menus, masses of fish, locally-reared game and even ostrich. Ramble at will past crackling fires, beams, gilt-framed mirrors, stone walls, cosy low ceilings and, eventually, the stone-flagged Farmer's Bar where you meet the "fair-minded, fun-loving locals" – one comes from as far as Birmingham to take his place at the bar; they'll have you playing darts in no time. As for Paul, "he's a tyrant to work for," said one of his staff with an enormous smile on his face. Bedrooms are just what you'd hope for: not grand, but perfectly traditional, with maybe a walnut bed or a cushioned window seat. Lose yourself in the Blackdown Hills or simply laze around inside with Princess Ida, the cat. If you like inns, stay here.

rooms	3: 2 doubles, 1 twin.
price	£50; singles £30.
meals	Lunch from £4. Dinner from £15.50.
closed	Christmas Day.
directions	From centre of Honiton, head north-east out of town. Stockland signed right just before junction with A30. Straight ahead for 6 miles to village.

Paul Diviani, John O'Leary & Heinz Kiefer

tel	01404 881361
fax	01404 881732
e-mail	reserve@kingsarms.net
web	www.kingsarms.net

map 2   entry 66

Combe House Hotel & Restaurant

Honiton, Nr. Exeter, Devon EX14 3AD

If the spirit of Combe House could be bottled and sprinkled over the world, good would surely come of it. As it is, Ruth and Ken have distilled their own worldly experience to create a sublime place to stay. Globe-trotting careers have seen them put Australia's Hunter Valley on the map and Ken cook in the Antarctic for three years. But what makes here so special is the modest way they apply themselves to each task, big or small. Their latest project has been the faithful restoration of a Georgian kitchen – for the first time in 50 years, a pendulum clock chimes on the hour at the top of the house. Throw a party here and try the best Devon produce, local as can be, (and maybe Victorian whim-wham trifle), with the chef finishing your main course on the huge, restored wood-burning range. The rest of the house is just as fabulous – meet history at every turn as Saxon, Elizabethan and Restoration eras meld into one: mullioned windows, oak panelling, ancestral portraits – not theirs! – luxurious bedrooms and trompe l'œil murals. All this on 3,500 acres with a "lost" arboretum. The long, wooded lane that brings you here will unravel all. Superb.

rooms	15: 12 twin/doubles, 1 four-poster, 2 suites.
price	£138–£190; suites £265; singles from £99. Half-board from £92 p.p.
meals	Lunch £15; 3 courses, £19. Dinner £32.50. Parties in Georgian kitchen, 4 courses, £38 p.p. plus room hire.
closed	Never.
directions	A30 south from Honiton for 2 miles; A375 for Sidmouth & Branscombe. Signed through woods.

Ruth & Ken Hunt

tel	01404 540400
fax	01404 46004
e-mail	stay@thishotel.com
web	www.thishotel.com

Alias Hotel Barcelona

Magdalen Street, Exeter, Devon EX2 4HY

This extraordinary place reinvents the British hotel experience. Alias Hotel Barcelona belongs to an exciting new breed which uses fresh design and classic memorabilia to put folk up in affordable style — without losing its sense of humour in the process. Barcelona is the brainchild of hotel visionary Nigel Chapman. Here, he has taken a former Victorian eye infirmary and turned it into a psychedelic ark of shape and colour that heals all the senses, even the most jaded. Nothing says 'Barcelona' directly, except the odd Jujol-inspired handrail and bedroom doors taken from Gaudi's Casa Mila. More, it's the vibrant buzz of the Catalan capital that's arrived in this terribly English city. There is so much to see that it is hard even to scratch the surface. The stunning collection of 50s and 60s furniture in the lobby, Café Paradiso with its rainbow-

coloured mural and authentic Naples pizza oven, the Kino cabaret club performing every weekend and elegant bedrooms that curve, angle and slope. Go see for yourself. *¡Arriva! ¡Arriva!*

rooms	46: 20 doubles/twins, 19 doubles, 7 singles.
price	£85–£105; singles £75.
meals	Continental breakfast included; full English £10.50. Lunch £12. Dinner £22.25.
closed	Never.
directions	M5, junc. 30, A379 for Exeter, then 3rd exit at Countess Wear r'bout, signed City Centre, for 2 miles to main traffic junc. Keep in right lane into Magdalen St. Hotel on right.

Fiona Dollan

tel	01392 281000
fax	01392 281001
e-mail	info@hotelbarcelona-uk.com
web	www.hotelbarcelona-uk.com

map 2   entry 68

Lord Bute Hotel

Lymington Road, Christchurch, Highcliffe, Dorset BH23 4JS

Lord Bute may have been an unpopular prime minister but this eponymous hotel restaurant is making amends... you need to book well in advance to eat excellent, locally-sourced food here – even Rick Stein recommends their Milford fishmonger. The new owners left their Special B&B to turn their tested talents to a bigger project. Actor Gary plans theatrical evenings, Simon has designs on the small garden where Far Eastern pieces and terracotta pots take pride of place. Black and white tiling, a Jacobean reception desk, elegant new chairs and blinds in the slim, sunny orangery, and deep sofas in the guest sitting room – this is all about classy comfort and having a good time. The restaurant remains traditionally smart – the grand piano is played each evening – with some stylish extras: mirrors and swathes of fabric. Good value bedrooms with reproduction mahogany furniture, muted colours and double-glazing to shield from road noise at the front. The totally tiled bathrooms are equally spotless and well-equipped. Take the path down to the beach behind next-door Highcliffe Castle, or fly to New York from nearby Hurn airport.

rooms	10 double/twins.
price	From £80; singles from £60.
meals	Dinner £25.95.
closed	Never.
directions	From Christchurch, A337 towards Lymington to Highcliffe. Hotel 200 yds past castle.

Gary Payne & Simon Box

tel	01425 278884
fax	01425 279258

Mortons House Hotel

Corfe Castle, Wareham, Dorset BH20 5EE

One day, the old railway will reach Wareham and collect you from your London train. Meanwhile, just enjoy the passing steam from the terrace of this wonderful 1590 manor house – the station is just below. Mortons was built from Purbeck stone in the shape of an 'E' to honour Queen Elizabeth I and overlooks the ruins of famous Corfe Castle. Bit by bit, these hugely enthusiastic owners are uplifting the whole hotel after rescuing it from dereliction. They've initiated a complete overhaul, signed up an award-winning chef and the garden is under review. Traditional bedrooms make good use of four-posters, 'hotel' furniture is being slowly replaced: one suite has its own private staircase and the finest views, another a fine four-poster and stone fireplace. What makes this place special is the unwavering friendliness of mostly local staff. Spend a wintry evening before a log fire among the oak panelling, or strike out along the coast in summer – the headlands and beaches are so clearly formed, they're used to teach coastal erosion to schoolchildren. The village is protected and perfect, the old 'capital' of the Isle of Purbeck… you've even a sunny micro-climate.

rooms	17: 11 doubles, 3 twins, 3 suites.
price	£118–£190; singles £75–£120. Half-board, 3 nights, £128–£148 p.p.
meals	Lunch £15. Dinner, 5 courses, £29.50. Bar meals from £7.50.
closed	Never.
directions	From Wareham, A351 to Corfe Castle. Hotel on left 50 yds from market square.

Andy & Ally Hageman, Ted & Beverly Clayton

tel	01929 480988
fax	01929 480820
e-mail	stay@mortonshouse.co.uk
web	www.mortonshouse.co.uk

map 3   entry 70

Innsacre Farmhouse

Shipton Gorge, Nr. Bridport, Dorset DT6 4LJ

This is a perfect place in 10 acres of orchard, valley and wooded hills, elegant without pretension and wrapped up in peace and quiet. Inside, 17th-century stone walls, low-beamed ceilings and warm French flair. Behind it all are Sydney and Jayne, two easy-going francophiles who share a gift for unwinding city-stressed souls. Come to relax – fine bedrooms with antique French beds, bold colours and crisp linen sheets will help unravel the tightest knot. There's a bar in the sitting room – Sydney is keen on his wines, knowledgeable too – piled high with books, with an open fire and soft, deep chairs to sink into. In summer, spill out onto the large terrace with your pre-dinner drink and watch the setting sun. The orchard is heavy, in season, with plums, apples and figs that Jayne turns into compotes – have them at breakfast along with cured ham sausages and American-style pancakes. Walk the fields and you may bump into the Jacob sheep – you can buy their undyed wool – or keep going and head for cliff walks, beaches and the Dorset Coastal Path... so rejuvenating.

rooms	4: 3 doubles, 1 twin.
price	£70–£85; singles from £55.
meals	Dinner £18.50. Late arrival supper £15.50.
closed	24 December–2 January.
directions	From Dorchester, A35 for Bridport for 13 miles, then left on 2nd road for Shipton Gorge & Burton Bradstock. Follow 1st driveway on left up to farmhouse.

Sydney & Jayne Davies

tel	01308 456137
fax	01308 456137

Bridge House Hotel

3 Prout Bridge, Beaminster, Dorset DT8 3AY

There is much here to make one happy – good food, award-winning hospitality and the inestimable beauty of Hardy country. At the heart of Bridge House is the food – traditional and as local as possible, and probably not for slimmers. You eat in the panelled, Georgian dining room, with a fine Adam fireplace and the palest of pink linen. The bedrooms, too, are solidly traditional, with padded headboards, floral duvet covers and curtains – no surprises but stacks of space. Peter is very much the convivial host; his good natured professionalism has won him many accolades and rightly so. The Pinksters have a gift for inspiring loyalty: their staff are local, they enjoy their work and they stay. The history of this ancient building gives it a sense of dignity and solidity as well; an Ancient Monument first, probably a 13th-century priest's house next, a dwelling house in the Tudor period which explains the variety of mullioned windows; later eras saw the creation of a priest's hole. Beaminster is a pretty village not far from the south coast and there's llama trekking nearby if you crave a little adventure.

rooms	14: 3 doubles, 9 double/twins, 1 single, 1 family.
price	£102-£130; singles £54-£93. Half-board (min. 2 nights) from £75 p.p.
meals	Lunch £11. Dinner, 4 courses, £29.50.
closed	Never.
directions	From Yeovil, A30 west, then A3066, signed Bridport, for 10 miles to Beaminster. Hotel at far end of village, as road bends to right.

	Peter Pinkster
tel	01308 862200
fax	01308 863700
e-mail	enquiries@bridge-house.co.uk
web	www.bridge-house.co.uk

map 2　entry 72

The Fox Inn

Corscombe, Nr. Dorchester, Dorset DT2 0NS

Martyn was master of a nearby hunt before he became landlord of the Fox. It's a nice little irony not lost on the ex-Army man, who's turned this 17th-century thatched inn into one of the most sought-after places to stay and eat in the south of England. Hospitality is first rate, food excellent and the setting is Hardy's Wessex at its most peaceful and beautiful. In days of yore, drovers on the way to market would wash their sheep in the stream opposite and stop for a pint of cider; the inn only received a full licence 40 years ago. Martyn and Susie are a delightful, stylish and amusing couple. They've kept the old feel of the inn, with clever additions like a slate-topped bar, a flower-filled conservatory with benches and a long table made from a single oak blown down during the storms of 1987. You're surrounded by eye-pleasing detail: stuffed owls in glass cases, blue gingham tablecloths, paintings, flowers, antlers, flagstones and fires in winter. Bedrooms have simple country charm with floral and mahogany touches; one in a converted loft is reached by stone steps. Special, indeed, and the sea isn't far, either.

rooms	4: 3 doubles, 1 twin.
price	£80–£100; singles £55–£75.
meals	Dinner, à la carte, about £20.
closed	Christmas Day.
directions	From Yeovil, A37 for Dorchester for 1 mile, then right, for Corscombe, for 5.5 miles. Inn on left on outskirts of village. Use kitchen door to left of main entrance if arriving before 7pm.

Susie & Martyn Lee

tel	01935 891330
fax	01935 891330
e-mail	dine@fox-inn.co.uk
web	www.fox-inn.co.uk

The Acorn Inn

Evershot, Dorchester, Dorset DT2 0JW

Thomas Hardy called this 400-year-old inn The Sow and Acorn and let Tess rest a night here; had he visited today; he might have let her stay longer. Martyn and Susie — as local as Hardy's literature — have balanced tradition with contemporary zing. The Acorn is almost two pubs in one: as much a place for locals to sup their ale as for foodies to sample some of the best food in Dorset — you're free to mix. The locals' bar still represents the heart of village life; black and white photographs of villagers cover the walls as stories are swapped by an open fire. Walk through to the dining room and the atmosphere suddenly changes to rural country house, with smartly-laid tables, warm yellows, terracotta tiles, soft lighting and elegant hamstone fireplaces — it's here the food is taken seriously, especially fresh local fish. Bedrooms creak with age *and* style: painted shutters, a bay window, a glimpse of the pub sign, uneven floors and beautiful drapes that soften dark oak four-posters — all work well together. Unspoilt Evershot, ancient woodland and rolling countryside provide ample walks. Hardy would approve.

rooms	9: 3 doubles, 3 twins, 3 four-posters.
price	£80–£120; singles £60–£80.
meals	Lunch from £3.75. Dinner, à la carte, about £20.
closed	Never.
directions	Evershot 1 mile off A37 midway between Yeovil and Dorchester.

Susie & Martyn Lee

tel	01935 83228
fax	01935 83707
e-mail	stay@acorn-inn.co.uk
web	www.acorn-inn.co.uk

Plumber Manor

Sturminster Newton, Dorset DT10 2AF

Best of all at Plumber is the family triumvirate of Brian in the kitchen, Richard behind the bar cracking jokes and Alison, who is simply everywhere. They know exactly how to make you feel at home. This has been *their* family home for 300 years, though ancestors have lived "in the area" since they arrived with William the Conquerer. Outside, there's a large, sloping lawn, a white bridge over the river and deckchairs scattered about the well-manicured garden. Inside, the house remains more home than hotel with huge family portraits crammed on the walls; everything in this house seems to be *big*. The atmosphere is relaxed and informal without a trace of pomposity. Stay in the main house if you can; bedrooms have had a recent makeover with fresh colours and fabrics, similar to those in the converted stables which are bigger but have less character. The stone path between the two came from a local river bed, and kept one guest amused for hours looking for dinosaur fossils... The enormous old sofa on the landing maybe the most uncomfortable ever made – but this is the *only* discomfort you'll find. The rest is irresistable. *Pets by arrangement.*

rooms	16: 2 doubles, 13 twin/doubles; 1 twin/double, with private bath.
price	£100–£155; singles from £85.
meals	Dinner £19–£24.50.
closed	February.
directions	From Sturminster Newton, follow signs to hotel and Hazlebury Bryan for 2 miles. Entrance on left, signed.

Richard, Alison & Brian Prideaux-Brune

tel	01258 472507
fax	01258 473370
e-mail	book@plumbermanor.com
web	www.plumbermanor.com

The Museum Inn

Farnham, Nr. Blandford Forum, Dorset DT11 8DE

This delightful part-thatched 17th-century inn owes its name to General Augustus Lane Fox Pitt Rivers, the 'father of archaeology'; it fed and bed folk who came to see his museum in the 1800s. He opened three museums in all to house his fabulous collection; only the Pitt Rivers Museum in Oxford survives today. No sign either of the yaks and zebu that the General once released into a nearby pleasure park. What you will discover is one of the best inns in the south of England. Vicky and Mark work well together to create a wonderfully warm and friendly place to stay: she does bubbly, he does laid-back. The smart refit has a lovely period feel, with flagstones, inglenook, fresh flowers and a mismatch of wooden tables and chairs. Leading from the restaurant is a gorgeous drawing room, with lots of books. Bright, comfortable bedrooms upstairs have antique beds and lots of prints; all are impeccably done. Chef Mark Treasure is as good as his name suggests, and sure to win more accolades for his imaginative cooking. Farnham is a pretty thatched idyll in the heart of Cranborne Chase: ideal for walks and horses.

rooms	8 doubles.
price	£75–£120; single occ. £65.
meals	Light lunch from £3.95. Dinner, à la carte, about £24.
closed	Christmas Day & New Year's Eve.
directions	From Blandford, A354 for Salisbury for 6.5 miles, then left, signed Farnham. Inn on left in village.

Vicky Elliot & Mark Stephenson

tel	01725 516261
fax	01725 516988
e-mail	AstorMuseumInn@aol.com
web	www.museuminn.com

map 3   entry 76

Rose and Crown

Romaldkirk, Barnard Castle, Durham DL12 9EB

Few country inns match one's expectations as well as the Rose and Crown. Built in the 1750s when Captain Bligh, Romaldkirk's famous son, was still a young sprite, this dreamy inn is superbly comfortable, gently informal and utterly unpretentious. In the small locals' bar, sit at settles and read the *Stockton Times*, or the *Teesdale Mercury*, warmed by an open fire, while a few trophies peer down. A shiny brass door latch reveals more: an elegant lounge where a grandfather clock sets a restful pace, and a bright, panelled dining room for more formal fare and breakfast; food is excellent and fantastic value. Bedrooms are vibrant, with slanting eaves, window seats, fun colours and the reassuring smell of proper furniture polish. Rooms in a nearby annexe suit walkers and pet owners. Outside, a village green, with church and unblemished stone cottages, opens onto countryside as good as any in Britain. Alison and Christopher are easy-going perfectionists – their hard work has made this the place to stay, the place to eat... a perfect antidote to England's fickle clime.

rooms	12: 5 doubles, 5 twins, 2 suites.
price	£90–£110; singles £65.
meals	Bar meals £5–£11. Dinner, 4 courses, £25.
closed	Christmas.
directions	From Barnard Castle, B6277 north for 6 miles. Right in village towards green. Inn on left.

Christopher & Alison Davy

tel	01833 650213
fax	01833 650828
e-mail	hotel@rose-and-crown.co.uk
web	www.rose-and-crown.co.uk

Seaham Hall Hotel

Lord Bryon's Walk, Seaham, Durham SR7 7AG

Seaham Hall is designed to make you feel *you* own the place – and we bet you never feel so spoiled. Perhaps the most remarkable thing about this ever so modern hotel is there are so few rooms for such a large building. Texture, shape and electronic gadgets knit together to create a stunning series of set-piece designs; every bedroom is separated from the world by two thick oak doors, and every bath fits two. The building was once a heart hospital; it was also where Lord Byron was married. You feel enormously good here. Get lost and cosy with a newspaper in the huge drawing room – the ceiling feels several double decker buses high. Tall French windows open onto a wide and formal garden terrace with stone steps leading to the bleak and beautiful north-east coast. The owner is a great patron of the arts; sculptures and paintings are added all the time. Pride of place goes to Charybdis, a water sculpture by William Pye, outside the front entrance. The cone-shaped spa is arguably the best in the country, the food is exceptional – and why bother to get dressed when breakfast in bed is all part of the service... just relax.

rooms	19: 13 doubles, 5 suites, 1 penthouse.
price	£145–£195; singles £135–£185; suites £255–£500.
meals	Continental breakfast included; full English £7.50. Dinner £34, à la carte, £30–£40.
closed	Never.
directions	A1(M), junc. 62, A690 through Houghton le Spring, A19 south on to Seaham. At seafront, left on B1287 for 2 miles. On left.

Tom & Jocelyn Maxfield

tel	0191 516 1400
fax	0191 516 1410
e-mail	reservations@seaham-hall.com
web	www.seaham-hall.com

map 10   entry 78

The Bell Inn & Hill House

High Rd, Horndon-on-the-Hill, Essex SS17 8LD

Christine is an original fixture in this Great Inn of England – her parents ran the Bell for years and she was born in one of the upstairs rooms. John is also a key figure, much admired in the trade, as is Joanne, their loyal manager of 16 years – a recent industry award for hospitality proved what folk had known a long time. Christine's beautifully decorated suites upstairs are by far the best places to stay – they're named after famous mistresses: Lady Hamilton, Madame du Barry and Anne Boleyn, who's said to be buried in the local church. The other bedrooms are next door in Hill House; all are comfortable. Dining areas suit the mood of the day: the breakfast room is light and airy, with elegant white table and chair coverings; the flagstoned bar, with oak panelled walls and French wood carvings – part of a huge collection built up by Christine's father – bustles with working folk at lunchtime; and the smart restaurant suits a quiet dinner in the evening. Waiters serve in white aprons and black ties – John sends them all on wine courses. The food rightly picks up awards, too, as should Christine's flower arangements. Great value and so close to London.

rooms	15: 7 doubles, 3 twins, 5 suites.
price	Twin/doubles £50-£60. Suites £75-£85.
meals	Breakfast £4.50-£7.50. Bar meals from £5.50. Dinner, à la carte, about £23.
closed	Christmas. No food on Bank Holidays.
directions	M25, junc. 30, A13 towards Southend for 3 miles, then B1007 to Horndon-on-the-Hill. On left in village.

Christine & John Vereker

tel	01375 642463
fax	01375 361611
e-mail	info@bell-inn.co.uk
web	www.bell-inn.co.uk

The New Inn At Coln

Coln St-Aldwyns, Nr. Cirencester, Gloucestershire GL7 5AN

Built by decree of Elizabeth I, this lovely coaching inn of roaring fire, low-beams and local cheer provides old-fashioned hospitality at its best. The New Inn At Coln is Brian and Sandra-Anne's life – you sense this in their relaxed, personal welcome. They and their staff take the time to talk you through a local walk, the ales on tap, the wonderful menu – chef Sarah Payton's food is "divine". Sandra-Anne's sumptuously designed bedrooms have everything – a four-poster here, a half-tester there, a romantic floral theme brilliantly developed. Those in the converted dovecote have views across meadows to where the River Coln meanders serenely. In summer, sip drinks lazily outside under the generous shade of parasols. With a little notice, brown trout fishing on the river at the bottom of the garden can be arranged. Golf, biking and horse riding are all nearby, or walk from the front door through this sleepy Cotswold village, past grazing cows and gliding swans, into some of England's loveliest countryside; nothing too dramatic, just a classic of its type, inspiration to the artist, the poet… and maybe you.

rooms	14: 10 doubles, 3 twin/doubles, 1 single.
price	£110–£140; singles £80–£95.
meals	Bar lunch from £8.50. Dinner £29.50.
closed	Never.
directions	From Oxford, A40 past Burford, B4425 for Bibury. Left after Aldsworth to Coln St-Aldwyns.

Brian & Sandra-Anne Evans

tel	01285 750651
fax	01285 750657
e-mail	stay@new-inn.co.uk
web	www.new-inn.co.uk

map 3   entry 80

The Swan Hotel at Bibury

Bibury, Gloucestershire GL7 5NW

The Swan must be the most photographed hotel in Britain; its setting by a bridge over a gentle river in a pretty village is pure Cotswold bliss. Inside is no less enchanting. Everywhere you look, something wonderful appears: Macintosh chairs, a baby grand piano in the lobby; the sky-blue panelling in the entrance hall is so impressive, it's been listed. Further on, the dining room is a spectacular monument to the decadent Twenties – high ceilings, claret wallpaper, oils and chandeliers make it a fabulous place to eat. Bedrooms are equally indulgent, with a mix of old and contemporary: maybe an Art Deco mirror or a ceramic bedside light the size of a barrel. Old Roberts radios, thick bathrobes in Italian-tiled bathrooms and the hotel's own spring water spoil further. Every room has something delightfully extravagant; the best look out the front. Retire at night to find the bed turned down, wake in the morning to find a newspaper waiting to be read. Walk in perfect countryside, or fish the hotel's beat – the trout farm opposite is an artistic triumph.

rooms	20: 9 doubles, 5 twins, 2 twin/doubles, 1 family, 3 four-posters.
price	£116–£260.
meals	Lunch from £5. Dinner £28.50; and à la carte.
closed	Never.
directions	From Oxford, A40 west, past Burford, then left on B4425 to Bibury. Hotel in village by bridge.

	Elizabeth Rose
tel	01285 740695
fax	01285 740473
e-mail	swanhot1@swanhotel-cotswolds.co.uk
web	www.swanhotel.co.uk

No. 12

Park Street, Cirencester, Gloucestershire GL7 2BW

No. 12 is that rare phenomenon in Britain, a small 'other place' run with enormous care and thought. Sarah wanted to create a welcome alternative to the diet of faceless, corporate hotels that she endured herself for many years as a senior marketing manager. She has succeeded admirably, lavishly converting this splendid, listed Georgian townhouse right down to the last detail – some beams date back to the early 1600s. Bedrooms mix antique and contemporary furniture, feather pillows, merino wool blankets and fine bed linen spoil further, and vast beds include a *bateau lit* and an antique brass. Ultra-modern bathrooms, almost minimalist in style, come with dressing gowns and Molton Brown smellies. Cranberry red walls and white china make a striking contrast in the dining room at breakfast, while checked sofas, fresh flowers and *Condé Nast Traveller* and *Vogue* in the sitting room suggest a smart clientèle. Old Cirencester, "capital of the Cotswolds" is equally splendid, a favourite destination for travellers since Roman times – civilised in every sense. *Children over 12 welcome.*

rooms	3 doubles.
price	£70; singles £50.
meals	Restaurants in Cirencester.
closed	Never.
directions	M4, junc. 15, A419 to Cirencester. Follow signs into town centre. House on right opp. museum.

Sarah Beckerlegge

tel	01285 640232
fax	01285 640233
e–mail	no12cirencester@ukgateway.net
web	www.no12cirencester.co.uk

map 3   entry 82

Heavens Above at
The Mad Hatters Restaurant

3 Cossack Square, Nailsworth, Gloucestershire GL6 0DB

In Carolyn's words, you "never know what's coming next" at this exceptional, fully organic restaurant with rooms. Arrive to a bowl of cherries one day, some fragrant sweet peas picked from the garden the next. She and Mike were smallholders once. They lived at the top of the hill, worked the land, kept livestock, made bellows and earned next to nothing. In the early Nineties, they came down the hill to open a restaurant. Locals flocked in, and still do. The food is quite delicious, consistently so, some still grown back up the hill: try fabulous fish soup, lamb with garlic and rosemary, and a mouth-puckering lemon tart. It's a place with real heart, not designed to impress, which is probably why it does, and full of warm, rustic charm: cookery books squashed into a pretty pine dresser, mellow stone walls, big bay windows, stripped wooden floors, simple ash and elm tables and exceptional art. Two bedrooms share a bathroom but that's soon to change. All are delightful — huge, like an artist's studio, with wooden floors, whitewashed walls and rag-rolled beams. Fabulous.

rooms	3: 1 twin; 1 double, 1 family, sharing bath.
price	£60; singles £35.
meals	Lunch from £6.50. Dinner, à la carte, £20–£25.
closed	Restaurant closed Sunday evening, Monday & Tuesday.
directions	M5, junc. 13, A419 east to Stroud, then A46 south to Nailsworth. Right at r'bout, then immediately left. On right, opp. Britannia pub.

Carolyn & Mike Findlay

tel	01453 832615
fax	01453 832615
e-mail	mafindlay@waitrose.com

The Priory

Priory Fields, Horsley, Stroud, Gloucestershire GL6 0PT

Suzie does good company and long, lazy meals with the odd glass or two so well that one guest even recommends the Priory hangover! A definite 'other place', this 1880s Cotswold stone house defies an obvious label; Suzie is someone you immediately warm to: she's such an exuberant hostess that you will want to feel a part of the fun and energy here. There's a well-stocked bar and deep feather-filled sofas to sink into and chat away by a log fire. Take your time over traditional English meals around a walnut table in the splendid terracotta dining room with sparkling chandelier, big mirrors, gold sconces and cut glass. Fresh flowers and plants are everywhere. Suzie has laboured heroically to transform a dilapidated home into a sophisticated country house. Her eclectic style and quirky sense of humour have brought together an elegant hotchpotch of treasures collected over the years – it's all very relaxing. The comfortable, smallish bedrooms come with impeccable bathrooms; some have tree-top views and all have the dawn chorus. The garden is being restored and the local pub is a pleasant stroll away. A great place for that special house party, too.

rooms	10: 6 doubles, 2 twins, 2 singles (1 with wheelchair access).
price	£75; singles £45. House party rates on application.
meals	Dinner by arrangement. Restaurants nearby.
closed	Never.
directions	M4, junc. 18, towards A46 north for Stroud. Enter Nailsworth on B4058, signed Horsley. Left at Bell & Castle pub. Entrance 200 yds on right.

	Suzie Lamplough
tel	01453 834282
fax	01453 833750
e-mail	theprioryhorsley@onetel.net.uk
web	www.theprioryhorsley.com

map 3   entry 84

Three Choirs Vineyards

Newent, Gloucestershire GL18 1LS

A fondness for cooking and the wine-making process will thoroughly equip you for the full-bodied and very English experience of Three Choirs. Thomas has run the vineyard with thoughtful and gentle reserve for almost almost a decade. There are 100 acres of grounds, of which 75 grow 16 varieties of grape; the rest have been left to encourage even more varieties of wildlife, including birds of prey that live around five ponds in the valley. The wine from here went to the wedding of Charles and Diana and still lubricates British embassies. The hotel and restaurant evolved more recently as a natural addition to the winery. The bedrooms are in a modern building and are crisply clean and functional, nothing quirky, but that's not what you're here for; each has French windows, with a small patio and cast iron furniture: relax with a glass of house wine and drink in the peaceful views that produced it. At breakfast, don't be embarrassed to ask for more wine with your smoked salmon and scrambled eggs – it's a house special. Tony the chef has won many accolades and runs cookery courses every month. Dick Wittington was born up the road – you may wonder what possessed him to leave.

rooms	8 twin/doubles.
price	From £85; singles £65. Half-board, 2 nights, £125 p.p.
meals	Lunch about 12.50. Dinner, à la carte, about £28.
closed	Christmas & New Year.
directions	From Newent, north on B4215 for about 1.5 miles, following brown signs to vineyard.

Thomas Shaw

tel	01531 890223
fax	01531 890877
e-mail	info@threechoirs.com
web	www.threechoirs.com

Hotel on the Park

Evesham Road, Cheltenham, Gloucestershire GL52 2AH

Symmetry and style to please the eye in the heart of the spa town of Cheltenham. The attention to detail is staggering – everything has a place and is just where it should be. The style is crisp and dramatic, a homage to the Regency period in which the house was built, but there's plenty of good humour floating around, not least in Darryl himself, who's brilliant at making you feel at home. He's the first to encourage people to dive in and enjoy it all. There are lovely touches too: piles of fresh hand towels in the gents' cloakroom, where there's a sink with no plug hole – you'll work it out; newspapers hang on poles, so grab one and head into the drawing room where drapes swirl across big windows. In the restaurant you'll come across Doric columns, Greek and Roman busts, lots of fun too. Upstairs, bedrooms are fabulous, crisp and artistic, all furnished to fit the period. The whole house is classically dramatic – a huge treat.

rooms	12: 6 doubles, 4 twins, 2 suites.
price	£107.50-£157.50; singles £85.50.
meals	Breakfast £7-£9.25. Dinner, à la carte, from £23.50.
closed	Never.
directions	From town centre, join one-way system, and exit signed Evesham. Continue down Evesham Road. Hotel on left opposite park, signed.

Darryl Gregory

tel	01242 518898
fax	01242 511526
e-mail	stay@hotelonthepark.co.uk
web	www.hotelonthepark.co.uk

map 3   entry 86

Alias Hotel Kandinsky

Bayshill Road, Montpellier, Cheltenham,
Gloucestershire GL50 3AS

Kandinsky, Russian painter, theorist and pioneer of the abstract — a fitting name for a hotel pushing back the boundaries of British hospitality. The first hotel to come from the Alias stable has hotel innovator Nigel Chapman's signature written all over it. Like its sister hotel in Exeter, Kandinsky gives free rein to Nigel's design-obsession with sitting down in the right chair in the right surroundings. Religious lithographs from Blake's *Marriage of Heaven and Hell* in the entrance hall suggest that what you're about to receive will prepare you for what you'll have to endure when you leave this vibrant port of call. Bedrooms are compact, stylish, with all mod cons. Puppets from Bali hang above reception. The bar and lounge with painted wooden floors and rugs is in the Raffles colonial style, as are bamboo plants in the conservatory. Gates from a French monastery lead to the restaurant with its trademark Italian pizza oven. The private club downstairs feels like a New York lounge, with soft lighting, black leather couches and 50s party dresses in the ladies loo that are there to be worn by all, and are! Welcome to the party.

rooms	48: 14 doubles, 26 twin/doubles, 8 singles.
price	£89–£115; singles £79. B&B 2 nights + 1 dinner from £104.50 p.p.
meals	Continental breakfast £7.75; full English £10.95. Lunch £14–£25. Dinner, à la carte, £20–£30.
closed	Never.
directions	M5, junc. 11, A40 to centre; left at r'bout end of Lansdown Rd for Montpellier. Road veers to left, hotel ahead.

Lorraine Jarvie

tel	01242 527788
fax	01242 226412
e-mail	info@hotelkandinsky.com
web	www.hotelkandinsky.com

The White Hart Inn & Restaurant

High Street, Winchcombe, Gloucestershire GL54 5LJ

The Swedes have arrived in Gloucestershire but there's nothing to fear – they come in peace, bearing a *smörgåsbord* of vibrant chic and warm hospitality. It's a far cry from the sixth century when this Cotswold village was the Saxon capital of Mercia; any mention of Scandinavians on the loose would have resulted in a call to arms! Not anymore. Locals have welcomed their arrival at this 16th-century coaching inn. Thanks to the discerning interior design of Nicole's mother Ursula, it feels more like a stylish rural hotel in Sweden: scrubbed wooden floors, sisal matting, big windows and Gustavian style blue-grey furniture in the restaurant. Bedrooms smell inviting; the best have views of the high street. One named after Swedish painter Carl Larsson has a stunning four-poster in the middle of the room, just as the artist did, with green checked fabric and fresh flowers. Nicole, who's half Swedish, employs solely Swedish staff on six-month stints to improve their English; all take it in turns to serve, clean, or cook authentic food: *sil*, marinated herring, is superb. They've even introduced Santa Lucia, a winter festival of song and candles.

rooms	8: 2 doubles, 4 twin/doubles, 2 four-posters.
price	£65–£125; singles £55–£115. Half-board (min. 2 nights) £75 p.p.
meals	Lunch about £10. Dinner, à la carte, about £25.
closed	Christmas Day.
directions	From Cheltenham, B4632 to Winchcombe. Inn on right.

	Nicole Burr
tel	01242 602359
fax	01242 602703
e-mail	enquiries@the-white-hart-inn.com
web	www.the-white-hart-inn.com

map 3   entry 88

Wesley House

High Street, Winchcombe, Gloucestershire GL54 5LJ

Wesley House, a 15th-century half-timbered townhouse, entices you off the street and seduces you once inside. Old timber-framed white walls, a terracotta-tiled floor and a large, open fire were made for lazy afternoons flicking through the papers. Downstairs is open-plan; the dining area stretches back in search of countryside — and finds it. French windows lead out to a small terrace where breakfast and lunch, or evening drinks, are enjoyed against a backdrop of the gentle Cotswold hills. Winchcombe was once the sixth-century capital of Mercia. Bedrooms have more of those ancient whitewashed, timber-framed walls that need little decoration: warm, smart, well-lit and compact, with good wooden beds, crisp cotton sheets, new carpets and the occasional head-cracking bathroom door; one room has a lovely balcony. Find fresh milk and coffee in every room, and indulge in breakfast in bed, with home-baked bread, croissants, pains au chocolat... even kumquat, orange and whisky marmalade. *Children over seven and babies welcome.*

rooms	5 doubles.
price	£75–£85; singles £55.
meals	Lunch from £6.95. Dinner, à la carte, £21.50–£31.
closed	Christmas.
directions	From Cheltenham, B4632 to Winchcombe. Restaurant on right.

Matthew Brown

tel	01242 602366
fax	01242 609046
e-mail	reservations@wesleyhouse.co.uk
web	www.wesleyhouse.co.uk

Lords of the Manor

Upper Slaughter, Nr. Bourton-on-the-Water, Gloucestershire GL54 2JD

The name is almost a linguistic form of time travel, the place a bastion of rural Englishness and the food out of this world – welcome to Lords of the Manor. The original house was built in 1650, with most of the later stuff added by the Victorians. The bar is more gentleman's club than hotel with old wooden floors, low lighting and the faint whiff of ancient logs on the fire. Take a leather sofa by a large bay window and let tradition swirl around you, staring out across rolling parkland – it's the perfect English hotel in the perfect English landscape. Progress tiptoes ever so discreetly here but to great effect – the restaurant is nicely contemporary, looking out onto a walled orchard, and head chef Toby Hill won a Michelin star in 2002, making it the only hotel in Gloucestershire to be awarded this coveted eating accolade. Bedrooms have a stately swagger, with heavily draped windows, big bunches of fresh flowers and welcoming decanters of sherry; they're split between the main house and the converted granary. Sleep easy, too: Slaughter comes from *scolostre*, meaning 'muddy place' – borrow wellies by the back door and squelch across to the village.

rooms	27: 19 twin/doubles, 2 singles, 3 four-posters, 3 suites.
price	£149-£299; singles from £99.
meals	Lunch £16.95. Dinner £40; à la carte, £50-£60. Picnic hamper available.
closed	Never.
directions	From Cirencester, A429 north about 16 miles, left for The Slaughters. In Lower Slaughter, left over bridge, into Upper Slaughter. Hotel on right in village, signed.

	Tracey Davies
tel	01451 820243
fax	01451 820696
e-mail	lordsofthemanor@btinternet.com
web	www.lordsofthemanor.com

map 3   entry 90

Dial House

The Chestnuts, Bourton-on-the-Water, Gloucestershire GL54 2AN

The 'Venice of the Cotswolds' and such a peaceful setting, with distinctive sandstone Georgian houses and the slow, meandering River Windrush idly drifting by. Bourton is popular with the Cotswolds' traveller, drawn to the genteel buzz of village life. There's lots going on, and right in its midst stands The Dial House, built in 1698 by architect Andrew Paxford – his and his wife's initials are carved on the front. Originally The Vinehouse, it was renamed after the large sundial above the front door. Inside, Jane and Adrian have created an oasis of old world charm, with Jacobean-style furniture, wonderful four-posters, old portrait paintings and impressive stone fireplaces lit in winter. Elegant, relaxed and friendly, it epitomises the traditional country-house hotel. The best bedrooms are in the main house, with lovely antiques, a little chintz to create the country feel, and views of the village and river through leaded window panes. Rooms in an extension look out onto the walled garden, a lovely spot to keep the world at arm's length for a while, and the classic English menu takes a lot of beating.

rooms	14: 3 four-posters, 9 doubles, 1 single, 1 suite.
price	£114. Half-board (min. 2 nights) £75 p.p.
meals	Dinner £14.95; and à la carte. Packed lunch available.
closed	Never.
directions	From Oxford, A40 to Northleach, right on A429 to Bourton-on-the-Water. Hotel set back from High St opp. main bridge in village.

Jane & Adrian Campbell-Howard

tel	01451 822244
fax	01451 810126
e-mail	info@dialhousehotel.com
web	www.dialhousehotel.com

The Fox Inn

Lower Oddington, Nr. Moreton-in-Marsh, Gloucestershire GL56 0UR

Amid the grandeur of old Cotswold country houses, The Fox evokes a wonderful sense of times past, gently at odds with the juggernaut of modern life. Low ceilings, worn flagstones, a roaring fire in winter, good food and an exemplary host induce quiet relaxation. After many years running restaurants and inns, some in London, Ian instinctively knows how to look after you. The information pack found in each delightful room is carefully researched, providing the complete loafer's guide to what to do and see. Bedrooms that fall into the 'charming inn' category sometimes leave a lot to be desired, but here they need no disclaimer; all are lovely in their own right, with antique beds, warm colours and prints of country scenes — the largest has views of the village and a lawned garden. The mellow bar is full of wooden furniture and walls of yellow ochre date back years. You breakfast in an elegant room painted a deep rose. Sit on a garden terrace from spring to autumn, thanks to awnings and outside heaters, and there's an 11th-century church nearby with magnificent frescoes. Good old-fashioned romance in good hands.

rooms	3 doubles.
price	£58–£85.
meals	Lunch from £4. Dinner, à la carte, about £17.50.
closed	Christmas & New Year.
directions	From Stow-on-the-Wold, A436 for Chipping Norton for 3 miles, then 2nd right after VW garage, for Lower Oddington. Inn 500 yds on right.

Ian McKenzie

tel	01451 870555
fax	01451 870669
e-mail	info@foxinn.net
web	www.foxinn.net

map 3   entry 92

Lower Brook House

Lower Street, Moreton-in-Marsh, Gloucestershire GL56 9DS

Lower Brook House started life as a B&B and evolved into an award-winning restaurant with rooms… and yet it's much more than that. Marie holds the key; so full of life-giving exuberance, she's not the sort of person to stand in the way of progress. Settle into coral sofas next to the huge inglenook fireplace, toss on a log and start *War and Peace*; never mind if ancient stone floors, timber-framed walls, fresh flowers everywhere and stacks of beautiful things distract you from the page. Next door in the restaurant, a gallery of family rogues hang on crimson walls, peering down at tables decorated with cut-glass crystal, hand-painted crockery and the best starched linen. In summer, eat breakfast and dinner in the garden – the latter by scented candle. Compact bedrooms, with mullioned windows and the odd exposed roof timber, are full of pampering paraphernalia: bathrobes, bowls of fruit, garden flowers. As for the food, maybe steamed fillet of sea bass or roast loin of venison, supported by the working kitchen garden – it's all delicious. Watch brown trout commuting up a nearby brook to pass the time.

rooms	7: 3 doubles, 2 twin/doubles, 2 four-posters.
price	£80–£145; singles from £75.
meals	Dinner about £21. Lunch by arrangement.
closed	Never.
directions	From Moreton-in-Marsh, A44 west, then right on B4479 into Blockley. House on right at bottom of hill, signed.

Marie Mosedale-Cooper

tel	01386 700286
fax	01386 700286
e-mail	lowerbrookhouse@aol.com
web	www.lowerbrookhouse.co.uk

The Churchill Inn

Paxford, Chipping Campden, Gloucestershire GL55 6XH

Above all, The Churchill is fun, an engaging mixture of the old and new that creates a relaxed, informal atmosphere. Walk into the bar, with stone floors and wooden tables, and find a hub of happy chatter. Leo and Sonya are proud of their creation – one guest described it as "Fulham in the country", and the locals seem to like it that way. Many were reluctantly starting to leave when our inspector arrived just after lunch. Bedrooms right above the bar are equally fun and stylish; two are small but good use of space won't leave you feeling hemmed in. "Frills and drapes are not us," says Sonya. Beams, old radiators and uneven floors obviously are. Add good fabrics, pastel colours and country views from the heart of this picture-perfect village and this is one place worth getting away for. The food is quite superb, too. One usually cantankerous Sunday critic conceded that the sticky toffee pudding was perfect. Such perfection might explain the prayer stool in one corner.

rooms	4 doubles.
price	£70; singles £40.
meals	Lunch from £10.50.
	Dinner from £14.50.
closed	Never.
directions	From Moreton-in-Marsh, A44 for Worcester & Evesham. Through Bourton-on-the-Hill, right at end to Paxford. Through Blockley, over railway and tiny bridge into Paxford. Inn is in village on right.

Leo Brooke-Little & Sonya Kidney

tel	01386 594000
fax	01386 594005
e-mail	info@thechurchillarms.com
web	www.thechurchillarms.com

map 3   entry 94

The Cotswold House Hotel

The Square, Chipping Campden, Gloucestershire GL55 6AN

Few brochures quite capture the spirit of a place, often losing their way in hackneyed cliché – Cotswold House's is one exception. It pulls out like a concertina, revealing a tantalising glimpse of what to expect behind the impressive colonnaded entrance of this 19th-century wool merchant's house. Ian and Christa's philosophy was to create a hotel where the bedrooms felt better than your own room at home – they've succeeded: National Trust colours, cashmere underblankets and Frette linen sheets on luxurious beds, French colognes and lotions in stylish bathrooms, fresh coffee percolators, Bang & Olufsen film and stereo systems, remote controls that move the TV to whatever angle you want... even a 'Pillow Menu'. Downstairs, relax in red and terracotta drawing rooms, with antiques, fresh flowers and paintings, or stroll in two acres of walled garden, with meandering paths and secluded spots; the vegetable garden supports a well-regarded menu in season. Wine, music and celebrity events are held through the year; the village has chi-chi shops to browse – and you can park for free. Go on, spoil yourself.

rooms	20: 2 doubles, 16 twin/doubles, 2 four-posters.
price	£120–£295.
meals	Brasserie meals from £9. Picnic £12–£15. Dinner £38.
closed	Never.
directions	From Oxford, A44 north for Evesham. 5 miles after Moreton-in-Marsh, right on B4081 to Chipping Campden. Hotel in village square by town hall.

Ian & Christa Taylor

tel	01386 840330
fax	01386 840310
e-mail	reception@cotswoldhouse.com
web	www.cotswoldhouse.com

The Malt House

Broad Campden, Chipping Campden, Gloucestershire GL55 6UU

You could imagine that one of the Famous Five lived in this substantial English house in the heart of an untouched Cotswold village, with climbing roses, magnolia trees and deckchairs on the lawn. A place that so echoes to the past, you almost expect the vicar to call for tea, or a post boy to bring a telegram to say the London train is running late. Still much in evidence is that very English ritual of sipping gin in a lovely setting: the manicured garden has its own 'gin and tonic' bench! A thatched summer house for afternoon tea, a walled kitchen garden that grows figs and a small brook completes the idyllic scene. The house itself has a mellow grandeur: polished wooden floors, ancient oak panelling, walls of shimmering gold and a 17th-century fireplace beneath a mantelpiece that rises to within a foot of the ceiling. Bedrooms vary, with mullioned windows, sloping floors, gilt mirrors, and muralled bathrooms; some have painted floorboards. Judi is very English, too. Friendly staff and good food, sourced locally and cooked by an American chef, will keep you smiling for days.

rooms	7: 2 doubles, 4 twin/doubles, 1 suite.
price	£100–£118.50; singles from £75. Suite from £115.
meals	Dinner, à la carte, £32.50.
closed	Christmas.
directions	From Oxford, A44, through Moreton-in-Marsh, then B4081 north to Chipping Campden. Entering village, 1st right, for Broad Campden. Hotel 1 mile on left.

	Judi Wilkes
tel	01386 840295
fax	01386 841334
e–mail	info@the-malt-house.freeserve.co.uk
web	www.malt-house.co.uk

map 3   entry 96

Hotel du Vin & Bistro

Southgate Street, Winchester, Hampshire SO23 9EF

Flair, high standards and exquisite attention to detail in an easy atmosphere… and all very French. There's a bistro with old wooden floors and tables, big windows that draw in light, a garden for *al fresco* dining in summer and a mirrored champagne bar in gold and blue, with *bergère* sofas to loll on like kings and queens for the night. Elsewhere, sweeping expanses of cream walls covered in prints and oils and handsome furniture. Bedrooms use strikingly simple colours, fine fabrics and Egyptian linen, beds are big and tempting and bathrooms have deep baths and 'smellies' specially made on a Scottish isle. Rooms are split between the bustling main house and the quieter Garden rooms; light sleepers should go for the latter. Food and wine are the hotel's raison d'être and staff are excellent – artisans who speak with passion about their work. Go completely *français* and play boules in the garden, or explore England's ancient capital. Winchester Castle is home to 'The Round Table of King Arthur'; Merlin crowned the 15-year-old Arthur at nearby Silchester, or so it's claimed.

rooms	23: 22 doubles, 1 suite.
price	From £105; suites £185.
meals	Breakfast £9.50–£13.50. Lunch & dinner £25–£30.
closed	Never.
directions	M3, junc. 11, signed Winchester South. At first r'bout, follow signs to St Cross & Winchester. Hotel on left after 2 miles.

Mark Huntley

tel	01962 841414
fax	01962 842458
e-mail	info@winchester.hotelduvin.com
web	www.hotelduvin.com

Westover Hall

Park Lane, Lymington, Hampshire SO41 0PT

A hotel, but family-run and without the slightest hint of stuffiness. It was built for the German industrialist Siemens in 1897 to be the most luxurious house on the south coast; a fortune was lavished on wood alone. It is still vibrant with gleaming oak and exquisite stained glass and it's hard to stifle a gasp when you enter the hall – it's a controlled explosion of wood. The Mechems are generous and open-minded, keen that people should come to unwind and treat the place as home. Private parties can take over completely and throw the rule book towards the window. Bedrooms are exemplary: some have sea views, all are furnished with a mix of the old and the contemporary; bathrooms are spotless. The whole place indulges you. Romantics can take to the bar or restaurant and gaze out to sea. The more active can dive outside and walk up the beach to Hurst Castle. Alternatively, sink into a sofa on the sunny balcony for great views of the Needles, or visit their nearby Mediterranean beach hut.

rooms	12: 8 doubles, 2 twins, 1 family, 1 single.
price	£145–£200. Half-board £97.50–£125 p.p.
meals	Light lunch £6–£12. Dinner £32.50.
closed	Never.
directions	From Lymington, B3058 to Milford-on-Sea. Continue through village. House on left up hill.

Nicola & Stewart Mechem

tel	01590 643044
fax	01590 644490
e-mail	info@westoverhallhotel.com
web	www.westoverhallhotel.com

 map 3   entry 98

Master Builder's House Hotel

Bucklers Hard, Beaulieu, Hampshire SO42 7XB

By the River Beaulieu in a timeless end-of-the-road idyll, Master Builder's has the feel of a well-heeled yacht club. The hotel shares this blissful location with two rows of cottages still lived in by workers of the nearby Montague Estate. Yachts and sailing boats glide past on their way to the Solent following the same route taken by Nelson's fleet two centuries before. It was here that the great shipwright Henry Adams built many of the warships which would go on to fight in the Battle of Trafalgar; ancient slipways that launched the ships still survive at the river's edge. Bedrooms in a wing named after Adams are uniformly done to a high standard, each with a king-size bed. More expensive bedrooms in the main part of the hotel have darker colour schemes and superb river views. There's a traditional pub, full of sailors in summer, a hall that seems to tumble down to the water, a restaurant with a view, and a terrace for *al fresco* meals. Beaulieu is a one-hour walk upstream past marshland teeming with birdlife and the New Forest stretches to the west. Also charter a boat to their other hotel on the Isle of Wight.

rooms	25 twin/doubles.
price	£165–£215; singles £120.
meals	Bar lunch from £4.95. Lunch £16.95. Dinner £29.50.
closed	Never.
directions	From Lyndhurst, B3056 south past Beaulieu turn-off, then 1st left, signed Bucklers Hard. Hotel signed left after 1 mile.

Samanatha Brinkman

tel	01590 616253
fax	01590 616297
e-mail	res@themasterbuilders.co.uk
web	www.themasterbuilders.co.uk

Hosting & Posting

Puddleston on Lugg, Moret on Lugg, Herefordshire

If you recognise this bizarre little hotel it is because you have seen it before — in our Italian book. It made such an impression on one of our readers that he bought it, lock stock and post-box, from the owner and had it carted back to Britain. We would like to relate that he was a purveyor of architectural oddities. But he was a property developer who thought he was on to a good thing in a country faced with a housing crisis. He went bust — deservedly — and the buildings were bought by the rather unusual current owner who thought he would make a go of it as a hotel. Keen to encourage beginners in the hotel business we are offering our support to this new venture. Odd they may be, but the interiors of this cluster of tiny buildings are remarkable: minimalist, each one like a dentist's waiting room. What could be more guaranteed to bring tears to the eyes? Note how each one faces out at a different angle. Clever. However, this first year is an experiment for the owners — and for us — so let us know how you get on. *Perfect for very small children whom you wish to separate.*

rooms	5 'box' rooms, each with subtly different 'widescreen' view.
price	5 1st class stamps for the lot.
meals	Dried, flatpacked and posted every other day.
closed	Only ever opened for those checking out.
directions	North on A49 from Hereford to Moret on Lugg. Tiny lane to Puddleston. If in doubt follow a post-office van or a local dog.

The Officer

tel	Correspondence by post only.
e-mail	box5@postboxonapost.eg
web	hosting.posting.postbox/~p_box_/

map 0   entry 100

Glewstone Court Country House Hotel & Restaurant

Glewstone, Ross-on-Wye, Herefordshire HR9 6AW

A relaxed country house, grand, yet nicely lived-in, with an authentic house-party feel, Glewstone is not the sort of place to stand on ceremony. Chill out in the drawing room bar, sink into a comfortable sofa and let Bill pour you a large gin and tonic – he looks after you with great style and panache. The centre of the house is early Georgian, with a Regency staircase that spirals up to a galleried and porticoed landing. Bedrooms are large, with quilted bedspreads, period furniture, and cupboards and walls decorated with Christine's pretty stencil work; the Rose Room is especially wonderful and the Victoria Room enormous. All look over fruit orchards to the Wye Valley and the Forest of Dean beyond. An ancient cedar of Lebanon dominates croquet lawn and fountain at the front of the house – there's even a modest helipad. Dine in the restaurant, the bistro, or outside in good weather. The relaxed dress code welcomes all styles, except baseball caps and mobile phones – and rightly so! Christine cooks brilliant food; most is grown locally and some is organic – the Hereford beef is exceptional. Heaven for those in search of the small, friendly and informal.

rooms	8: 5 doubles, 1 single, 2 junior suites.
price	£90-£105; singles £45-£60.
meals	Lunch & dinner in bistro about £17. Dinner in restaurant £26. Sunday lunch £15.
closed	25-27 December.
directions	From Ross-on-Wye, A40 towards Monmouth, then right 1 mile south of Wilton r'bout, signed Glewstone. Hotel on left after 0.5 miles.

Christine & Bill Reeve-Tucker

tel	01989 770367
fax	01989 770282
e-mail	glewstone@aol.com

Kilverts Hotel

The Bullring, Hay-on-Wye, Herefordshire HR3 5AG

Those wanting to stay in the thick of this literary outpost bang on the Welsh border could do no better than check into Kilverts. The hotel sits in narrow streets full of bookshops, art galleries and antique shops that wind round the town's crumbling castle which peers over all. Hay is the secondhand bookshop capital of Britain, and holds an internationally famous literary festival every May. If you've been searching for that elusive book, this is the place to come. The front terrace of the hotel is also the place to people-watch with a drink or a meal; the bar is a cosy retreat if the weather drives you inside, with stone floor, wooden tables, local ales and home-made pizzas. The more formal restaurant has a mural on the wall of a ballroom in chaos! The menu is the same wherever you eat and has daily specials. There's also the quieter garden out back – it's the biggest undeveloped plot in the town. Upstairs, go for one of two lovely beamed attic rooms at the top: one has an 18th-century oak tester; the rest have few surprises but all are comfortable. Colin is a likeable chap, as is Tired Ted the hotel cat, and the countryside seduces with every visit.

rooms	11: 6 doubles, 2 twins, 3 twin/doubles.
price	£70–£90; singles £50.
meals	Bar meals from £3.25. Lunch & dinner, à la carte, about £19.
closed	Christmas Day.
directions	On entering Hay continue past NatWest Bank, then take next right turn & continue downhill for approx. 40 yds. Kilverts on right. Car park at rear.

	Colin Thomson
tel	01497 821042
fax	01497 821580
e-mail	info@kilverts.co.uk
web	www.kilverts.co.uk

map 2   entry 102

Penrhos Hotel

Kington, Herefordshire HR5 3LH

Penrhos is magnificent by any standards, but as you enter the cruck hall – a stone-flagged medieval masterpiece – bear in mind it was a pile of medieval rubble 20 odd years ago. Daphne and Martin did most of the renovation themselves, ensuring the tiniest details were historically accurate. The effect is jaw-dropping: tapestries on the walls, a 14th-century snug sitting room with a wooden ceiling, and a huge fireplace where they burn great knotted logs; walk in, look up and see the sky. Outside, a stone barn, cow byre and puddleduck pond. The highlight is the hall where you eat at night by candlelight from hewn wooden slabs made from a giant elm that fell near the house during the storms of 1987. Daphne cooks, between running a school of food and health, and the restaurant is fully organic, with no red meat, reflecting their eco-friendly philosophy; they host a yearly 'green cuisine' festival. Upstairs, bedrooms have immense character, big and bright, with views over hills; downstairs, French windows look onto a pretty garden. Bring your boots and walk. Heaven.

rooms	15: 9 doubles, 4 twins, 2 four-posters.
price	£95–£120; singles from £65.
meals	Dinner, 4 courses, £31.50.
closed	January.
directions	From Leominster, A44 for Kington. Hotel 1 mile before Kington on left, 200 yds up drive, signed.

Martin Griffiths & Daphne Lambert

tel	01544 230720
fax	01544 230754
e-mail	martin@penrhos.co.uk
web	www.penrhos.co.uk

Priory Bay Hotel

Priory Drive, Nettlestone, Isle of Wight PO34 5BU

Medieval monks thought Priory Bay special, so did Tudor farmers and Georgian gentry, all helped to mould this tranquil landscape into a rural haven. Parkland rolls down from the main house and tithe barns to a ridge of trees. The land then drops down to a long, clean sandy beach and a shallow sea; it's as Mediterranean as Britain gets, and all owned by the hotel. Fishermen land their catch here for the freshest mackerel breakfasts. Huge rooms in the house mix classical French and contemporary English styles. The sun-filled drawing room has wonderfully tall windows – exquisite rococo-style chairs obligingly face out to sea, and afternoon cream teas by the winter log fire are a treat. The dining room has a mural of the bay on the wall, and elaborate flower decorations at each table. Bedrooms in the main house are luxurious; some have a fresh and modern feel, others oak panelling, maybe a crow's nest balcony and telescope. Bedrooms in nearby outbuildings are less enticing but much cheaper. Andrew is a humorous host, and a supporter of the organic movement – they grow as much as they can. The grounds also support falcon and red squirrel, and the odd golfer.

rooms	26: 16 twin/doubles, 10 family.
price	£90-£250; singles from £50. Half-board £65-£120 p.p.
meals	Lunch & dinner £25. Picnic hampers available.
closed	Never.
directions	From Ryde, B3330 south through Nettlestone, then left up road, signed to Nodes Holiday Camp. Entrance on left, signed.

Andrew Palmer

tel	01983 613146
fax	01983 616539
e-mail	reception@priorybay.co.uk
web	www.priorybay.co.uk

map 3   entry 104

The George Hotel

Quay Street, Yarmouth, Isle of Wight PO41 0PE

The position is fabulous, with the old castle on one side, the sea at the end of a sunny garden, and the centre of Yarmouth, the island's oldest town, just beyond the front door. Handy if you're a corrupt governor intent on sacking ships that pass. Admiral Sir Robert Holmes moved here for that very reason in 1668, demolishing a bit of the castle to improve his view. The house has been rebuilt since Sir Robert's day but a grand feel still lingers: the entrance is large, light and stone-flagged; a drawing room next door panelled, with kilim-covered sofas. Six newly refurbished bedrooms were done in Colefax and Jane Churchill prints, while the bigger, more expensive bedrooms are beautifully panelled; one has a huge four-poster, and two have timber balconies with views out to sea. Meals can be taken outside in the garden bar; or else eat in the buzzy, cheerful, yellow-and-wood brasserie, or the sumptuous, burgundy dining room. Dig even deeper into your pocket and charter a private boat to take you to lunch at their other hotel on the mainland.

rooms	17: 15 twin/doubles, 2 singles.
price	£165–£215; singles from £120.
meals	Lunch & dinner in brasserie from £25. Dinner in restaurant, 4 courses, £45.
closed	Restaurant closed Sunday & Monday.
directions	Take Lymington ferry to Yarmouth, then follow signs to town centre.

	Jacki Everest
tel	01983 760331
fax	01983 760425
e-mail	res@thegeorge.co.uk
web	www.thegeorge.co.uk

Hotel du Vin & Bistro

Crescent Road, Royal Tunbridge Wells, Kent TN1 2LY

You enter immediately, and literally, into the spirit of the place – chatter spills from the bars and bistro into an ocean of wood below a faraway ceiling; the enormous hall is the hub of the place, and though magnificent bedrooms will tempt a linger, you'll be irresistibly drawn back to join the fun downstairs. The Burgundy bar buzzes with local life; open fires and facing sofas lead inevitably to 'later' dinners. The yellow-walled, picture-crammed bistro is distinctly French, with more wooden floors, while hops that tumble from the windows pay tribute to Kent. Afterwards, wander into the Havana room – the bullet holes are fake – for a game of billiards and a cigar, or take coffee in the Dom Perignon room where huge hand-painted copies of the Impressionists hang boldly. Bedrooms come in different sizes – the biggest is *huge* – and all have fantastic bathrooms; you sleep on Egyptian linen, naturally. A modern masterpiece.

rooms	36 doubles.
price	From £85.
meals	Breakfast £9.50–£13.50. Lunch & dinner £25–£30.
closed	Never.
directions	M25, A21 south for 13 miles, then A264, signed Tunbridge Wells, into town. Right at lights into Calverley Rd, then left at mini-r'bout, into Crescent Road.

Matt Callard

tel	01892 526455
fax	01892 512044
e-mail	info@tunbridgewells.hotelduvin.com
web	www.hotelduvin.com

map 4   entry 106

Romney Bay House

Coast Road, New Romney, Kent TN28 8QY

Designed by Clough Williams-Ellis – creator of Portmeirion – for American star Hedda Hopper, this atmospheric dreamscape is as stunning as the photograph above suggests. Inside, the whole house has a lingering 1920s house-party feel. There's an honesty bar full of colour, a drawing room with deep sofas to sink into and a pretty dining room and conservatory to sample Jennifer's wonderful cooking – don't miss tea. Everything has been thought out and is just right, a perfect home from home. Unwind with a book in front of the fire, go for long beachside walks, or simply fall in love with the sheer romance of the place – nothing disappoints. The library look-out upstairs has a telescope – spy on France on a clear day – as well as more books and lots of games. Bedrooms are elegant, full of everything you need: pretty furniture, half-testers, sleigh beds, beautiful bathrooms and most have views out to sea. Jennifer is full of enthusiasm, and Helmut has a great sense of humour. A very special place indeed.

rooms	10: 8 doubles, 2 twins.
price	£85–£140; singles £60–£95.
meals	Light lunch at weekends from £5.50. Cream tea £5. Dinner, 4 courses, £32.
closed	Christmas. Restaurant closed mid-June.
directions	M20, junc. 10, A2070 south, then A259 east through New Romney. Right to Littlestone, then left at sea and continue for 1 mile.

Helmut & Jennifer Gorlich

tel	01797 364747
fax	01797 367156

Wallett's Court Country House Hotel

Westcliffe, St Margaret's at Cliffe, Dover, Kent CT15 6EW

Wallett's Court is *old*; Odo, half-brother of William the Conqueror, lived on the land in Norman times, then Jacobeans left their mark in 1627. When Chris and Lea renovated in 1975, the house gave up long-held secrets: tobacco pipes fell from a ceiling and 17th-century paintings were found in a blocked-off passageway, still hanging on the wall. Gavin, their son, now runs the business with the same passion and commitment. It's a hotel that feels warm and genuine... even the ghost is impeccably well-behaved. Old features catch the eye: ancient red-brick walls in the drawing room, an oak staircase with worn, shallow steps in the hall. Bedrooms in the main house are big, with heaps of character; those in the barn and cottages are good and quiet; and above the spa complex – indoor pool, sauna, steam room and spa – four excellent, contemporary rooms have been recently added. There's tennis, a terrace with views towards a distant sea and white cliffs within a mile for breezy walks, towering views, rolling mists and wheeling gulls. Great food, too; puddings to diet for. Popular with golfers.

rooms	16: 13 doubles, 2 twins, 1 family.
price	£90–£150; singles £75–£110.
meals	Lunch £17.50. Dinner £27.50.
closed	Christmas.
directions	From Dover, A2/A20, then A258 towards Deal, then right, signed St Margaret's at Cliffe. House 1 mile on right, signed.

Chris, Lea & Gavin Oakley

tel	01304 852424
fax	01304 853430
e-mail	stay@wallettscourt.com
web	www.wallettscourt.com

map 4 entry 108

The Walpole Bay Hotel

Fifth Avenue, Cliftonville, Kent CT9 2JJ

Edwardian through and through... and as much a museum as a hotel, The Walpole is just as it always was, if not more so, splendidly faded and run with true devotion. It's been Jane and Peter's long ambition to preserve that period between the wars when genteel English folk flocked to the seaside in their best attire. Step back in time as you walk up marble steps to a beautiful wrought iron veranda with wicker chairs and old sedans. Inside, swirly carpets, flowery wallpaper, huge palms, working gas lights, original po's, Lincrusta panelling and old photos of guests posing outside with their charabancs; many of the museum's artefacts were donated. The ballroom with its sprung maple floor ballroom is retro heaven – 20s and 40s nights are recommended! The 1927 gated Otis lift travels three floors to bedrooms with sea views; the balconies are next to be restored. Jane and Peter live in the butler's quarters and are as fun as the hotel is authentic – everything fits so well, you can't help falling for its nostalgic charm. There's lots to do as well. Visit the extraordinary shell grotto, or stroll along the Thanet coastline and find an 80-million-old fossil.

rooms	42: 34 doubles, 3 four-posters, 5 suites.
price	£60–£105; singles £40–£75.
meals	Lunch from £3.50. Dinner, à la carte, from £15. Afternoon tea from £3.50.
closed	Never.
directions	From Margate, to Cliftonville along coast road with beach on left, past Winter Gardens and Lido. Fifth Ave. on left after Butlins Hotel. Hotel on right opp. indoor bowls centre.

Jane & Peter Bishop

tel	01843 221703
fax	01843 297399
e-mail	info@walpolebayhotel.co.uk
web	www.walpolebayhotel.co.uk

Hotel Continental

29 Beach Walk, Whitstable, Kent CT5 2BP

Of course oysters are the thing – George V was so impressed with their curative powers that he gave the foreshore, yards from The Continental, to the Oyster Fishery Company. They're still regarded as the best in the country, just as the hotel's Oyster Fishery is rated as one of the best fish restaurants: try roasted sea bass with rosemary and garlic, or griddled ballourni with chilli jelly; the setting is casually chic, with parquet flooring, white tablecloths and blackboard menus. Bedrooms are uncluttered and airy, some with sea views, all painted a quiet sunny yellow, with checked curtains and blue carpets; nothing fussy, perfectly comfortable. For complete privacy with plenty of space and more clean lines, stay in one of the converted Fisherman's Huts right down on the sea front, or in the Anderson Shed, a converted boat shed with two double rooms and a kitchen – breakfast at the hotel is included. Once the pride of the north Kent coast, Whitstable still feels authentic, though today it's as easy to get a cappuccino as a bag of fish and chips. Gaze on lots of boat activity, or take in a flick – the hotel owns the Imperial Oyster Cinema, too.

rooms	29: 5 doubles, 15 twin/doubles, 3 family, 6 huts.
price	£55-£125; singles Sunday-Thursday £49.50-£69.50.
meals	Dinner, à la carte, about £18.50.
closed	Christmas Eve & Christmas Day.
directions	M2 for Margate, then A229 to Whitstable. Turn to town centre at Longreach r'bout down Long Road. Hotel on left after bowling alley.

	Jamie Robb & James Green
tel	01227 280280
fax	01227 280257
web	www.oysterfishery.co.uk

map 4　entry 110

The Ringlestone Inn

Ringlestone Hamlet, Nr. Harrietsham, Kent ME17 1NX

Two old sisters once ran The Ringlestone; if they liked the look of you, they'd lock you in; if they didn't, they'd shoot at you. Michael and his daughter Michelle have let that tradition slip, preferring to run their 1635 ale house with a breezy conviviality. Glass tankards dangle above the bar, a woodburner throws out heat from the inglenook and old *Punch* cartoons hang on the original brick and flint walls between oak beams and stripped wooden floors. They stock 30 fruit wines and liqueurs as well as excellent local ales to sup in settles or on quirky, tiny, yet very comfy chairs. Across the lane in the farmhouse, bedrooms are perfect: oak furniture, sublime beds, crisp linen and big, luxurious bathrooms. The food is delicious – try a Ringlestone pie – and in the garden you can play *pétanque*; they hold competitions here. The inn has a children's licence, they sometimes host vintage car rallies, there's good walking and Leeds Castle is close. As for Michael's breakfasts, they'll keep you going for a week.

rooms	3: 2 twin/doubles, 1 four-poster.
price	£99–£109; singles £89.
meals	Breakfast £10–£14. Lunch from £6. Dinner £8–£25.
closed	Christmas Day.
directions	M20, junc. 8. Left after 0.25 miles at 2nd r'bout to Hollingbourne. Through Hollingbourne, up hill, then right at brown 'Knife and Fork' sign. Pub on right after 1.5 miles.

Michael Millington-Buck

tel	01622 859900
fax	01622 859966
e-mail	bookings@ringlestone.com
web	www.ringlestone.com

The Inn at Whitewell

Whitewell, Clitheroe, Lancashire BB7 3AT

Richard was advised not to touch this inn with a bargepole, which must qualify as among the worst advice ever given, because you'll be hard-pressed to find anywhere better than this. The inn sits just above the River Hodder with views across parkland to rising fells in the distance. Long ago, merchants used to stop at this old deerkeeper's lodge and fill up with wine, food and song before heading north through notorious bandit country; superb hospitality is still assured but the most that will hold you up on the road today is a stubborn sheep. Back at the inn, Richard, officially the Bowman of Bowland, wears an MCC tie and peers over half-moon glasses with a soft, slightly mischievous smile on his face, master of all this informal pleasure. The bedrooms are a triumph of style, warm and fun, some with fabulous Victorian showers, others with deep cast iron baths and Benesson fabrics; all have great art and Bose music systems, and ones that look onto the river are bigger. The long restaurant and an outside terrace drink in the view, too. There's also seven miles of private fishing, even their own well-priced Vintner's. But book early – it's very popular.

rooms	17: 11 twin/doubles, 5 four-posters, 1 suite.
price	£87–£108; singles £63–£99; suite £125.
meals	Bar meals from £5.50. Dinner, à la carte, from £23.50.
closed	Never.
directions	M6, junc. 31a, then B6243 east through Longridge, then follow signs to Whitewell for 9 miles.

Richard Bowman

tel	01200 448222
fax	01200 448298

map 6   entry 112

La Gaffe

107-111 Heath Street, Hampstead, London NW3 6SS

Genuine Italian hospitality and great value mark out La Gaffe amid the wealth and Georgian splendour of leafy Hampstead. Bernardo and Androulla Stella opened the restaurant in 1962, adding rooms in 1976. Today it's run with the same ineffable charm by their sons, Lorenzo and Salvatore. The list of celebrities who've eaten here is too long to mention, but actors Peter O'Toole and David Soul are still regulars. The hotel is made up of five former shepherd's cottages built in 1734, well before Hampstead became a desirable address. It's the highest point in London; views from the Heath just across the road are wonderful. The village itself is full of terraced cafés, trendy boutiques and charming backstreets, including Church Row – said to be the most beautiful in London. Compact bedrooms have pretty floral fabrics; those at the back look onto a quiet square and two have steam baths. The restaurant has murals and faux-Roman walls which suit its classic style of Italian cooking – the olive oil, cheese and hams come from an uncle's farm in Abruzzo. A family-run gem, and popular with locals. Don't miss the meatballs.

rooms	18: 4 four-posters, 6 doubles, 4 twins, 4 singles.
price	£90-£125; singles £65.
meals	Lunch & dinner, à la carte, 2 courses, £15-£18.
closed	Never.
directions	Tube: Hampstead. Bus: 46, 268. Parking: £10 a day on-street.

Lorenzo Stella

tel	020 7435 8965
fax	020 7794 7592
e-mail	la-gaffe@msn.com
web	www.lagaffe.co.uk

Portobello Gold

95-97 Portobello Road, Notting Hill, London, London W11 2QB

Portobello Gold is a cool little place in the heart of Ladbroke Grove, one of London's trendier districts for musicians. It's a bar, a restaurant, an internet café and a place to stay. Bedrooms are basic, with small shower rooms and good beds. Ideal if the hippy in you is still active, or you're after a cheap, quirky place to stay in London, but not for those who want luxury. Downstairs, sit out on the pavement in wicker chairs and watch Portobello life amble by, or hole up at the bar for a beer with the locals, just as Bill Clinton did on his last visit to Britain as US president. Tiled floors, an open fire and monthly exhibitions of photography and modern art fill the walls. At the back, the conservatory restaurant with its retractable glass roof feels comfortably jungle – dine on Irish rock oysters, sashimi – or Thai Moules to the sweet song of four canaries. Linda writes about wine, so expect to drink well. Michael is a cyber-visionary, hence the fold-away computers in the bar – internet use is free to guests. Ideal for the Notting Hill Carnival in August and Portobello antique market held every Saturday.

rooms	5: 2 doubles; 3 doubles, all with shower, sharing wc; 1 apartment for 4.
price	£40–£85; singles £50–£55. Apartment £120–£180.
meals	Continental breakfast included; full English £5.50. Bar meals from £6. Dinner £20–£25.
closed	Never.
directions	Tube: Notting Hill. Bus: 12, 27, 28, 31, 52, 328. Parking outside: £25 per 24 hrs.

Michael Bell & Linda Johnson-Bell

tel	020 7460 4910
fax	020 7460 4911
e-mail	mike@portobellogold.com
web	www.portobellogold.com

map 4   entry 114

Miller's

111a Westbourne Grove, London W2 4UW

This is Miller's, as in the antique guides, and the collectables on show in the first-floor drawing room make it one of the great spots in London for undemanding hedonists. The week I visited, guests included Marianne Faithful, the top brass of a Milan fashion house, a professional gambler and an opera singer who was giving guests lessons. Breakfast is taken communally around a 1920s walnut table in a drawing room where, at ten o'clock on the morning I visited, a fire was smouldering in a huge carved-wood fireplace. You get an idea of what to expect when you step in off the street and pass an 18th-century sedan chair stuffed under the stairs, as if discarded, but in the drawing room, to give you a taster: a gilt-framed Sony Trinitron, a Tibetan deity (well, his statue), a 1750s old master's chair, a couple of hundred candles, flower pots embedded with oranges, a samurai sword, busts and sculptures, oils by the score, globes, chandeliers, plinths, rugs, sofas… Aladdin was a pauper if you compare his cave to this one. Bedrooms upstairs are equally embellished, just a little less cluttered. Perfection never came so cheap.

rooms	6 doubles.
price	£140–£195.
meals	Continental breakfast only.
closed	Never.
directions	Tube: Bayswater, Queensway, Notting Hill Gate. Bus: 7, 23, 28, 31, 70. Nearest car park £25 for 24 hrs.

Martin Miller

tel	020 7243 1024
fax	020 7243 1064
e-mail	enquiries@millersuk.com
web	www.millersuk.com

L'Hotel

28 Basil Street, London SW3 1AS

L'Hotel is well-named – it has the feel of a small Parisian hotel, but chief among its many bounties is Isabel, who, in her short reign (long live the Queen), has proved it is not only what you do, but how you do it that matters. Her way is infectious; she is kind and open and nothing is too much trouble. The hotel's not bad either. Downstairs there's a great little restaurant/bar for breakfast, lunch and dinner – the social hub of the place – where the odd note of jazz rings out. You can have breakfast down here – excellent coffee in big bowls, pains au chocolat, croissants – or they'll happily deliver it to your room where you can laze about on vast beds that are covered in Egyptian cotton, with Nina Campbell fabric on the walls, little box trees on the mantlepiece, original art on the walls and an occasional open fireplace. Turn left on your way out and Harvey Nicks is a hundred paces; turn right and Harrods is closer. If you want to eat somewhere fancy, try the Capital next door. It has a big reputation, is owned by the same family, and Isabel will book you in. A very friendly, very pretty place.

rooms	12: 11 twin/doubles, 1 suite.
price	£165–£175; suite from £190.
meals	Continental breakfast included, full English from £6. Lunch & dinner £6–£15.
closed	Never.
directions	Tube: Knightsbridge. Bus: 14, 19, 22, 52, 74, 137, C1. Parking: £25 a day off-street.

	Isabel Murphy
tel	020 7589 6286
fax	020 7823 7826
e-mail	reservations@lhotel.co.uk
web	www.lhotel.co.uk

map 4   entry 116

The Sloane Hotel

29 Draycott Place, Chelsea, London SW3 2SH

You get an inkling of what to expect at The Sloane by walking into its reception hall: a faux leopard-skin sofa, a mountain of vintage luggage, an ancient admiral's uniform, a gilded marble fireplace and a huge cabinet in one corner with ornate columns and pediment; nothing in the room is less than breathtaking. Nor, for that matter, is the rest of the hotel. On our tour we stopped first in a bedroom with a mirrored wall behind an 18th-century walnut bed, with rich claret wallpaper and 16 pictures on one wall. It was an extraordinary room (a standard double), so I asked if people often described it as "opulent". "Not this one, but the others, yes", came the reply. And things do get more opulent. I saw nowhere quite like The Sloane in my travels; it is a treasure-trove of beautiful things. Look out for faux fur blankets, four-poster beds draped in raw silk, antiques that span five centuries, exquisite *Lelièvre* wallpaper, porcelain pots, armchairs and sofas dressed in the finest fabrics; the place is an A-Z of designers old and new. There's a twist, too – you can buy the lot. The beds, apparently, are extremely popular. Amazing.

rooms	22: 16 doubles, 6 suites.
price	£175-£250; suites from £280.
meals	Breakfast £9-£12.
closed	Never.
directions	Tube: Sloane Square. Bus: 11, 19, 22, 137, 211, C1. Parking: nearest car park £21 per 24 hrs.

	Miguel Pita
tel	020 7581 5757
fax	020 7584 1348
e-mail	reservations@sloanehotel.com
web	www.sloanehotel.com

The Victoria

10 West Temple Sheen, London SW14 7RT

Mark, ex-Conran, now proprietor extraordinaire, was consoling the waitress, who had toothache, as he made the coffee, his eyes scanning his empire to make sure everything was just so. Which it was: I couldn't see a teaspoon out of place. This is the result of much hard work; last year Mark and Clare transformed the place into a cool, contemporary gastro pub, with airy rooms, wooden floorboards, tongue and groove panelling and purple cushions on the sofas. It's got local tongues wagging, the good folk of Sheen keen to come and try the food. Their efforts will be well-rewarded, the menu appearing as apples did to Eve. Treat yourself to saffron and tomato quiche, Toulouse sausage and mash with onion gravy, and poached pear in red wine. After which you can retire to stylish bedrooms: white walls, Egyptian cotton, halogen lighting, beechwood beds, goose down pillows, multi-coloured blankets and high pressure showers. Great value for money, and with the Sheen Gate entrance to Richmond Park close by, you can walk off your indulgence lost to the world. A great little place.

rooms	7: 5 doubles, 2 twin/doubles.
price	£92.50–£115; singles from £82.50.
meals	Lunch and dinner £5–£20.
closed	Never.
directions	Train: Waterloo to Mortlake. Buses: 33 & 337.

Mark & Clare Chester

tel	0208 876 4238
fax	0208 878 3464
e-mail	mark@thevictoria.net
web	www.thevictoria.net

map 4   entry 118

Eleven Didsbury Park

Didsbury Village, Manchester M20 5LH

Welcome to a warm 21st-century hotel experience, a townhouse hotel that celebrates the urban minimalist style without paring down your comfort in the process. Unlike more brand-conscious contemporaries hell-bent on creating a new hotel order, Eleven Didsbury Park does design without the attitude. Eamonn has blended modern design with the sparing beauty of Georgian influences from his homeland – he hails from Co. Kerry – to create a hotel full of relaxed, uncluttered style, where simplicity delights the eye and old luxuries balance new. Lovely big bedrooms mix the best Egyptian linen and rich, earthy, handmade fabrics with mirror de-misters and hi-fi gizmos. In summer, the pretty garden with its terrace of tables and chairs feels like a country estate: peaceful and full of birdsong, and the surrounding buildings are masked by exuberant growth. Didsbury is a lush, leafy suburb, just a short bus ride from Manchester's mini-revival – exciting modern architecture, regenerated docklands and the Lowry Museum await. A courtesy four-wheel drive will also take you to local restaurants and bars.

rooms	14: 2 doubles, 10 twin/doubles, 2 suites.
price	£79.50–£165.50.
meals	Breakfast £8.50–£10.50. Room service until 10.30pm, £2.95–£8.95. Restaurants in Manchester.
closed	Never.
directions	From Manchester city centre, A34 south for 4 miles, then right on A5145 Wimslow Rd. Didsbury Park 4th on right, house 200 yds on left.

Eamonn & Sally O'Loughlin

tel	0161 448 7711
fax	0161 448 8282
e-mail	enquiries@elevendidsburypark.com
web	www.elevendidsburypark.com

Didsbury House

Didsbury Park, Didsbury Village, Manchester M20 5JT

Stylish Eleven Didsbury Park made a name for itself on the 'boutique hotel' circuit; now along comes a bigger, more stylish version in a converted Victorian villa. Didsbury House seduces the moment you enter: beautiful inlaid parquet floors and an original carved wooden staircase that carries the eye upwards to a magnificent stained-glass window. Planners and building regulations may have thwarted Eamonn and Sally's wilder ambitions at their first hotel down the street but here in this 1840 merchant's house their ideas run rampant: the luxurious attic suite has separate his and her roll-top baths as well as his and her seats in a gigantic shower cubicle, while in every gorgeous room, baths fit two. Two split level 'duplex' rooms add further intrigue; a walkway spans a central atrium above your head; a sitting room, with ostrich-egg-shaped lights and pewter bar, leads outside through French windows; a floor below, the gym and spa. But best of all should be the planned roof-top terrace, with hot tub and jungle ferns and bamboo in big clay pots. Contemporary interior design given a free rein, run with down-to-earth Mancunian humour. Superb.

rooms	26: 20 twin/doubles, 6 suites.
price	£99.50–£150; suites £175–£250.
meals	Continental breakfast £9.50, full English £11.50.
closed	Never.
directions	From Manchester city centre, A34 south for 4 miles, then right on A5145 Wimslow Rd. Didsbury Park 4th on right, hotel on corner.

Eamonn & Sally O'Loughlin

tel	0161 448 2200
fax	0161 448 2525
e-mail	enquiries@didsburyhouse.co.uk
web	www.didsburyhouse.co.uk

map 6   entry 120

Strattons

4 Ash Close, Swaffham, Norfolk PE37 7NH

It's not just the feel of rural France, or the spectacular interiors that make Strattons so special – it's also the greenest hotel in Britain. "Everything is home-made, recycled, bought locally, restored, renewed, recovered and rethought," Vanessa says of this splendid Palladian villa. Enter a peaceful courtyard, a minute's walk from the market square, to gardens reassuringly unmanicured, full of urns and terracotta pots. Les and Vanessa met at art school, and have covered every square inch with wonderful ideas: mosaics, murals, marble busts, bronze sculptures, piles of books, bunches of dried roses, rugs on wooden floors – it feels like a small, and wildly original French château. Bedrooms are exquisite: a carved four-poster, a tented bathroom, Indian brocade, stained glass, trompe l'œil panelling and sofas by a log fire; two suites added in 2002 are heaven. Dine in the pure and simple lower-ground floor bistro, with white-painted brickwork, crisp linen, voile curtains and gilt-framed paintings. Vanessa's fresh and local cooking style has won many awards. E M Forster dreamed of a "holy trinity of soil, soul and society" – they've got it pretty close here.

rooms	8: 4 doubles, 1 twin, 1 four-poster, 2 suites.
price	£100–£130; singles from £75; suites £170.
meals	Dinner, 4 courses, £35.
closed	Christmas.
directions	Ash Close runs off north end of market place between W H Brown estate agents and Express cleaners.

Vanessa & Les Scott

tel	01760 723845
fax	01760 720458
e-mail	strattonshotel@btinternet.com
web	www.strattons-hotel.co.uk

The Norfolk Mead Hotel

Coltishall, Norwich, Norfolk NR12 7DN

You *can* paddle your canoe from the bottom of the garden all the way along the River Bure to the Broads, though it involves a few miles of exertion. A better idea is to stay closer to home and potter lazily about in one of the hotel's rowing boats. Norfolk Mead is in a great position, with 12 acres of lawns, mature trees, a walled garden and a swimming pool… there's even a one-acre fishing lake. Come for the owners, the food and the easy-going luxury of a lovely old Georgian country house – the sort you dream of. The bedrooms, all different, are super-comfortable, with the best quality linen and every tiny, frivolous need anticipated. The food is just as good, all fresh and local, maybe samphire from Blakeney, or home-made ice cream. A fine entrance hall with high-backed sofas and an open fire unwind you immediately. Big, gracious, beautifully proportioned, yet perfectly relaxing. And if that's not enough, Jill and Don's daughter, Nicky, will provide a massage or manicure. Expect to be pampered.

rooms	12: 7 doubles, 3 twins, 2 suites.
price	£85–£140; singles £70–£90. Half-board from £65 p.p.
meals	Dinner £25. Sunday lunch £14.50.
closed	Never.
directions	From Norwich, B1150 north to Coltishall, over humpback bridge, then 1st right before church down drive, signed.

Jill & Don Fleming

tel	01603 737531
fax	01603 737521
e-mail	info@norfolkmead.co.uk
web	www.norfolkmead.co.uk

map 8   entry 122

Beechwood Hotel

Cromer Rd, North Walsham, Norfolk NR28 0HD

There's an old-fashioned perfectionism about the Beechwood – it is impeccable, professional and immensely well-mannered. Agatha Christie was a frequent guest when it was a private house and it is not difficult even now to imagine quiet conspiratorial conversations over dinner. The atmosphere is that of a traditional country-house hotel but with imaginative flourishes: bold black and white tiling in one bathroom, with a splendid, old roll-top bath painted black on the outside – the cistern is still, quite rightly, high on the wall, the down-pipe gleaming. Curtains in the dining room are richly pelmeted, the separate tables elegant and attractive. The food is British with a strong Mediterranean influence: *fettucine* with a wild mushroom, stilton and tarragon sauce, roast Scottish salmon on a saffron rissotto, haddock, prawn and chive cakes... all sound delicious. The bread is home-made and organic ingredients are used whenever possible. In the bedrooms, curtains match the bedspreads; in the smart sitting room, old leather sofas and armchairs demand to be wallowed in. Above all, there is space – and peace.

rooms	10: 8 doubles, 1 twin, 1 four-poster.
price	£90–£160; singles £66. Half-board £60 p.p.
meals	Lunch £14. Dinner £28.
closed	Christmas.
directions	From Norwich, B1150 to North Walsham. Under railway bridge, then left at next traffic lights. Hotel 150 yds on left.

Lindsay Spalding & Don Birch

tel	01692 403231
fax	01692 407284
e-mail	enquiries@beechwood-hotel.co.uk
web	www.beechwood-hotel.co.uk

The Lifeboat Inn

Ship Lane, Thornham, Norfolk PE36 6LT

They want you to be comfortable, relaxed and well-fed and there's every reason you should be. The Lifeboat Inn is ideal for some away-from-it-all, traditional and unpretentious good cheer – there's not enough of it about. It's been an alehouse since the 16th century, they know how to serve a decent pint – Adnams, Greene King, Woodfordes – and use locally-sourced food whenever possible to good effect in both the beamy bar and the more formal, richly coloured restaurant. Try the bar for its staples: steaming cauldrons of Norfolk mussels and chips and real ale-battered fish; and the restaurant for dishes with a more sophisticated air. The bedrooms are pine-furnished, not huge but entirely functional and well-equipped; most have mind-clearing views over the marsh to the sea. North-west Norfolk is a great place for being outdoors. Come when the wind blows, and the hall fire flickers around damp dogs, while the odd stuffed animal looks on. Bask in the sheltered courtyard when it's sunny and let the children run. Staff are kind and unfussy, the atmosphere easy. But book ahead – people do know about this place.

rooms	14: 3 doubles, 11 double/twins.
price	£70–£96; singles £50–£63. Half-board (min. 2 nights) from £96 p.p.
meals	Lunch £8.50. Dinner £24.
closed	Never.
directions	From King's Lynn, A149 via Hunstanton to Thornham. In village, left into Staithe Rd & follow road round to right. Inn on right.

Angela Coker

tel	01485 512236
fax	01485 512323
e-mail	reception@lifeboatinn.co.uk
web	www.lifeboatinn.co.uk

map 8   entry 124

Saracens Head

Wolterton, Erpingham, Norfolk NR11 7LZ

Food, real ale, good wines, a delightful sheltered courtyard and walled garden, Norfolk's bleakly lovely coast – this is why people come here. But the food is the deepest seduction. Robert and his team cook up "some of Norfolk's most delicious wild and tame treats". Typical starters are Morston mussels with cider and cream, or fricassée of wild mushrooms. Expect pigeon, Cromer crab, and venison. Then Robert works his own magic on old favourites such as bread and butter pudding, and the less familiar nutty banana and marsala crumble. The bar is as convivial as a bar could be, a welcome antidote to the garish pub bars of our age; piped music and fruit machines – Robert will have none of them. There's a parlour room where residents can sit, with a big open brick fireplace, deep red walls, colourful plastic tablecloths and candles in old wine bottles, a black leather banquette along two walls. Bedrooms are plain, modest and comfortable with pine beds, quilted bedspreads and courtyard views. The whole mood is of quirky, committed individuality – slightly arty, slightly unpredictable and in the middle of Norfolk's nowhere. Great stuff.

rooms	4: 3 doubles, 1 twin.
price	£65; singles £35–£40.
meals	Bar meals from £3.95. Dinner about £17.
closed	Christmas Day.
directions	From Norwich, A140 past Aylsham, then left, for Erpingham. Straight through village to Calthorpe. Over x-roads. On right after about 0.5 miles.

Robert Dawson–Smith

tel	01263 768909
fax	01263 768993

Elderton Lodge & Langtry Restaurant

Gunton Park, Thorpe Market, Norfolk NR11 8TZ

Shades of Scotland embrace this peaceful north Norfolk shooting lodge set in a deer park with Gunton Tower graceful in the distance. Gunton Hall is just over the brow and was a favourite with Edward VII and Lilly Langtry. The local railway station was built specially to deliver their champagne – 1,000 cases at a time! Pictures of Lilly Langtry hang on the walls, as does a letter she wrote. The house echoes to her time: tasselled lamps, old rugs, leather sofas, trophies and oils – all the deep country trimmings. For new owners Mike Parsey and Pat Roofe, Norfolk is a homecoming. Mike has returned from 20 years in Africa and Pat, a pilot, has landed back where he was brought up. Elderton exudes comfort. Splash out on the more expensive rooms, as they're bigger and full of Edwardian antiques, rich fabrics and plush headboards. In most rooms, you can lie in bed and look out across parkland to the tower. Enjoy candlelit dinners in the warm and elegant restaurant, and breakfast amid hanging ferns in the Victorian, tiled conservatory. Deer graze all around and there's a varied programme of special interest weekends, too. *Children over five welcome.*

rooms	11: 9 doubles, 2 twins.
price	£95–£115; singles from £60. Half-board from £55 p.p.
meals	Lunch, 3 courses, £12.95. Dinner £19.50; and à la carte.
closed	Never.
directions	From North Walsham, A149 north for 3 miles. Hotel on left, signed.

Mike Parsey & Pat Roofe

tel	01263 833547
fax	01263 834673
e-mail	enquiries@eldertonlodge.co.uk
web	www.eldertonlodge.co.uk

map 8   entry 126

The Falcon Hotel

Castle Ashby, Nr. Northampton, Northamptonshire NN7 1LF

Follow the example of Purdy, The Falcon's gorgeous black labrador, and live life at a contented plod when you stay here. Stone-built and originally a farmhouse dating back to 1594, the inn lies opposite the castle after which this dreamy village is named. The Easticks came here after Michael decided he needed another change – he has already been a farmer and a racing driver, among other things. These days, he is quite happy being a hotelier, making sure the cellar bar is full of beer, the oils hang symmetrically, the fire crackles with huge logs and guests get well fed in the pretty stone-walled restaurant; much of the produce comes from their vegetable garden. In summer, eat outside and watch cows saunter up to the dairy as sheep graze beyond; the garden is full of flowers. Bedrooms are split between the inn and a cottage next-door-but-one – the octogenarian ex-postmistress lives in between. All received a makeover recently, with country cottage fabrics, bright yellows and blues, bathrobes, fresh flowers and gentle village views. Wander round the spectacular castle grounds or mooch in nearby craft shops… no need to hurry.

rooms	16: 13 twin/doubles, 3 singles.
price	£85–£125; singles from £69.50. Half-board from £75 p.p.
meals	Lunch £14.95. Dinner £24.50.
closed	Never.
directions	From Northampton, A428 towards Bedford for about 6 miles, then left, for Castle Ashby. Inn in village.

Michael & Jennifer Eastick

tel	01604 696200
fax	01604 696673
e-mail	falcon.castleashby@oldenglishinns.co.uk

The Tankerville Arms Hotel

Cottage Road, Wooler, Northumberland NE71 6AD

A cheery Northumbrian welcome awaits at this 17th-century inn — honest, unpretentious, and full of warmth. The charm of the Tankerville is that it's not trying to be anything it isn't. Anne has been involved in running the place for more than two decades and does so in a calm, friendly way; most of the staff are well-established, too. The inn lies at the foot of the Cheviot hills just inland from miles of wild and unspoilt coastline. Inside, décor is smart and homely: a grandfather clock and Regency antiques add splendour to the reception area; a lovely collection of paintings and prints of maps, cattle and the local landscape give character to the bar, restaurant and sitting rooms. Immaculate bedrooms are done in a traditional hotel style, with shiny new bathrooms. Brighten long, winter nights next to an open fire, or choose a nice sheltered spot in the garden to catch some summer rays. Lindisfarne island, where Christianity in England was founded, is close by — look out for St Cuthbert's 'beads' on the beach, but do check the tide times.

rooms	16: 6 doubles, 6 twins, 2 singles, 2 family.
price	£85–£90; singles £49.
meals	Light lunch from £4.50. Dinner from £14.95.
closed	Christmas.
directions	From Newcastle, A1 north of Morpeth, then A697 to Wooler. Inn just north of village on right.

Anne Park

tel	01668 281581
fax	01668 281387
e-mail	enquiries@tankervillehotel.co.uk
web	www.tankervillehotel.co.uk

map 10   entry 128

The Pheasant Inn

Stannersburn, Kielder Water, Northumberland NE48 1DD

A really super little inn, the kind you hope to chance upon: not grand, not scruffy, just right. The Kershaws run it with huge passion and an instinctive understanding of its traditions. The stone walls hold 100-year-old photos of the local community; from colliery to smithy, a vital record of their past heritage – special indeed. The bars are wonderful; brass beer taps glow, anything wooden – ceiling, beams, tables – has been polished to perfection and the clock above the fire keeps perfect time. The attention to detail is staggering. Robin and Irene cook with relish, again nothing fancy, but more than enough to keep a smile on your face – game pies, salmon and local lamb as well as wonderful Northumbrian cheeses. Bedrooms next door in the old hay barn are as you'd expect: simple and cosy, super value for money. You are in the Northumberland National Park; hire bikes and cycle round the lake, sail on it or go horse riding. No traffic jams, no hurry and wonderful Northumbrian hospitality – they really are the nicest people.

rooms	11: 6 doubles, 4 twins, 1 family.
price	From £60; singles from £35. Half-board from £48 p.p.
meals	Bar meals from £6. Dinner £15-£20.
closed	Never.
directions	From Bellingham, follow signs west to Kielder Water and Falstone for 7 miles. Hotel on left, 1 mile short of Kielder Water.

Walter, Irene & Robin Kershaw

tel	01434 240382
fax	01434 240382
e-mail	thepheasantinn@kielderwater.demon.co.uk
web	www.thepheasantinn.com

Falkland Arms

Great Tew, Chipping Norton, Oxfordshire OX7 4DB

In a perfect Cotswold village, the perfect English pub. Five hundred years on and the fire still roars in the stone-flagged bar under a low-slung timbered ceiling that drips with jugs, mugs and tankards. Here, the hop is treated with reverence; ales are changed weekly and old pump clips hang from the bar. Tradition runs deep; they stock endless tins of snuff with great names like Irish High Toast and Dr Kalmans. In summer, Morris Men stumble on the lane outside and life spills out onto the terrace at the front, and into the big garden behind. This lively pub is utterly down-to-earth and in very good hands. The dining room is tiny and intimate with beams and stone walls; every traditional dish is home-cooked. The bedrooms are snug and cosy, not grand, but fun. Brass beds and four-posters, maybe a heavy bit of oak and an uneven floor — you'll sleep well. The house remains blissfully free of modern trappings, nowhere more so than in the bar, where mobile phones meet with swift and decisive action.

rooms	5 doubles.
price	£65–£80; singles £40.
meals	Lunch from £4. Dinner from £8.
closed	Christmas & New Year. Inn open all year for food & drink.
directions	From Chipping Norton, A361, then right onto B4022, signed Great Tew. Inn by village green.

Paul Barlow-Heal & Sarah-Jane Courage

tel	01608 683653
fax	01608 683656
e-mail	sjcourage@btconnect.com
web	www.falklandarms.org.uk

map 3   entry 130

The Feathers Hotel

Market Street, Woodstock, Oxfordshire OX20 1SX

Once a draper's, then a butcher's, this serene English townhouse hotel has stayed true to its roots, with the finest fabrics and award-winning food its proud standard. Follow labyrinthine corridors under mind-your-head beams to the four original staircases that once led their separate ways before these four 17th-century houses became one: open fires, stone floors, oil paintings, beautiful antiques and an elegant upstairs sitting room point to a luxurious past. A pretty terraced bar, Johann the parrot and tumbling, colourful flowers at windows that frame the bustle of old Woodstock. The restaurant is part library, half-panelled with soft yellow walls and low ceilings. Bedrooms are beautiful; some are smaller than others, but all have period furniture, towelling bathrobes, purified water and home-made shortbread; most have marble bathrooms and one suite has a steam bath. Relax with backgammon in the study while devouring sinful afternoon teas, take to the sky in a hot-air balloon, or drift down the Thames in a chauffeured punt – all can be arranged. Blenheim Palace is on your doorstep as well.

rooms	20: 8 doubles, 8 twins, 4 suites.
price	£135–£185; singles from £99. Suite £235–£290.
meals	Lunch from £17.50. Dinner about £38; menu gourmand, 6 courses with champagne & port, £65.
closed	Never.
directions	From Oxford, A44 north to Woodstock. In town, left after traffic lights. Hotel on left.

Peter Bate

tel	01993 812291
fax	01993 813158
e-mail	enquiries@feathers.co.uk
web	www.feathers.co.uk

The Lamb Inn

Sheep Street, Burford, Oxfordshire OX18 4LR

The Lamb must be one of the finest inns in Britain with surely the best address – especially considering the owners' name! The inn dates back to 1420 when it used to be a dormy house. In the old bar, the footsteps of monks and thirsty locals have worn a gentle groove into the original stone floor. Make a grand tour and you'll come across four fires, two sitting rooms, rambling corridors, lots of polished brass and silver, thick rugs, mullioned windows, old parchments and a settle with a back high enough "to keep the draught off a giant's neck". Ferns hang luxuriantly above smart, candlelit tables in the pillared restaurant – the food is sheer perfection. Bedrooms are just as good, with plump-cushioned armchairs, heavy oak beams, brass beds, half-testers, four-posters and antiques of every hue and colour. Out back, a courtyard leads to a secluded walled garden. The whole place has a mellow magic, rather like Richard and Caroline: they've been here 19 years and the locals, sensibly, won't let them leave until they've matched the 40 years chalked up by the previous owners.

rooms	15: 11 doubles, 3 twins, 1 four-poster.
price	£130–£150; singles from £75.
meals	Dinner £29.50.
closed	Christmas Day & Boxing Day.
directions	From Oxford, A40 west to Burford. Sheep Street is 1st left down High Street.

Caroline & Richard De Wolf

tel	01993 823155
fax	01993 822228

map 3   entry 132

Burford House

99 High Street, Burford, Oxfordshire OX18 4QA

Burford House is a delight, small and intensely personal, full of elegant good taste and so relaxing. Small enough for Simon and Jane to influence every corner, which they do with ease and good cheer. "If only all hoteliers were like them," said our inspector. Classical music and the scent of fresh flowers drift through beautiful rooms; oak beams, leaded windows, good fabrics, antiques, simple colours, log fires, immaculate beds, roll-top baths and a little garden for afternoon teas; all in this pretty Cotswold town. And there's an honesty bar, with home-made sloe gin and cranberry vodka, and sipped from cut-glass tumblers, no less. Hand-written menus promise ravishing breakfasts and tempting lunches, and they will recommend the best places for dinner. Both are happy in the kitchen: Simon cooks and Jane bakes, and Cotswold suppliers provide honey, jams, smoked salmon and farmhouse cheeses. Jumble the cat is 'paws on', too. Unwind, then unwind a little more. Enchanting river walks start in either direction through classic English countryside. Guests return time after time. A perfect little find.

rooms	8: 3 doubles, 2 twins, 3 four-posters.
price	£95-£130; singles from £80.
meals	Light lunch & afternoon tea only. Dinner in Burford and nearby villages.
closed	2 weeks in January/February. Restaurant closed Sunday & Monday.
directions	On right in centre of Burford.

Jane & Simon Henty

tel	01993 823151
fax	01993 823240
e-mail	stay@burfordhouse.co.uk
web	www.burfordhouse.co.uk

Old Parsonage Hotel

1 Banbury Road, Oxford, Oxfordshire OX2 6NN

It must have been a good year for cooks. Edward Selwood, the chef of nearby St John's College, completed his grand house in 1660 and the vast oak front door still hangs. Inside, sympathetic design details and use of materials have kept the old-house feel and the intimacy of a private club; Oscar Wilde reputedly had digs here. The hall has fine stone flags, huge original fireplace – log-stocked in winter – and urns of dried flowers. Bedrooms have distinctive florals and checks, some in the old house have fireplaces and panelling; all have glorious bathrooms. There's a first-floor roof garden, lush with plants, for tea or sundowner, and a snug sitting room downstairs for those seeking quiet. All roads seem to lead to the Parsonage bar/restaurant, the hub of the hotel; newspapers hang on poles, walls are heavy with pictures and people float in all day long for coffee, drinks and good food. First-class service from real people too – they'll do just about anything they can to help. Much comfort, not a whiff of pretension, and strolling distance from the dreaming spires.

rooms	33: 30 twin/doubles, 3 suites.
price	£155–£190; singles £130; suites £200.
meals	Lunch & dinner from £15.
closed	24–27 December.
directions	From A40 ring road, south at Banbury Road r'bout to Summertown city centre. Hotel on right next to St Giles church.

Philip Mason–Gordon

tel	01865 310210
fax	01865 311262
e-mail	info@oldparsonage-hotel.co.uk
web	www.oxford-hotels-restaurants.co.uk

map 3   entry 134

The Old Bank

92-94 High Street, Oxford, Oxfordshire OX1 4BN

The original safe, too heavy to remove, now guards the wine cellar. Built of mellow golden stone, the hotel is in the heart of old Oxford, flanked by colleges and cobbled streets. Rooms at the top have views across the fabled skyline of dreaming spires, towers and domes, a sublime panorama of architectural splendour. Downstairs, the big old tellers' hall has been turned into a 'hip' bar and restaurant – the hub of the hotel, with stone floors, a zinc-topped bar, huge modern oils on the walls and big arched windows that look out onto the High Street. In summer, eat on the deck at the back, beneath umbrellas or in the shade of lime trees in a tiny private garden. Bedrooms are superb and just as contemporary, stylishly clean-cut with natural pastel colours, the best linen, velvet and silk; some have big bay windows or views to the back, and they're full of 21st-century gadgetry. A five-minute stroll will take you through Merton College, the Meadows and down to the river. Perfect.

rooms	40: 36 twin/doubles, 2 singles, 2 suites.
price	£155-£300; singles from £135.
meals	Breakfast £8-£11. Lunch & dinner £8.75-£25.
closed	25-26 December.
directions	Cross Magdalen Bridge for city centre. Keep left through 1st set of lights; 1st left into Merton St. Follow road right, then 1st right into Magpie Lane. Car park 2nd right.

Ian Hamilton

tel	01865 799599
fax	01865 799598
e-mail	info@oldbank-hotel.co.uk
web	www.oxford-hotels-restaurants.co.uk

Crazy Bear

Bear Lane, Stadhampton, Oxfordshire OX44 7UR

A wow factor in spades, The Crazy Bear was originally the pub then spread along the terrace to create possibly the jazziest village street in England. You know your room is going to be fabulous as you're led along the zebra-striped carpet to one of the amazing copper-coated doors. No two rooms match; all are flamboyantly weird and full of funky technicolour style. There's a cone-shaped headboard, a mirrored ceiling, a sunken bath, a metal bed in the Art Deco style and all the bathrooms are tiled floor-to-ceiling with great lighting and good towels; extras include Bose stereos and a fruit and sweets bowl, and groups can stay in a whole cottage that sleeps five. But onto the food, and drink... champagne on tap, literally, and a huge clam shell full of fresh oysters on the bar — shame not to try both together! They also do excellent home-made frozen vodkas and there's a humidor of fat cigars. The food is exceptional — modern British with French service upstairs, authentic Thai food with matching staff downstairs. Jet ski, fly in a helicopter, or people-watch — there's no end to what you can get up to here. Fabulous.

rooms	12: 7 doubles, 4 suites, and 1 cottage.
price	£100–£160; singles £80–£100; suites £210–£250.
meals	Continental breakfast included, full English £10. Lunch £10. Dinner £13.50 (except weekends). Dinner, à la carte, £26–31.
closed	Christmas Day & Boxing Day.
directions	M40, junc. 7, A329 for 4 miles to Stadhampton. Hotel on left.

Jason Hunt

tel	01865 890714
fax	01865 400481
e-mail	sales@crazybearhotel.co.uk
web	www.crazybearhotel.co.uk

map 3   entry 136

The Old Trout Hotel

29-30 Lower High Street, Thame, Oxfordshire OX9 2AA

Good food and good humour are served up in equal measure at this long, low, thatched, higgledy-piggledy former merchant's house. Thame gets a special mention in the Domesday Book: corn and butter were being traded here as far back as 1203 and street names reveal bustling markets past. The Old Trout is named after a recent prime minister: not hard to guess which; much harder to tell that this restaurant with rooms is run by a consortium of foodies. Committed staff are on a mission to care for you. Our inspector arrived to find the general manager bidding farewell to the lunch crowd – they didn't want to leave! The place has a worn, timeless feel, with stone flagstones and a hotchpotch of well-buffed furniture; whoever owns this place remains the caretaker of a cherished institution that has been here forever. Go for bedrooms in the main house: one has the smallest hotel door in Britain and perhaps the tallest four-poster? All have bags of character and, most notably, sloping floors. The food is a big draw. The head chef is French and cooks "with latitude". Eat *al fresco* in the courtyard with a pond full of huge koi carp.

rooms	6: 1 double, 1 single, 4 four-posters.
price	£85–£95; singles £65. Half-board Friday & Saturday £125 for 2.
meals	Lunch £12. Dinner about £25.
closed	Never. Restaurant closed Sunday lunchtime.
directions	M40, junc. 8, then A418 to Thame. Hotel on right.

	Matt Granger
tel	01844 212146
fax	01844 212614
e-mail	theoldtrout@inncompany.co.uk

Stonor Hotel

Stonor, Oxfordshire RG9 6HE

Lying on the edge of the Chiltern Hills, The Stonor has the feel of deep country – you wouldn't think it was so close to London. Footpaths lead out to hills and forest, red kites circle above the deer park at Stonor House, which is open to the public, and lanes lead up to pretty villages. Key notes at the hotel are tiptop service, elegance and relaxed informality. Being close to Henley-on-Thames, the hotel also has strong links with the Royal Regatta; the grand, flagstoned bar has two crossed oars on the ceiling and old rowing photos. Sit in comfortable leather sofas and armchairs and take it all in over a quiet drink. The restaurant is more formal, with elegant furniture and lovely oil paintings. Eat from a menu that changes with the seasons, and uses fresh and local ingredients. The bedrooms tend to be huge, with antiques, and lots of extras; find your bed turned down, a morning paper delivered to your room and lots of peace and quiet. Rooms on the ground floor lead into a pretty walled garden. In summer, dine outside by candlelight, or breakfast among the roses. A beautiful setting in which to spoil yourself.

rooms	11: 4 doubles, 7 twin/doubles.
price	£145–£175; singles £120.
meals	Bar meals from £4. Dinner £25–£30.
closed	Never.
directions	M40, junc. 6, B4009 to Watlington, B480 for Nettlebed. Left after 2 miles for Stonor. Inn in village.

	Peter Brunn
tel	01491 638866
fax	01491 638863
e-mail	info@mystonor.com
web	www.stonor-arms.co.uk

map 3   entry 138

Thamesmead House Hotel

Remenham Lane, Henley-on-Thames, Oxfordshire RG9 2LR

Patricia's eye for a news story has proved equally adept at creating a wonderful place to stay in the home of the Royal Regatta. The former arts correspondent has transformed a "seedy" 1960s Edwardian guest house into a chic getaway just a short amble from the centre of Henley-on-Thames; the walk over the famous three-arched bridge (1786) is easily the best introduction to this charming town. Soak up lazy, idyllic river views in both directions, then walk along towpaths or mess about in a rowing boat. Thamesmead is small but perfectly formed. Elegant bedrooms are decorated in a comfortably crisp Scandinavian style; mustard yellows, terracotta and soothing blues, big Oxford pillows to sink into, modern art on the walls, an extraordinary fossil fireplace in one, and painted wooden panelling in the bathrooms. The breakfast/tea room is relaxing, with Thompson furniture – spot the distinctive carved mouse motif – and French windows that let in lots of light, and maybe a gentle summer's breeze. Presiding over all is the erudite and fun-loving Patricia, a Dubliner to the core.

rooms	6: 4 doubles, 1 twin/double, 1 single.
price	£115–£140; singles £95–£115.
meals	Afternoon tea. Restaurants in Henley.
closed	Never.
directions	From M4 junc. 8/9, A404 (M) to Burchett's Green, then left on A4130, signed Henley (5 miles). Before bridge, turn right just after Little Angel pub. House on left.

Patricia Thorburn-Muirhead

tel	01491 574745
fax	01491 579944
e-mail	thamesmead@supanet.com
web	www.thamesmeadhousehotel.co.uk

Phyllis Court Club Hotel

Marlow Road, Henley-on-Thames, Oxfordshire RG9 2HT

Classically English right down to the rose emblem, with the sort of strict protocol you'd expect from a private member's club, Phyllis Court is a class apart. Founded almost a century ago to create somewhere spiffing for bright young things from the city to zoom up in their new motor cars to, it still attracts the great and the good, including royalty. It isn't hard to see why. Apart from the grandstand – it's bang opposite the finishing line of the Royal Regatta – the manor house itself is a grandly self-effacing place: tweed, tennis and *The Telegraph* blend with a sense of fun. Members number some 3,000 today, and run the place with great pride. There *are* 'rules' but Muirfield it isn't! The club is named after the old English word for a red rose, 'fyllis'; a rose was paid to the Crown each year to rent the land in the 14th century. Once moated, Phyllis Court was rebuilt in the 17th century, then again in the 18th and 19th. Bedrooms are easy on the eye with no surprises but full of spoiling touches. The long drive sweeps past lawn and croquet 'courts'. There are gorgeous river walks, and Henley buzzes with day-trippers just as it always has. Hurrah!

rooms	17: 9 doubles, 8 twin/doubles.
price	£126.50–£155; singles £108–£121.25.
meals	Lunch from £15.94. Dinner £22.94.
closed	Never.
directions	From Henley-on-Thames, A4155 towards Marlow. Club on right.

	Sue Gill
tel	01491 570500
fax	01491 570528
e-mail	enquiries@phylliscourt.co.uk
web	www.phylliscourt.co.uk

map 3   entry 140

Pen-y-Dyffryn Country Hotel

Rhydycroesau, Nr. Oswestry, Shropshire SY10 7JD

Staggeringly beautiful scenery surrounds this old rectory, commissioned in 1845 by its first rector, Robert Williams, who compiled the first Celtic dictionary. He was said to be a stuffy character – the very opposite of Miles and Audrey, whose relaxed and easy-going manner suffuses the house with unpretentious charm. The entrance hall doubles as a bar; the bar itself an old *chiffonier* – "a posh sideboard," says Miles – with menus tucked away in the drawers. The bedrooms are 'comfy old house', with good fabrics and some with hand-painted furniture. One little double has its own flight of stairs, while the two 'old stable' rooms are big and contemporary, with private terraces; nearly all the rooms have spectacular views. There's a sitting room to curl up in, a restaurant for all tastes, organic beers and wines and a front terrace on which to sip long drinks and savour that view. The five acres of Pen-y-Dyffryn start at the top of the hill and roll down to Wales; the river at the foot of the beautiful valley marks the natural border.

rooms	10: 4 doubles, 4 twins, 1 single, 1 family.
price	£90–£118; singles £70.
meals	Dinner £25.
closed	Christmas & 1–14 January.
directions	From A5, head to Oswestry. Leave town on B4580, signed Llansilin. Hotel 3 miles on left just before Rhydycroesau.

Miles & Audrey Hunter

tel	01691 653700
fax	01691 650066
e-mail	stay@peny.co.uk
web	www.peny.co.uk

Cleobury Court

Cleobury North, Shropshire WV16 6RW

It's been quite a spending spree since Bill and Christina took over this former dower house. Francophiles both, they've collected furniture, tapestries and prints on their travels across the Channel. There's also a hint of the East as Christina ran a Balinese shop. The colour schemes are hers, such as the pale lemon sitting room carpet, fabrics, boldly floral, dramatically swathed. She makes the curtains and upholsters, too. Bill's more in charge of the food – good, local – and the garden. There are two suites: Ludlow, with its open country views, has a smart sitting room, a huge specially-made four-poster and a big, luxurious bathroom. The more intimate Garden suite has twin beds, set together under a super king-size half-tester, a charming Regency-striped sitting room, and a roll-top bath. The cosy double is blue and white in a French style. Be pampered in the manner of a private home rather than a hotel – Bill, who's Canadian, and Christina, a Londoner, are both extremely hospitable. Play the grand piano, or billiards, or stretch yourself in the gym. Ludlow is a short drive, or walk up Brown Clee from the back door.

rooms	3: 1 double, 2 suites.
price	£75; suites £90–£99; singles from £60.
meals	Dinner £18.50; give 24 hrs notice.
closed	Occasionally.
directions	From Bridgenorth, B4364 to Cleobury North. On right 0.5 miles from Cleobury Court signpost.

Bill & Christina Mills

tel	01746 787005
fax	01746 787005
e-mail	info@cleoburycourthotel.co.uk
web	www.cleoburycourthotel.co.uk

map 6   entry 142

Mr Underhill's at Dinham Weir

Dinham Bridge, Ludlow, Shropshire SY8 1EH

With Chris and Judy at the helm, Mr Underhill's started life in Suffolk, travelled 18,000 frustrating miles around England looking for a new home, then finally found one at the foot of Ludlow Castle. A moveable feast in every sense, they brought their Michelin star, too. Its position right on the River Teme is dreamy and worth all the bother. In summer, eat outside in the courtyard garden and watch the river drift by. The restaurant is long, light and airy, modern, warm and fun, and there's lots of glass to draw in the view. Bedrooms are at the other end of the house – the only noise you hear is the river – and almost Shaker in style: simple fabrics, crisp linen, king-size beds, a canopied four-poster without the posts, and more river views. Judy has cleverly designed the smaller rooms so they feel bigger; all are good and restful. Back downstairs, you're bound to meet Mungo and Toby, two British blues, and heirs to Frodo's empire after whose alias, as Tolkien-lovers will confirm, the restaurant is named. Good people with huge commitment.

rooms	6: 4 doubles, 2 twin/doubles.
price	£75–£120; singles £65–£85.
meals	Dinner £30.
closed	Occasionally. Restaurant closed Tuesday.
directions	Head to castle in Ludlow centre, then take 'Dinham' Rd to left of castle and follow down short hill, right at bottom before crossing river. On left, signed.

Chris & Judy Bradley

tel	01584 874431
fax	01584 874431
web	www.mr-underhills.co.uk

Porlock Vale House

Porlock Weir, Somerset TA24 8NY

Exmoor National Park runs into the sea here, tiny lanes ramble down into lush valleys while headlands rise to meet the waves. From the hotel – spurn two feet and wheels, saddle up a horse and ride off into the sunset. Well, maybe not, but this is an exceptional riding school, so come to jump, to brush up your dressage, or to hack across the moors. All levels from beginner to Olympic medallist welcome, so don't be shy. You don't have to ride; come to sit out on the terrace and watch the deer eat the garden, or walk down across fields and paddle in Porlock Bay. Whatever you do, you'll enjoy coming back to the simple splendour of this relaxed country house. Good, hearty food in the dining room, crackling log fires and leather sofas in the hall, books and games scattered about the place. Bedrooms are big, bright and comfortable with sofas if there's room; most have sea views and the bigger rooms are huge. Make sure you see the beautiful Edwardian stables; you may find the blacksmith at work in the yard, and the smell of polished leather in the tack room is just fantastic. Smashing people.

rooms	15: 9 doubles, 5 twins, 1 single.
price	£80–£130; singles £45–£85. Half-board £55–£89 p.p.
meals	Lunch from £5. Dinner £22.50.
closed	Mid-week in January & early February.
directions	West past Minehead on A39, then right in Porlock, for Porlock Weir. Through West Porlock, signed right.

Kim & Helen Youd

tel	01643 862338
fax	01643 863338
e-mail	info@porlockvale.co.uk
web	www.porlockvale.co.uk

map 2　entry 144

The Crown Hotel

Exford, Somerset TA24 7PP

Entering Hugo and Pamela's mildly eccentric world in the middle of Exmoor is guaranteed to be entertaining – don't be surprised to find a horse propping up the bar! The Crown is their latest venture, following on from the success of the Rising Sun in Lynmouth. These generous hosts have an in-built knack of looking after you. "People work so hard these days, they deserve to be spoilt," says Pamela, a scientist by trade and big-hearted by nature. Hugo is a gentleman of the old school, impeccably dressed beneath a shock of white hair. He sharpens his wits playing bridge with seasoned oldies who "clout me over the head if I make a foolish bid". You're in unspoilt, horsey country where laid-back locals draw just comparison with the easy-going outlook of rural Ireland. The building itself is Exmoor's oldest coaching inn, set in front of the village green – its angled eaves and peaked roof look like a crown from the front. It's very much work in progress inside. The Jeune way is gradually transforming floral bedrooms while good service and imaginative cooking is making a difference downstairs. Watch this place – it's destined to get better and better.

rooms	17: 8 doubles, 4 twins, 3 singles; 2 doubles, both with private bath.
price	£95-£110; singles £47.50. Half-board £70-£77.50.
meals	Lunch, 3 courses, £18.50. Dinner £25. Bar meals from £3.95.
closed	Never.
directions	M5, junc. 25, A38 to Taunton, A358 towards Minehead, then B3224 to Exford, via Wheddon Cross. Hotel by village green.

Hugo & Pamela Jeune

tel	01643 831554
fax	01643 831665
e-mail	info@crownhotelexmoor.co.uk
web	www.crownhotelexmoor.co.uk

The Royal Oak Inn

Withypool, Exmoor National Park, Somerset TA24 7QP

The drive to this oasis of luxury through twisting lanes shrouded in early morning mist leaves a magical impression of Exmoor which is impossible to shake – not that you'd want to. Look on any map and Withypool is the point at which all roads across the Moor meet. A small, forgotten place made immune to outside cares by the barren embrace of stone and bog, and heather that blazes a respendent purple in summer – there's no better place to flee. The 300-year-old Royal Oak will indulge you completely. Gail has a background in producing adverts for television but she isn't exaggerating when she says her bedrooms are "the nicest on the Moor". Full of graceful style and simple good taste, they are divided between the main inn and two superb cottages across the courtyard, also let as holiday homes: *toile de Jouy* fabrics and wallpaper, tongue-and-groove-panelled bathrooms, maybe an antique half-tester, or an old slipper bath, and dyed sheepskin rugs to cosset tired feet. The food is excellent, the welcome warm and the bar bustles with country brio. Walk to Tarr Steps, but heed Jake the barman's advice: an Exmoor mile is longer than an ordinary mile. Wildly invigorating.
Two gorgeous self-catering cottages next to inn also available, sleep 4-6, £600-£700 p.w.

rooms	8: 6 doubles, 2 twin/doubles.
price	£90–£110; singles £60–£70.
meals	Lunch from £4.75. Dinner about £20.
closed	Christmas Day.
directions	M5, junc. 27. A4361 to Tiverton, then right on A396, for Bampton & Dulverton. At Exbridge, left on B3222 to Dulverton & onto Withypool.

Gail Sloggett

tel	01643 831506/7
fax	01643 831659
e-mail	enquiries@royaloakwithypool.co.uk
web	www.royaloakwithypool.co.uk

 map 2   entry 146

Langley House Hotel & Restaurant

Langley Marsh, Taunton, Somerset TA4 2UF

A golden grasshopper welcomes you to the understated luxury of Langley House. Many years ago, it used to hang outside a merchant bank in the City of London, which is appropriate because Stuart used to hang out with merchant bankers before he and Sue opted recently to make hospitality their full-time careers. An air of quiet professionalism pervades, the Warnocks preferring to run things with a light touch in the classic hotel tradition, without the visible signs; it's more like entering a well-oiled English country house where discreet staff treat you with the utmost courtesy. The house was originally two 15th-century farm cottages, joined in 1720 to create a gentleman's residence. The entrance hall used to be an alleyway; now it leads to a cosy dining room, with swirls of green foliage print on the walls, candles at each table and a view of the pretty cottage garden, floodlit at night. Their food already has a good reputation. Relax in a big, comfy drawing room, or lounge at a small bar. Upstairs, bedrooms bloom with William Morris and Sanderson patterns; all are nicely done, with casual good taste. Popular with shooting parties.

rooms	8: 4 doubles, 2 twin/doubles, 1 four-poster, 1 family suite.
price	£100–£140; singles from £85.
meals	Dinner, 4 courses, £32.50.
closed	Never.
directions	From Taunton, B3227 to Wiveliscombe town centre, then right signed Langley Marsh. Hotel on right after 0.5 miles.

Stuart & Sue Warnock

tel	01984 623318
fax	01984 624573
e-mail	info@langleyhousehotel.co.uk
web	www.langleyhousehotel.co.uk

Bindon Country House Hotel

Langford Budville, Wellington, Somerset TA21 0RU

An extraordinary, beautiful building, Bindon hides on the edge of woodland where rare and colourful wild flowers flourish. Five years ago, it was a derelict mansion full of dust and cobwebs; now it's full of Mark and Lynn's enthusiasm. What strikes you most, entering through the large glass front door, is the crispness of it all: the tiled entrance hall, the stained glass, the wall tapestries, the plaster mouldings on the ceiling, the galleried staircase, the glass-domed roof... absolutely pristine. Keep going into the snug panelled bar, past the wrought iron candlesticks, for coffee served with piping hot milk and delicious home-made biscuits. In summer, move outside through open hall doors and sit by a magnificent stone balustrade that looks over rose gardens down to an old dovecote. Bright bedrooms come in different sizes: two oval rooms at the front of the house are *huge*, with dusky pink furniture, patterned wallpaper depicting genteel garden scenes, a high brass bed and Victorian baths; the others are large and very comfortable. Add gorgeous food and a luxuriously-heated pool for a hidden treasure.

rooms	12: 11 twin/doubles, 1 four-poster.
price	£95–£195; singles £85. Half-board (min. 2 nights) from £60 p.p.
meals	Lunch £12.95. Dinner, 5 courses, £29.95.
closed	Never.
directions	From Wellington, B3187 for 1.5 miles, then left at sharp S-bend for Langford Budville. Right in village for Wiveliscombe, then 1st right. House on right after 1.5 miles.

Lynn & Mark Jaffa

tel	01823 400070
fax	01823 400071
e-mail	stay@bindon.com
web	www.bindon.com

map 2   entry 148

Orchards Restaurant at Wrexon Farmhouse

Dipford Rd, Angersleigh, Taunton, Somerset TA3 7PA

The axiom that some people are made for each other surely applies to the immensely likeable owners of Orchards Restaurant. Norman and Julie have known each other since they were toddlers and this charming, established restaurant in an old Somerset crofter's cottage marks a lifetime of unswerving devotion. Relax with an aperitif by a wood stove in a cosy bar, or sit out in summer in a courtyard full of honeysuckle and rosemary. Herbs, salads, apples, damsons and plums grow on four acres for the table. Norman is a no-frills cook, preferring classic English methods to current trends: fish from Brixham, roast duckling, pavlovas and home-made ice creams are house specialities – the dessert trolley is a big favourite. In the restaurant, tables lit by candlelight fit snugly around gnarled beams and an elm trunk that seems to grow upstairs. You stay in a barn next door and breakfast arrives at the time of your choosing. As for the traffic, you'll be too busy enjoying yourself to notice the march of the nearby motorway. The cottage's thick walls insulate and the prevailing wind blows the sound in the other direction!

rooms	1 apartment for 2-3.
price	£69; singles £55.
meals	Continental breakfast £6.75. Dinner, à la carte, about £25. Lunch for groups of 12 or more.
closed	Restaurant closed Sundays & Mondays.
directions	From Taunton centre, follow signs to Trull; right after Queen's College, into Dipford Road, signed Angersleigh. 2 miles on right, just after bridge over M5.

Norman & Julie White

tel	01823 275440
e-mail	mail@orchardsrestaurant.co.uk
web	www.orchardsrestaurant.co.uk

Greyhound Inn

Staple Fitzpaine, Taunton, Somerset TA3 5SP

The Greyhound typifies the classic English country pub, walls bedecked with ad hoc collages of pictures and fishing memorabilia that create an atmosphere of warmth and hospitality. Let the eye wander, while sitting at old, wooden tables, worn nicely from frequent use and decorated simply with vases of wild flowers. A roaring hearth in winter, a flagstoned bar busy with friendly locals – ask after Mr Flack and Mr Grabham – and a good meal, with fish delivered daily from Brixham and meat from within four miles. Then "retreat in good order", as one boxing print wisely suggests, to clean, comfortable bedrooms; more hotel than individual. Ivor and Lucy bought the inn about two years ago, leaving careers in the pharmaceutical industry. "We still work long hours but we see each other now," says Ivor, a relaxed host, seemingly made for the job of community landlord. The Back Room restaurant promises much, with new chef Stephen Frost at the helm. What a spot, too, in deepest rural Somerset; walks through forestry lead to Castle Neroche and stunning views from the Blackdown Hills. Henry VIII's heart is even said to be buried in the churchyard. *Children over 12 welcome.*

rooms	4: 2 doubles, 1 twin, 1 twin/double.
price	£75–£90; singles £49.95.
meals	Lunch from £4. Dinner, à la carte, about £20.
closed	Never.
directions	M5, junc. 25, A358 towards Ilminster for 4 miles, then right, for Staple Fitzpaine. Left at T-junction. Village 1.5 miles further. Inn on right at x-roads.

Ivor & Lucy Evans

tel	01823 480227
fax	01823 481117
e-mail	stay@the-greyhoundinn.com
web	www.thegreyhoundinn.fsbusiness.co.uk

map 2   entry 150

Little Barwick House

Barwick Village, Yeovil, Somerset BA22 9TD

Emma and Tim belong to a vanguard of British hoteliers blending depth of experience with a new-found freedom to experiment and do their own thing. Little Barwick is a delightful restaurant with rooms that produces superb food in a relaxed atmosphere: flair, lots of ability and a rare sense of vocation and commitment are all in evidence. Step out of your car and the smell of something irresistible is likely to waft your way. They make whatever they can – marmalades, chutneys, sorbets, ice creams, breads, shortbreads, jams – even pasta. The house is full of variation as well. Emma has given the graceful Georgian interior a fresh, contemporary makeover: natural colours, stripped wooden floorboards and polished stone floors are the order of the day; anything stuffy or frilly has been banished. The bedrooms are all different, with spoiling touches. In winter, a three-day stay is incredible value; indulge yourself at breakfast with house champagne by the glass... go on, you're worth it.

rooms	6: 4 doubles, 2 twins.
price	£93–£103. Half-board from £78.50 p.p.
meals	Lunch from £12.95. Dinner £29.50.
closed	2 weeks in January. Restaurant closed Sunday & Monday evening, & Tuesday lunchtime.
directions	From Yeovil, A37 south for Dorchester, then left at 1st r'bout by Red House pub. Down hill, past church, house on left after 200 yds.

Emma & Tim Ford

tel	01935 423902
fax	01935 420908
e-mail	reservations@barwick7.fsnet.co.uk
web	www.littlebarwickhouse.co.uk

Glencot House

Glencot Lane, Wells, Somerset BA5 1BH

Jacobean elegance spills from this beautiful late-Victorian mansion into its 18-acre parkland setting. Inside, it's just as you would expect: four-poster beds, carved ceilings, walnut panelling, magical hallways filled with ancient furniture and bric-a-brac, plants and flowers everywhere. The drawing room is the magnet of the house; you'll meet the other guests here, all staring at the ceiling. The room is panelled top-to-toe with a mix of four woods and there's an inglenook fireplace the size of a room; in winter the flames leap six feet high. Hard to believe it has all mod-cons, too. Glencot was rescued from a state of dilapidation by Jenny and her husband; long hours of toil have brought it back to life. Don't miss the garden: a magnificent terrace with stunning stone balustrade and wide, gracious steps sweeps you down to the River Axe. There are fountains, a

waterfall and an old stone bridge to take you over to the cricket pitch where the village team plays in summer. *Pets by arrangement.*

rooms	13: 2 doubles, 3 twins, 3 singles, 5 four-posters.
price	£90–£115; singles from £68.50.
meals	Dinner from £26.50. Packed lunch from £3.50.
closed	Never.
directions	From Wells, follow signs to Wookey Hole. Sharp left at finger post, 100m after pink cottage. House on right in Glencot Lane.

	Jenny Attia
tel	01749 677160
fax	01749 670210
e-mail	relax@glencothouse.co.uk
web	www.glencothouse.co.uk

map 2   entry 152

The George

Norton St. Philip, Bath, Somerset BA3 6LH

Once an ostler would have calmed your snorting steed after its urgent canter across the Downs, directing you under the massive stone arch, across the cobbled courtyard and into the snug bar where logs crackled and ale was poured under darkened oak beams... The George must have been like that. The building is one of Somerset's finest, brilliantly converted, a 13th-century inn in continuous use — reputed to be an English record. During the English Civil War it sided with the rebels, harbouring the Duke of Monmouth, Charles II's illegitimate son; the Duke was later defeated at the Battle of Sedgemoor in 1685. There are restored 15th-century wall paintings, timber and stone everywhere, an ancient balconied corridor, and rear views across the cricket pitch to the church. The village street passes in front, but quietly at night. Eat well in a large beamed dining room, or a snug alcove; the bar bench is a 700-year-old monk's writing table — not often do you see the legs of the person serving your beer! Bedrooms are magnificently redone with reproduction beds and furniture, bare floorboards in some, luxury in all...

rooms	8: 5 doubles, 3 four-posters.
price	£80–£110; singles from £60.
meals	Bar meals from £3.95. Dinner about £18.
closed	Christmas Day & Boxing Day.
directions	From Bath, A36 south, then A366 west for 1 mile. Inn in village.

David & Tania Satchell

tel	01373 834224
fax	01373 834861
e-mail	info@thegeorgeinn-nsp.co.uk
web	www.thegeorgeinn-nsp.co.uk

Ounce House

Northgate Street, Bury St Edmunds, Suffolk IP33 1HP

An extremely handsome 1870 red-brick townhouse minutes from the heart of one of England's prettiest ancient towns. Bury St Edmunds has a rich history; the Romans were here, its Norman abbey attracted pilgrims by the cartload, and the wool trade made it rich in the 1700s. A gentle, one-hour stroll takes you past 650 years of architectural wonder – special indeed. Ounce House is more house than hotel, pristine and full of fine antiques. Enjoy sumptuous breakfasts around a mighty-sized mahogany dining table and slump in leather armchairs around a wildly ornate carved fireplace. Light floods in all day through the double doors between the drawing and dining rooms. Elsewhere, a snug library has an honesty bar, while fine, homely bedrooms are packed with books, mahogany furniture, local art and piles of magazines; the room at the back of the house has a pretty view of the garden. The Potts can arrange tickets to the Theatre Royal, pick you up from the train station, or help you decide between the 35 restaurants within five minutes of the house.

rooms	3: 2 doubles, 1 twin.
price	£85–£95; singles £60–£70.
meals	Restaurants in Bury St Edmunds.
closed	Never.
directions	A14 north, then central junction for Bury St Edmunds, following signs to centre. At 1st r'bout, left into Northgate St. On right at top of hill.

Simon & Jenny Pott

tel	01284 761779
fax	01284 768315
e-mail	pott@globalnet.co.uk
web	www.ouncehouse.co.uk

map 4   entry 154

Pipps Ford

Needham Market, Suffolk IP6 8LJ

Richard Hakluyt, the Elizabethan chronicler, once had the "Manor at Pipps". It is still a fine Suffolk house, beamed and whitewashed and now with a conservatory – a riot of vines and other climbing plants, like a smart greenhouse and an entertaining place to dine. And you dine well – on tiger prawns in coconut with coriander and lemon, or bream, partridge, lamb... even talapia. The atmosphere in this easy-going and cosy house encourages conversation. Once through the narrow hall you are into a big sitting room with some fine furniture and a grand piano (another is sometimes used for private meetings). The dining room is dark red, low-beamed and wooden floored. The bedrooms in the main house – there are some in a barn – are full of fabric and chintz, floral patterns and plain carpets, traditional and endearingly cottagey. The floors are characterfully crooked and rooms have very English views over the lovely garden. The house is on its own, with walks along the old canal and so much of lovely Suffolk to see beyond. *Children over five welcome.*

rooms	7 doubles.
price	£65-£80; singles £49.50.
meals	Dinner from £22.50.
closed	2 weeks over Christmas & New Year. No dinner on Sunday.
directions	From Ipswich, A14 north to r'bout where A140 joins A14. 1st left at r'bout down private track, signed to house.

Raewyn Hackett-Jones

tel	01449 760208
fax	01449 760561
e-mail	b+b@pippsford.co.uk
web	www.pippsford.co.uk

The Great House

Market Place, Lavenham, Suffolk CO10 9QZ

A little pocket of France in a pretty corner of England, The Great House pulls off that rare trick of being a hotel that feels like a home. Régis and Martine are charming, as are their French staff. The house is authentic, too, with an 18th-century front and a 15th-century interior that is utterly lovely and full of surprises. The bedrooms have antique desks and chests of drawers, fresh flowers and superb marble in perfect bathrooms: one has a big Jacobean oak four-poster — like an island in a sea of rugs; another in the roof has sofas and armchairs from which to marvel at the huge beamed timbers. Most have their own private sitting area and some have views over this bustling, historic market town. It's simply impossible to escape the generosity and good taste of it all, and that's never more true than in the restaurant — essence of France in the middle of Suffolk. The sheer splendour of the food brings guests back again and again; the cheese board alone is a work of art. Catch the early sun in the courtyard for breakfast, or eat supper *al fresco* on warm and lazy summer nights. Fabulous.

rooms	5 doubles.
price	£90–£150; singles from £70. Half-board from £64.95 p.p.
meals	Lunch from £11. Dinner from £21.95.
closed	January. Restaurant closed Monday.
directions	From Sudbury, A134 towards Colchester for about 2 miles, then left, signed Lavenham. Hotel is in the market place.

Régis & Martine Crépy

tel	01787 247431
fax	01787 248007
e-mail	info@greathouse.co.uk
web	www.greathouse.co.uk

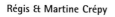

map 4 entry 156

The White Hart Inn

High Street, Colchester, Suffolk CO6 4JF

Michel Roux's 'other place' is exquisite on all counts; the way things are done here is second to none. The service is remarkable. Staff here do have a sense of pride in their work – this sometimes seems a rarity in Britain these days (although not in this book, of course...). The inn dates from the 15th century and has kept its timber-framed walls and beams. Inside has been opened up a bit, not enough to lose its rambling feel, but just enough to make it light and airy. Feast on "scrumptious food", to quote an enraptured guest, and sup from a vast collection of New World wines. "People like to travel when they drink," says Michel. Exemplary bedrooms have a striking yet simple country-style elegance; yellow walls and checked fabrics, crisp linen and thick blankets, excellent bathrooms, angled beams (two rooms almost have vaulted ceilings), piles of cushions, sofas or armchairs, and wonderful art; some have wildly sloping floors and one has original murals that may be the work of Constable's brother. Superb.

rooms	6 doubles.
price	£82; singles £69.
meals	Lunch from £9.95. Dinner about £24.
closed	Restaurant closed Monday.
directions	Nayland is signed right 6 miles north of Colchester on the A134 (no access from A12). In village centre.

	Michel Roux
tel	01206 263382
fax	01206 263638
e-mail	nayhart@aol.com
web	www.whitehart-nayland.co.uk

The Pier at Harwich

The Quay, Harwich, Suffolk CO12 3HH

It's easy to underestimate the charms of Harwich – the "oldest recorded town in England" – but The Pier stands against that current and has never looked better. Owners the Milsoms recently took over the next-door pub to carve out a handsome lounge: loads of space, seagrass matting, simple bold colours and deep sofas around an open fire. The upstairs restaurant takes the pick of the views over the harbour, the Stour and Orwell estuaries and fresh fish is, of course, what you should eat. Chris and Vreni Oakley – he's the seafood expert, she's front of house and his absolutely charming Swiss-born wife – have been here nearly 25 years; they clearly love the place and go out of their way to see that guests do too. Informal eating – checked tablecloths, plastic chairs – takes place in the Bistro and on the buzzing quayside. Bedrooms are beautifully done: more seagrass, painted tongue and groove panelling, great colour, good quality fabrics – splash out on the Mayflower suite for the best views. The hall and bar have a modern feel with leather-look seating and a maritime sprinkling of ship's wheels and brass portholes. Book a mooring.

rooms	14 doubles.
price	£80–£150; singles £62.50–£75. Half-board (min. 2 nights) from £100 p.p.
meals	Lunch £16. Dinner, à la carte, £25–£28.
closed	Never.
directions	M25, junc. 28, A12 to Colchester bypass, then A120 to Harwich. Head for quay. Hotel opposite pier.

Chris & Vreni Oakley

tel	01255 241212
fax	01255 551922
e-mail	info@pieratharwich.co.uk
web	www.pieratharwich.com

map 4   entry 158

The Dolphin

Peace Place, Thorpeness, Aldeburgh, Suffolk IP16 4NA

Thorpeness is a one-off, the perfect antidote to 21st-century holidays. The village was the turn-of-century brainchild of GS Ogilvie, who set out to create a holiday resort for children, free of piers and promenades, with safety assured. His master stroke is the Meare — a 64-acre lake, never more than three feet deep, inspired by Ogilvie's friend, J M Barrie, creator of *Peter Pan*. Children can row, sail and canoe their way up creeks and discover islands that may have a lurking (wooden) crocodile round the corner. The Dolphin — in the middle of the village — is a great little inn. It has three very good bedrooms in cottage style with old pine furniture, soft colours and spotless bathrooms; and two lively bars, open fires, wooden floors in the dining room and outside, a terrace and lawn for barbecues and *al fresco* dinners. Tennis at the Country Club, a great golf course, an unspoilt sand and pebble beach, a summer theatre company and even a "house in the clouds". A paradise for families and excellent value for money.

rooms	3 twin/doubles.
price	£60-£65; singles £45.
meals	Lunch & dinner from £10.
closed	Never.
directions	From A12 at Farnham, A1094 to Aldeburgh seafront. Turn left and follow coast road for 2 miles into Thorpeness. Inn on right, signed.

Tim Rowan-Robinson

tel	01728 454994
fax	01728 454971
e-mail	info@thorpeness.co.uk
web	www.thorpeness.co.uk

Bailiffscourt Hotel

Climping, Sussex BN17 5RW

Everything about Bailiffscourt is exhilarating. It is beautiful to the eye, too, the architect having searched high and low for its soft, golden Somerset sandstone. The gardens and grounds are a simple paradise and as you stroll in peace from barn to coach house you feel as if you are walking around an ancient monastery. Inside, rooms are big and have a perfect medieval atmosphere, set off brilliantly by bold colours, rich fabrics and large tapestries on the walls. There are mullioned windows, heavy, ancient beams, even an entire ceiling of wood in the restaurant. Bedrooms are perfect too, with carved four-posters, oak chests, waterfalls of cushions, 600-year-old doors, fabulous bathrooms and decanters of sherry. Best of all is the truth – Bailiffscourt, incredibly, is a 'genuine fake', built in the 1930s from innumerable medieval bits and bobs. One of the buildings was moved here brick by brick; only the 13th-century chapel is authentic. It is quite magnificent; there's even a beach at the end of the garden. Come and revel in it all.

rooms	32 doubles.
price	£160–£330; singles from £140.
meals	Lunch from £15.50.
	Dinner, 4 courses, £37.50.
closed	Never.
directions	From Littlehampton, A259 west. At the brown sign for Bailiffscourt, left into Climping St and up lane to hotel. Entrance last on right.

Sandy & Anne Goodman

tel	01903 723511
fax	01903 723107
e-mail	bailiffscourt@hshotels.co.uk
web	www.hshotels.co.uk

map 3   entry 160

Ockenden Manor

Ockenden Lane, Cuckfield, Sussex RH17 5LD

If some hotels flatter to deceive, Ockenden Manor does the reverse, its handsome Tudor front providing no clue to the awesome cathedral proportions that await inside. The change of scale is so sudden and surprising, it feels as if you've walked into a different building. In a way, you have, because what you see was rebuilt after a fire burnt down most of the original Tudor house in 1608. Enter a long hall that leads to an even grander drawing room with impossibly high ceilings. The dining room has original oak panelling from the floor up to a ceiling of carved floral motifs; stained-glass windows depict family crests and look onto well-loved gardens, small but perfect for a cream tea. Back inside, Sandy and Anne have filled the giant spaces with exquisite good taste: stunning furniture, vases of fresh flowers, decanters of port, cut-glass crystal and antique prints in the bar. Smart bedrooms, named after the children of previous owners, are decorated with Colefax & Fowler and Zoffany; some are in the house, the rest are in a 1990 addition. Close to Gatwick, but much more than an airport stopover.

rooms	22: 11 doubles, 4 twins, 1 single, 6 four-posters.
price	£160-£330; singles from £105.
meals	Lunch from £10. Cream tea £7.50. Dinner, à la carte, £38.
closed	Never.
directions	A23 south from M23, then B2115 south-east to Cuckfield. In village, right, opp. Talbot Inn, into Ockenden Lane. Hotel signed.

	Sandy & Anne Goodman
tel	01444 416111
fax	01444 415549
e-mail	ockenden@hshotels.co.uk
web	www.hshotels.co.uk

The Griffin Inn

Fletching, Nr. Uckfield, Sussex TN22 3SS

The Griffin is the sort of inn worth moving house to be near; perfect almost because of the occasional touch of scruffiness. The Pullan family run it with gentle passion as a true local; regulars were queuing up before opening time when we arrived on a chilly Tuesday morning in January. Inside, six open fires, obligatory 500-year-old beams, oak panelling, settles, red carpets, black and white photos on the walls... this inn has been allowed to age. There's a small club room for racing on Saturdays and two cricket teams play in summer. Bedrooms are perfect, tremendous value for money and full of uncluttered country-inn elegance: uneven floors, lots of old furniture, rag-rolled walls, free-standing Victorian baths, huge shower heads, crisp cotton linen and thick bathrobes; rooms in the coach house are quieter. Good food is guaranteed – the inn was voted best dining pub in Sussex. Over the summer months, jazz bands play in the garden against the backdrop of a 10-mile view across Ashdown Forest to Sheffield Park; and they lay on a spit-roast barbecue as well. Wonderful.

rooms	8: 1 twin, 7 four-posters.
price	£70–£120.
meals	Lunch from £7. Dinner £20.
closed	Christmas Day.
directions	From East Grinstead, A22 south, then right at Nutley, signed Fletching. Straight on for 2 miles into village.

Bridget, Nigel & James Pullan

tel	01825 722890
fax	01825 722810
web	www.thegriffininn.co.uk

map 4   entry 162

Stone House

Rushlake Green, Heathfield, Sussex TN21 9QJ

One of the bedrooms has a huge bathroom with enough room for a sofa and two chairs around the marble bath, but does that make it a suite? Jane thought not. The bedroom is big, has a beautiful four-poster, floods with light and, like all the rooms, has sumptuous furniture and seemingly ancient fabrics, all typical of the generosity of both house and owners. Stone House has been in the Dunn family for a mere 500 years and Peter and Jane have kept the feel of home. Downstairs, amid the splendour of the drawing room, there's still room for lots of old family photos; across the hall in the library, logs piled high wait to be tossed on the fire. Weave down a corridor to ancient oak panelling in the dining room for Jane's cooking – she's a Master Chef. Having eaten, walk out to the superb, half-acre walled kitchen garden and see where it's all grown – they're 99% self-sufficient in summer. There are 1,000 acres to explore and you can fish for carp. Indulgent picnic hampers for Glyndebourne, including chairs and tables, can be arranged.

rooms	7: 3 twin/doubles, 1 single, 2 four-posters, 1 suite.
price	£115–£225; singles £75–£90.
meals	Lunch, by arrangement, £24.95. Dinner £24.95.
closed	Christmas & New Year.
directions	From Heathfield, B2096, then 4th turning on right, signed Rushlake Green. 1st left by village green. House on left, signed.

Peter & Jane Dunn

tel	01435 830553
fax	01435 830726
web	www.stonehousesussex.co.uk

Little Hemingfold Hotel

Telham, Battle, Sussex TN33 0TT

The south east of England is much underrated in terms of rural beauty; drive up the bumpy track that leads to Little Hemingfold and you could be miles from the middle of nowhere. People who want to get away to the simplicity of deep country will love it here. It's comfortably rustic, a little like renting a remote country cottage, though here you don't have to cook or clean; open fires, *bergère* sofas and armchairs, books and games, lots of flowers and floods of light. Breakfast in the yellow dining room is under beams; at night the candles come out for delicious home-cooked dinners. The bedrooms are all over the place, some in the main house, others across the small, pretty courtyard. They are fairly earthy, four having woodburning stoves – again that feel of deep country – with a four-poster perhaps, maybe a sofa, glazed-brick walls and simple bathrooms. Outside, a two-acre lake to row and fish or swim in, a grass tennis court (the moles got the better of the croquet lawn), woodland to walk in and lots of peace and quiet.

rooms	12: 10 twin/doubles; 2 family with private bath.
price	£88–£95; singles £54–£82.50. Half-board £62–£69.50 p.p.
meals	Dinner, 4 courses, £24.50.
closed	January–February.
directions	From Battle, A2100 for Hastings for 1.5 miles. Hotel signed left by 'sharp left' road sign, 0.5 miles up farm track.

Allison & Paul Slater

tel	01424 774338
fax	01424 775351

map 4   entry 164

Jeake's House

Mermaid Street, Rye, Sussex TN31 7ET

Rye, one of the Cinque Ports, is a perfect town for whiling away an afternoon; wander aimlessly and discover the tidal river, old fishing boats, arts and crafts shops and galleries. Jeake's House is in the heart of old Rye on a steep, ancient cobbled street. The house has a colourful past as wool store, school and home of American poet Conrad Potter Aiken. The galleried dining room, once an old Baptist chapel, is now painted deep red and is full of plants, busts, books, clocks and mirrors — perfect for those who like to make a grand entrance at breakfast! Jenny is engagingly easy-going and has created a lovely atmosphere. Rooms full of beams and timber frames are pretty, generously draped and excellent value. Some have stunning old chandeliers, others four-posters, and a mind-your-head stairway leads to a big attic room with views over roof tops and chimneys to open country. Downstairs, a small library keeps away the rainy day blues, the hearth is lit in winter and musicians will swoon at the working square piano. Relax into it all with a drink from the honesty bar. A super little hotel. *Children over 12 welcome.*

rooms	12: 10 doubles, 1 suite; 1 single, sharing bath.
price	£66–£110; singles £34–£70.
meals	Restaurants in Rye.
closed	Never.
directions	Enter Rye & follow signs to town centre under arch into High St, then 3rd left at Lloyds Bank & 1st right into Mermaid St. House on left. Private parking nearby, £3 a day.

Jenny Hadfield

tel	01797 222828
fax	01797 222623
e-mail	jeakeshouse@btinternet.com
web	www.jeakeshouse.com

The Howard Arms

Lower Green, Ilmington, Warwickshire CV36 4LT

Once upon a time Robert and Gill ran the Cotswold House Hotel in Chipping Campden with a mix of flair, quirkiness and professionalism. After a deserved sabbatical, they decided to cast their fairy-dust over this old inn, with magical results. The Howard buzzes with good-humoured babble, as well-kept beer flows from the flagstoned bar. An irresistible dining room at the far end has unexpected elegance for a pub, with great swathes of bold colour and some noble paintings. Gorgeous bedrooms are set discreetly apart from the joyful throng, mixing period style and modern luxury beautifully: the double oozes olde worlde charm; the twin is more folksy, with American art and patchwork quilts; and the half-tester is almost a suite, full of classy antiques — all individual and all huge by pub standards. The village is a surprise, too, literally tucked under a lone hill, with an unusual church surrounded by orchards and an extended village green. Round off an idyllic walk amid buzzing bees and fragrant wild flowers with a meal at the inn — folk come a long way to sample the food. Stratford and the theatre are close.

rooms	3: 1 twin, 2 doubles.
price	£85–£96; singles from £52.
meals	Lunch & dinner £8.50–£20.
closed	Christmas Day.
directions	From Moreton-in-Marsh, north on A429 for about 5 miles, then left, signed Darlingscott and Ilmington. Pub in village centre.

Robert & Gill Greenstock

tel	01608 682226
fax	01608 682226
e-mail	howard.arms@virgin.net
web	www.howardarms.com

map 3   entry 166

The Fox and Goose

Armscote, Nr. Stratford-upon-Avon, Warwickshire CV37 8DD

Sue is one of those irrepressible innkeepers with an instinctive feel for what works. She took on a pub that had seen better days, stripped it back to its bare walls, pulled up the carpets, put in earthy wooden floors, then coated the walls with Farrow & Ball paints. The feel is fresh, informal, vibrant – it's a 'happening' place. Purple, crushed-velvet stools in the stone-flagged bar, shutters on all the windows, an open fire, woodburning stove, heavy oak beams – fixtures and fittings from the 17th century, blended with 21st-century style. She also added an excellent dining room for food that's "not too fancy, but very well cooked" – maybe Thai chicken, rib-eye steaks or home-made pasta; on Sundays, choose from goose, beef and lamb, all roasted to perfection. Bedrooms above the restaurant are spectacular, though fairly compact: bold blues, reds and yellows, stripped wooden floors and big, comfy beds with padded 'jester hat' headboards. Grab a disc from reception for the CD player, light the candles in the bathroom, fill the tub, and take in your glass of wine...

rooms	4 doubles.
price	£80; singles £40.
meals	Lunch & dinner £4.50–£25.
closed	Christmas Day & New Year's Day.
directions	From Stratford-upon-Avon A3400 south for 8 miles, then right for Armscote just after Newbold-on-Stour. In village.

Sue Gray

tel	01608 682293
fax	01608 682293
web	www.foxandgoose.co.uk

The Red Lion

High Street, Lacock, Wiltshire SN15 2LQ

The dashing Mr Darcy was sensible enough to stop here during the BBC's filming of *Pride and Prejudice* – and how comforted he was by the inn's warm, beamed embrace. The Red Lion dates from the early 1700s, and may well have been known to the impressionable Jane Austen; big open fires, tankards hanging above the bar, rugs on flagstones, bare wooden floors – not a lot has changed. Order a drink and sit down to fine home-cooked food, amid timber frames, old settles, a row of branding irons and hanging Victorian birdcages; you may have to ask about the more bizarre farming tools on display. Climb the shallow tread of the stairs to small but excellent bedrooms in a Georgian style; old oak dressers, half-testers, crowns above beds, antique furniture, a beam or two. Breakfast – the full Wiltshire – is eaten in a pretty, first-floor room that looks out onto the High Street. In summer, eat outside in the atmospheric courtyard garden, with country views. This beautifully preserved National Trust village was built around the 13th-century Abbey and on the old cloth route between London and Bristol. A historic port of call.

rooms	4: 3 doubles, 1 twin.
price	£65–£75; singles from £45.
meals	Lunch from £6. Dinner about £15.
closed	Never.
directions	Lacock is just off A350 between Chippenham and Melksham. Inn on High Street.

Chris & Sarah Chappell

tel	01249 730456
fax	01249 730766

map 3   entry 168

The Angel Inn

Hindon, Wiltshire SP3 6DJ

It's impossible not to eat well at The Angel. The robust, modern English cooking draws folk from far and wide. Penny's latest venture at this 1750 coaching inn in the heart of Wiltshire follows a wonderful Georgian conversion in Oxfordshire; she seems much more at home in her present surroundings. Over lunch, watch a mixed crowd of retired-military and likeable loafers file in for their medicinal pint. There's a great atmosphere: you might be asked to help with the crossword – that is, if Penny can't help. She's the first port of call for most things here: hands on, ever-present and a smiling stickler for things to be done just right, and why not! Downstairs, she's cast her magic wand over bar and restaurant; upstairs is next. We expect great things of the bedrooms, judging by the jazzy red walls and wooden floors of the bar. Further on, under the bust of a plaster angel, the linear and more formal restaurant is softened by impressively large black and white photographs of scenes taken within five miles of the inn – the tree surrounded by wild garlic is beautiful. Terrific.

rooms	7: 4 doubles, 1 twin, 1 family, 1 four-poster.
price	£50-£75; singles from £50.
meals	Lunch, à la carte, about £14. Dinner, à la carte, about £22.
closed	Restaurant & bar closed Sunday evening.
directions	From A303, Hindon signed left about 7 miles after main A36 Salisbury turn-off. Inn at x-roads in village.

	Penny Simpson
tel	01747 820696
fax	01747 820869
e-mail	eat@theangel-inn.co.uk
web	www.theangel-inn.co.uk

The Compasses Inn

Lower Chicksgrove, Tisbury, Wiltshire SP3 6NB

The first impression on arriving at Compasses is of having found the perfect English pub; so is the second. Lying at the heart of a dreamy village of thatched and timber-framed cottages, this lovely inn seems so content with its lot it could almost be a figment of your imagination. Over the years, 14th-century foundations have gradually sunk into the ground. Its thatched roof is like a sombrero, shielding bedroom windows that peer sleepily over the lawn outside. Duck instinctively into the sudden darkness of the bar and experience a wave of nostalgia as your eyes adjust to a long wooden room, with flagstones and cosy booths divided by farmyard salvage: a cart-wheel here, some horse tack there; at one end is a piano, at the other, a brick hearth. The pub crackles with Alan's energy and enthusiasm; he's fairly new to the trade, but his genuine hospitality more than compensates. People come for the food as well: figs baked in red wine, topped with goat's cheese and chorizo, or grilled fish from the south coast. Bedrooms have the same effortless charm and the sweet serenity of Wiltshire lies just down the lane. Modest, ineffably pretty, and great value.

rooms	4: 2 doubles, 2 twin/doubles.
price	From £55; singles £40.
meals	Lunch from £4. Dinner, à la carte, about £20.
closed	Monday except Bank Holidays, then closed Tuesday.
directions	From Salisbury, A30 west, 3rd right after Fovant, signed Lower Chicksgrove, then 1st left down single track lane to village.

	Alan Stoneham
tel	01722 714318
fax	01722 714318

map 3   entry 170

Howard's House

Teffont Evias, Nr. Salisbury, Wiltshire SP3 5RJ

Howard's has been a favourite of ours for years — luxurious without boasting, modest in its success, the sort of place where the sun shines, even in January. With one toe in deep country, this attractive 1623 stone house is the last building in a quiet village of soaring church spire and gently rising hills. Step inside the warm flagstoned entrance hall to mullioned windows of odd shapes and sizes, masses of space, flowers everywhere and bold colours throughout. Mustard and red walls draw you into the sitting room to relax by a huge stone fireplace — you'll find *Tatler*, *The Economist* and *Classic Car* on the table. Strong yellows and blues lift the crisp, modern dining room, and pastel hues dominate faultless bedrooms with floral fabrics, fresh fruit, home-made biscuits, bathrobes and big towels. French windows lead to patios with tables and chairs. The immaculate garden has clipped hedges, croquet lawns, sensory herb patches, fountain and pond. Bill entertains with aplomb and the modern British cooking is consistently good. Beautiful Wiltshire starts right outside.

rooms	9: 6 doubles, 1 twin/double, 1 family, 1 four-poster.
price	£145–£165; singles from £95.
meals	Dinner, £23.95; à la carte, about £27.
closed	Christmas.
directions	From Salisbury, A350, then B3089 east to Teffont. In village, right at sharp left-hand bend, following brown hotel sign. Entrance on right after 0.5 miles.

Bill Thompson

tel	01722 716392
fax	01722 716820
e-mail	enq@howardshousehotel.co.uk
web	www.howardshousehotel.co.uk

The Mill at Harvington

Anchor Lane, Evesham, Worcestershire WR11 5NR

Not a bad house for a miller; he baked Birmingham's bread until 1898 when the river froze over, breaking the mill's waterwheels, a fate from which it never recovered. But he left a legacy: Russian pine beams – imported for the great weight they could support – with shipping marks branded in Cyrillic. The house dates from the 1700s though you enter through the Chestnut Tree, a bright 1990s addition with glass walls and a trim wooden roof. Like the rest of the house, it looks out onto the huge lawned garden that runs down to the River Avon. In summer, there's a liberal sprinkling of parasoled tables; pick one up and plonk it wherever you like, then sit back and watch canal boats chug by. Alternatively, sink into deep sofas in the sitting room or hang your head out of one of the bedroom windows – they all look 'the right way'. Rooms are "comfortable, not luxurious," says Simon, who always wears a bow-tie; good fabrics, drapes and king-size beds prove his point. *Children over 10 welcome.*

rooms	21: 16 doubles, 5 twins.
price	£89–£129.
meals	Light lunch from £10. Dinner £23.
closed	24-29 December.
directions	From Evesham, A46 north, then B4088 to Norton. At r'bout by Norton Grange pub, right, for Bidford, then right after 1.5 miles over bridge, signed to hotel. Entrance on left after 0.5 miles.

Simon & Jane Greenhalgh

tel	01386 870688
fax	01386 870688
e-mail	millatharvington@aol.com

map 3   entry 172

The Cottage in the Wood

Holywell Road, Malvern Wells, Worcestershire WR14 4LG

Walk along a path through the woods, dappled with light, and emerge in a clearing in this very English jungle. There, The Cottage gazes across the wide, flat Severn Valley to the distant Cotswolds. Walk all the way to the breezy top of the Malvern Hills – England's oldest rock and a 'forgotten corner' much loved by Elgar. It is enough just to be here, but to find such an endearingly friendly, book-lined and log-fired country-house hotel is heart-warming. Furniture, curtains, carpets and wallpapers are polished, swagged, patterned and lined, and distinctly pre-modern. The service is magnificent, the sort you only get when a large and talented family is at the helm. Dominic's cooking is as good as his father's hotel-keeping, and his sister's front of house. Local produce is used in an eclectic, modern and imaginative way and portions are unusually generous: try chilled cucumber soup with seared langoustines, or maybe honey-roast quail on broad beans and bacon. Relax in the main house, drink in the views and John's well-chosen wines, and play basketball from your bath. There's lots of humour as well as old-fashioned professionalism.

rooms	20: 17 doubes, 1 twin/double, 2 four-posters.
price	£98–£160; singles £79–£92. Half-board (min. 2 nights) £68–£108 p.p.
meals	Lunch from £15.50. Packed lunch £7.50. Dinner, à la carte, about £30.
closed	Never.
directions	M5, junc. 8, M50, junc. 1, A38 for Worcester, then left after 3 miles on A4104 for Upton upon Severn. Right after bridge on B4211, then left after 1.5 miles on B4209.

John & Sue Pattin

tel	01684 575859
fax	01684 560662
e-mail	reception@cottageinthewood.co.uk
web	www.cottageinthewood.co.uk

The Weavers Shed
Restaurant with Rooms

Knowl Road, Golcar, Huddersfield, Yorkshire HD7 4AN

Stephen's reputation for producing sublime food goes from strength to strength at The Weavers Shed, a restaurant with rooms firmly fixed on the wish lists of foodies all over the country. His passion stretches as far as planting a one-acre kitchen garden; it now provides most of his vegetables, herbs and fruit. You may get warm mousse of scallops, Lunesdale duckling and warm rhubarb tartlet, the latter home-grown, of course. The old mill owner's house sits at the top of the hill, with cobbles in the courtyard and its own lamp post by the door. Inside, whitewashed walls are speckled with menus from famous restaurants, a small garden basks beyond the windows and, at the bar, malts and eaux-de-vie stand behind a piece of wood that look as if it came from an ancient church, but actually came from the Co-op. Earthy stone arches and plinths in

the Sardinian-tiled restaurant at the back give the feel of a Tuscan farmhouse. Elsewhere, gilt mirrors and comfy sofas and big, bright, brilliantly priced bedrooms that hit the spot with complimentary sherry, dried flowers, bathrobes and wicker chairs.

rooms	5: 3 doubles, 1 twin/double, 1 four-poster.
price	£60-£70; singles from £45.
meals	Lunch from £9.95. Dinner about £25.
closed	Christmas & New Year. Restaurant closed Saturday lunchtime & Sunday.
directions	From Huddersfield A62 west for 2 miles, then right for Milnsbridge and Golcar. Left at Kwiksave; signed on right at top of hill.

Stephen & Tracy Jackson

tel	01484 654284
fax	01484 650980
e-mail	info@weaversshed.co.uk
web	www.weaversshed.co.uk

map 6   entry 174

Weaver's

15 West Lane, Haworth, Yorkshire BD22 8DU

If you don't know what a Clun or a Lonk is, use it as an excuse to make a trip to this unusual restaurant with rooms — the answer is somewhere on the walls. The rambling eccentricity here is superb; nothing has a place, yet everything is exactly where it should be. The front bar has the intimate feel of an old French café, with heavy wood, marble-topped tables, atmospheric lighting and comfy chairs, while the lively restaurant at the back seems in step with the Charleston era. None of this was intended, of course. Eat the best and most unpretentious food imaginable — smoked haddock soup, Pennine pie, home-made ice cream... even Yorkshire feta. It's outstanding value and people come back time and again. Bedrooms are as full of surprises and understated originality: French beds, dashes of bright colour, the odd bust, antique furniture — everything is just right. Rooms at the back overlook the Brontë Parsonage. Colin runs front of house — from the kitchen — with true Yorkshire sass: straight-talking, down-to-earth, and blessed with a wicked sense of humour. Worth a long detour, for the organic breakfast alone.

rooms	3: 2 twin/doubles, 1 single, all with private bathrooms.
price	£80; singles £50-£60.
meals	Dinner £12.50-£25; à la carte about £25; bar supper about £12.50.
closed	26 Dec-9 Jan, & 1 week in June. Restaurant open Tuesday-Saturday evenings & Sunday lunchtime.
directions	A6033 to Haworth, follow signs to Brontë Parsonage Museum. Use museum car park. Restaurant near passageway to high street.

Colin & Jane Rushworth

tel	01535 643822
fax	01535 644832
e-mail	weavers@amserve.net
web	www.weaversmallhotel.co.uk

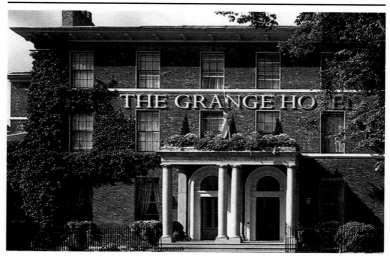

The Grange Hotel

1 Clifton, York, Yorkshire YO30 6AA

Half a mile from the city wall where the ancient Minster stands, this lovely hotel casts its spell immediately. The Grange is everything a big townhouse hotel should be: gracious, elegant, sumptuously grand, with a warmth that will unravel the tightest knot. Jeremy and Vivien rescued the Georgian building from years of municipal neglect. Effortless style runs throughout: stone floors, Doric columns and urns erupting with flowers greet you in the hall. Leather sofas in the morning room ask to be worn in some more, and the gorgeous vaulted brasserie in the old cellars with red banquettes in snug corners is an unexpected surprise. The formal dining room has a mural covering wall and ceiling showing a race scene through the open flaps of a blue and white-striped pavilion. The horse-racing link is apropos: York's course, with its tight bends, is considered one of the most exciting in Britain. The hotel is always full on race days — it's said the optimists meet here! Bedrooms are also full of flair: bold greens and reds, a silky purple four-poster, writing paper on the desks and rich fabrics. Those after history need only step outside.

rooms	33: 9 doubles, 18 twin/doubles, 3 singles, 2 four-posters, 1 suite.
price	£135–£195; singles from £105; suite £230.
meals	Lunch from £7.95. Dinner £28.
closed	Never.
directions	From York ring road, A19 south into city centre. Hotel on right after 2.5 miles, 400 yds from city walls.

	Jeremy & Vivien Cassel
tel	01904 644744
fax	01904 612453
e-mail	info@grangehotel.co.uk
web	www.grangehotel.co.uk

map 7   entry 176

Cutlers on the Stray

19 West Park, Harrogate, Yorkshire HG1 1BL

The knife, fork and spoon are put to many uses at this hugely enjoyable brasserie with rooms. Secondhand cutlery has been contorted into candle-holders, key fobs, works of art, even the hotel logo features the threesome, the spoon doubling up cleverly as a room key. But Cutlers isn't just a smart motif. It's also about unbending good taste, unswerving service and food cooked with an imaginative twist just yards from the Stray, a 'C'-shaped swathe of green that envelopes Yorkshire's famous spa town – wheat grew here during the Second World War. Originally a coaching inn, then a hotel, it's been a place to stay for more than 200 years; an advert from 1877 bears an uncanny likeness: "In every way commodious... combining the accommodation of a first-class hotel with the domestic comforts of home." Rick and Susan have added more flair than pomp though. Stylish bedrooms in warm Mediterranean oranges and yellows have nice surprises: Medusa light fittings, Italian armchairs, CD players; six look onto the Stray, three have balconies. Susan is great company with a natural enthusiasm for getting things right that rubs off on friendly staff. Popular with ladies who lunch.

rooms	19: 11 doubles, 6 twins, 2 suites.
price	£85–£110; singles £75–£100; suite £120–£140.
meals	Lunch £6.50. Dinner, à la carte, about £22.50.
closed	Never.
directions	Entering Harrogate on A59, right at Prince of Wales r'bout, signed town centre. Hotel 100 yds on right.

Susan Symington & Rick Hodgson

tel	01423 524471
fax	01423 506728
e–mail	info@cutlers-web.co.uk
web	www.cutlers-web.co.uk

The Boar's Head Hotel

Ripley Castle Estate, Harrogate, Yorkshire HG3 3AY

When the Ingilbys decided to reopen The Boar's Head, the attic at the castle got a shakedown and the spare furniture was sent round. The vicar even came to bless the beer taps — you'll find them in Boris's bar, Boris being the eponymous head. Elegant fun is the net result and there's something for everyone. Lady Ingilby has done a brilliant job with the décor. The sitting rooms and hall have crisp yellow Regency wallpaper, big old oils, roaring fires and gilt mirrors. The restaurant is a deep, moody crimson, candlelit at night, and you drink from blue glass. There are games to play, newspapers to peruse, menus to drool over and a parasoled garden where you can sip long summer drinks. Up the staircase, past more ancestors, to bright smartly done bedrooms, with floral fabrics, antique furniture, fresh flowers, sofas, tumbling crowns above big beds and rag-rolled bathrooms; those in the coachman's loft in the courtyard have the odd beam and pretty pine panelling. Visit the castle gardens as a guest of the hotel; umbrellas and wellies are there for you to use on rainy days.

rooms	25: 4 doubles, 21 twin/doubles.
price	£120; singles £99-£120. Half-board (min. 2 nights) from £80 p.p.
meals	Dinner, à la carte, £18.50-£26. Lunch and dinner in bistro from £8.95.
closed	Never.
directions	From Harrogate, A61 north for 3 miles, then left at r'bout, signed to Ripley & castle.

Sir Thomas & Lady Emma Ingilby

tel	01423 771888
fax	01423 771509
e-mail	reservations@boarsheadripley.co.uk
web	www.boarsheadripley.co.uk

map 7   entry 178

The Red Lion

By the Bridge at Burnsall, Nr. Skipton, Yorkshire BD23 6BU

Family-run and family-friendly, The Red Lion is an inn for all ages, full of olde-worlde charm and fun. Even the resident ghost in the 12th-century cellars has a sense of humour, amusing itself by turning off the beer taps from time to time! Elizabeth keeps a matriarchal eye on things, ensuring spirits a floor above don't get out of hand either, while son-in-law Jim cooks seriously good food. The net result is cosy, unpretentious, thoroughly comfortable, and humming with happy locals. The sitting room, with comfy sofas and a woodburning stove, has books for all, from guides to kids' adventure stories. Bedrooms above the inn have lots of character, with beams and low, slanting ceilings, while rooms in a next-door annexe are larger; one has a big brass bed and an open fire, another a highchair and baby listener. Originally a ferryman's inn, it was made redundant by the beautiful stone bridge that spans the wide and shallow river; its gentle meander matches the pace of this small, sleepy village set in a glorious English landscape. The Burnsall fell race — eight minutes up, four minutes down — starts outside the front door.

rooms	11: 5 doubles, 4 twin/doubles, 1 family, 1 single.
price	£95–£120; singles from £47.50. Half-board £70 p.p.
meals	Lunch & dinner from £7.50. Dinner in restaurant £24.95.
closed	Never.
directions	From Harrogate, A59 west to Bolton Bridge; B6160 to Burnsall. Hotel next to bridge.

Elizabeth & Andrew Grayshon

tel	01756 720204
fax	01756 720292
e-mail	redlion@daelnet.co.uk
web	www.redlion.co.uk

The Yorke Arms

Ramsgill-in-Nidderdale, Nr. Harrogate, Yorkshire HG3 5RL

It takes a lot of nous to establish one of the best restaurants in Britain, let alone one up a small country lane in the middle of the Yorkshire Dales. The Yorke Arms is near perfection; exquisite food, wonderful rooms and beautiful countryside make it irresistible. The oldest part was built by monks in the 11th century, the rest added in 1750 when it became a coaching inn. The interior is absolutely charming, with polished flagstone floors, low oak beams, comfy armchairs, open fires and antique tables; in summer, eat under a pergola near a burbling beck. Classy rooms continue the theme; attention to detail is guaranteed. Bill, affable and considerate, is a natural host, while Frances scintillates the palette in the kitchen, using fish from the east and west coasts and meat and game from the Dales. Wander from the hamlet of Ramsgill to nearby Gouthwaite reservoir – formed during the Industrial Revolution to supply the city of Bradford with water – or work up an appetite visiting Brimham Rocks or Stump Cross Caverns. *Kennels for pets £5 per night.*

rooms	14: 7 doubles, 3 twin/doubles, 3 singles, 1 cottage suite.
price	Half-board £85–£150 p.p.
meals	Lunch about £20. Dinner included; non-residents about £25–£30.
closed	Occasionally in January & November. Restaurant closed Sunday evenings to non-residents.
directions	From Ripley, B6165 to Pateley Bridge. Over bridge at bottom of High St, 1st right into Low Wath Rd to Ramsgill (4 miles).

Bill & Frances Atkins

tel	01423 755243
fax	01423 755330
e-mail	enquiries@yorke-arms.co.uk
web	www.yorke-arms.co.uk

map 6   entry 180

Simonstone Hall

Hawes, Yorkshire DL8 3LY

Drool over the picture of Simonstone, knowing it's just as good inside. This is a glorious country house, built in the 1770s as a shooting lodge for the Earl of Wharncliffe. The drawing room is magnificent – gracious and elegant – with a wildly ornate fireplace, painted panelled walls and a flurry of antiques. Its triumph is the huge stone-mullioned window through which Wensleydale unravels – a place to stand rooted to the spot. Elsewhere, find stone-flagged floors, stained-glass windows and old oils and trophies. There's a big warm traditional bar – almost a pub – with hanging fishing nets, clocks and mirrors, and if you don't want to eat in the panelled dining room you can have excellent bar meals here. Bedrooms are superb. It's well worth splashing out and going for the grander ones – they indulge you completely; four-posters, mullioned windows, stone fireplaces, oils – the full aristocratic Monty. Breakfast on the terrace with those fabulous views.

rooms	20: 9 doubles, 4 twin/doubles, 5 four-posters, 2 suites.
price	£90–£220; singles from £60.
meals	Lunch from £5. Dinner about £25.
closed	Never.
directions	From Hawes, north for Muker for about 2 miles. Hotel on left, at foot of Buttertubs Pass.

Jill Peterson

tel	01969 667255
fax	01969 667741
e-mail	e-mail@simonstonehall.demon.co.uk
web	www.simonstonehall.com

The Blue Lion

East Witton, Nr. Leyburn, Yorkshire DL8 4SN

The Blue Lion has a big reputation locally; so big it followed our inspector round Yorkshire – "you must go there," everyone said. Paul and Helen came here 10 years ago, mixing the traditions of a country pub with the elegance of a country house. There's a dreamy atmosphere inside; no-one seems in a hurry to leave, nothing seems so pressing to spoil drawing out the pleasure a little longer – add superlative food and it's not hard to see why it's such a favourite with locals. Aproned staff, polished beer taps, stone-flagged floors, open fires, newspapers on poles, big settles to sit at, huge bunches of dried flowers hanging from beams and splashes of fresh flowers. The two restaurants have boarded floors and shuttered Georgian windows, two coal fires, gilt mirrors and candles everywhere. Bedrooms are comfortable rather than luxurious: those in the main house have bold dashes of colour, padded headboards and wooden beds; in the stables, exposed beams, old pine furniture, regal colours and maybe a brass bed. East Witton has a interesting plague tale to tell and Jervaulx Abbey is a mile away. Come and take your time.

rooms	12: 9 doubles, 2 twins, 1 family.
price	£69–£89; singles £54.
meals	Bar meals from £7. Dinner about £25.
closed	Never.
directions	From Leyburn, A6108 for 3 miles to East Witton.

Paul & Helen Klein

tel	01969 624273
fax	01969 624189
e-mail	bluelion@breathemail.net
web	www.thebluelion.co.uk

map 6   entry 182

Crab Manor at The Crab and Lobster

Asenby, Thirsk, Yorkshire YO7 3QL

Circle the globe in 12 nights at this exceptional place, full of fairground thrills and surprises, original in every way. Each room is inspired by a famous hotel around the world, and you're given a hotel passport on arrival so you can collect the set. All are superb: free-standing baths in Italian-tiled bathrooms, wood carvings, cherubs on the walls, massive wooden antique beds, elephant hats, crushed-velvet cushions, mosquito nets; three in the tropical beach house have saunas and hot tubs. There are deep, leather armchairs in the lavish sitting room, a secret beer tap in the hall – find where it is and drink as much as you like for free! – and the eight-foot tall yeti on the landing talks. Eat in the conservatory amid terracotta pots, plinths and busts, or stroll through the garden along lantern-lit gravel paths to The Crab and Lobster where all is just as whacky; the ceilings, a riot of memorabilia, include a deep sea diver. Everything you see was designed by the wildly imaginative David Barnard; the hotel is now in new hands but there's no plan to change a thing, which should reassure fans of the one-hole golf course. Brilliant fun.

rooms	12: 9 four-posters, 3 doubles.
price	£130–£160; singles from £100.
meals	Lunch from £12. Dinner about £35.
closed	Never.
directions	A1(M), junc. 41, then A168 for Thirsk. Left after 2 miles, for Topcliff. Left again, for Asenby, then left, signed 'village only'. 1st right. House on right.

Mark Spenceley

tel	01845 577286
fax	01845 577109
e-mail	enquiries@crabmanor.fsnet.co.uk
web	www.crabandlobster.co.uk

Island House

The Island, Thistlethwaite-on-the-Thwack, Yorkshire SOT INY

An Englishman's home is his castle, apparently. Well, castles are getting hard to find and we have to make do with the next best thing. Combine our passion for status and security with the new housing crisis and you get some unusual results. Brown-field sites are now all the rage. Homes, and hotels, are becoming smaller and smaller as profits are squeezed and as our family units break up into smaller and smaller groups. Some of the more eccentric among us, however, are still prepared to do their own thing and seek the security and status of the castle in their own way. Witness Ian and Nerdie's island hotel retreat. No chance of any surprises from across the water. The one tree is gargantuan enough to shade the house. Disturbance from coots and ducks is guaranteed but not from humans. Note the big green satellite dish, installed for guests who cannot take the isolation. Come to do nothing at all, other than a quick stroll around the island. A big plus is that you can do your ablutions in the lake, and there are unlikely to be other guests to embarrass you. Another is the near-miraculous luxury of the bedrooms. How on earth they fit still mystifies us. *Why not leave your children there? They'll love it.*

rooms	Accommodation for feet only.
price	A pocketful of small change.
meals	Quarter-board.
closed	Height restrictions apply – confirm when booking.
directions	From York take A12 north to Thistlethwaite. In village ask for the Thwack. Once there, face east and yell. Ian will row out to meet you.

Ian & Nerdie Sular

tel	0123456789
e-mail	tinyhouse@tinyweenymail.itsy.bitsy
web	www.tinyhouseontinyisland./&t?=*-1/~

map 0   entry 184

The Abbey Inn

Byland Abbey, Coxwold, Yorkshire YO61 4BD

The monks of Ampleforth who built this farmhouse would surely approve of its current devotion to good food; whether they'd be as accepting of its devotion to luxury is another matter. But one monk's frown is another man's path to righteousness. The Abbey Inn is a delightful oasis next to a ruined 12th-century abbey – lit up at night – that indulges the senses. They measure success in smiles up here; Jane loves to see the look on people's faces as they enter the Piggery restaurant, a big flagstoned space, lit by a skylight, full of Jacobean-style chairs and antique tables, that demands your joyful attention. Bedrooms are jaw-dropping, too. Abbot's Retreat has a huge four-poster while a bust of Julius Caesar in the gorgeous black and white tiled bathroom strikes a nice, decadent note – order a bottle of bubbly and jump in the double-ended bath. Priors Lynn has the best view – right down the aisle of the abbey; all have bathrobes, aromatherapy oils, fruit, home-made biscuits and a "treasure chest" of wine. Come and enjoy it all.

rooms	3 doubles.
price	£80–£120.
meals	Light lunch from £5. Dinner, à la carte, about £16.
closed	Restaurant closed Sunday night & Monday lunchtime.
directions	From A1 junc. 49, A168 towards Thirsk for about 10 miles, then A19 towards York at r'bout. Left after 2 miles, signed Coxwold. Left in village, signed Byland Abbey. Inn opposite abbey.

Jane & Martin Nordli

tel	01347 868204
fax	01347 868678
e-mail	jane@nordli.freeserve.co.uk
web	www.bylandabbeyinn.co.uk

The Star Inn

Harome, Nr. Helmsley, Yorkshire YO62 5JE

You know you've 'hit the jackpot' as soon as you walk into The Star – it ticks over with such modest ease and calm authority. Andrew and Jacquie arrived in 1996, daughters Daisy and Tilly not long after, and the Michelin star in 2002. It's been a formidable turnaround given this 14th-century inn had an iffy local reputation when they took over, yet there's no arrogance; the brochure simply says: "He cooks, and she looks after you"... and how! Andrew began cooking at the age of 10 when his mother fell ill and remembers washing bags of crabs in the bath. His food is rooted in Yorkshire tradition, refined with French flair and written in plain English on ever-changing menus: try dressed Whitby crab, beef from two miles away, Ryedale deer, or maybe Theakston ale cake. Fabulous bedrooms, all ultra-modern yet seriously rustic, are just a stroll away. Thatched and 15th-century Black Eagle Cottage has three suites; the rest are in Cross House Lodge, a breathtaking new barn conversion; the largest room has its own snooker table. There's also the Mousey Thompson bar, the roof mural, the deli and the Coffee Loft – just possibly the most enchanting attic in the world. Brilliant.

rooms	11: 6 doubles, 2 twins, 3 suites.
price	£120–£195.
meals	Continental breakfast included; full English £15. Lunch from £3.50. Dinner, à la carte, £25.
closed	Never.
directions	From Thirsk, A170 towards Scarborough. Through Helmsley, then right, signed Harome. Inn in village.

Andrew & Jacquie Pern
tel 01439 770397
fax 01439 771833

map 7   entry 186

The White Swan

Market Place, Pickering, Yorkshire YO18 7AA

Mix the boundless energy of a former futures trader with the magical beauty of the North Yorkshire Moors and amazing things can happen. Victor gave up a job in the City to take over this old coaching inn from his parents and it's obvious wandering round that he and Marion left the stress behind and brought a lot of style. They've refurbished the place throughout with simple good taste. Duck in through the front door to find cosy tap rooms that nicely contrast: the snug bar with deep burgundy walls and open fire and the light dining room, with porthole mirrors and plaques from champagne cases on each table. Further on, the sitting room and formal restaurant add more indulgent options. Bedrooms upstairs are clutter-free and extremely elegant: good fabrics, Penhaligan smellies, antique beds, maybe a frilly armchair to sit on and look over the pretty courtyard. The food is just as good – the head chef has been with the Buchanans for years; breakfast inspired one traveller to write a poem, now framed on the wall. Rievaulx Abbey is close, the steam railway even closer and a local pub has a tombstone in its roof. Full of surprises. *Pet surcharge: £7 per pet.*

rooms	12: 5 doubles, 2 twins, 3 twin/doubles, 2 suites.
price	£100–£110; singles £70–£80; suite £120–£150.
meals	Lunch about £15. Dinner about £25.
closed	Never.
directions	From Thirsk, A170 to Pickering. Entering town, left at r'bout, then 1st right up Market Place. On left.

Victor & Marion Buchanan

tel	01751 472288
fax	01751 475554
e-mail	welcome@white-swan.co.uk
web	www.white-swan.co.uk

Crathorne Hall

Crathorne, Nr. Yarm, Yorkshire TS15 0AR

An immensely imposing house, built in 1903 and still going strong as a grand hotel in the country. It is enclosed within acres of splendid gardens; it would be fine to sit at one end of the long tree-lined lawn with a glass of wine, living as once Stanley Baldwin's private secretary did during the abdication crisis. The comfort is as magnificent as the décor, with swathes and swathes of flowery fabrics, acres of carpets and every manner of gadget to make the modern traveller feel at home. There are trouser presses in the bedrooms and those special coat hangers that one cannot steal. You may have a welcoming teddy-bear on the bed but you will sleep deeply for no expense has been spared. The food is excellent, perhaps a touch 'minceur' but irreproachable: try feuillette of quail and wild mushrooms, and pannacotta with bruschetta. The welcome is that of a city hotel, with a personalised message on your TV and labels on your staff, but Crathorne will make you feel very grand. New manager Iain Shelton ran the wonderful Lords Of the Manor in the Cotswolds and will work his magic here too.

rooms	37: 25 doubles, 3 twin/doubles, 4 singles, 2 four-posters, 3 suites.
price	£140–£170; singles £113; suites £190-230. Half-board from £90 p.p.
meals	Lunch £19.50. Dinner £27.50; and à la carte.
closed	Never.
directions	A19, then A67, following brown signs to hotel.

	Iain Shelton
tel	01642 700398
fax	01642 700814
e-mail	enquiries@crathornehall.com
web	www.crathornehall.com

map 7   entry 188

Courtesy of the Atlantic Hotel

CHANNEL ISLANDS

"My calm sleep is the last memory of that day."
ITALO SVEVO

Atlantic Hotel

St Brelade, Jersey JE3 8HE

Perfect peace, perfect luxury – and sunsets across a golden sea leave a lasting memory of The Atlantic. At first sight, it may look big, modern, almost brashly confident, but enter and you'll find the virtues we consider so important: warmth, personality and individual attention. In the past few years, Patrick has given the hotel built by his father in the early 70s an impressive makeover, creating the 21st-century equivalent of those wonderfully grand old hotels of the Edwardian age. It is bold, beautifully run by loyal and friendly staff, irrepressibly comfortable, and understated. Classic and contemporary blend well, balancing antiques, urns, fountains, a wrought iron staircase and specially commissioned furniture upholstered in warm, rich fabrics. The bedrooms are big, modern, pale and cool, with bathrooms of white marble, pale oak and polished chrome; many have sliding doors to balconies with ship-style balustrading and lovely sea views. Dine on smoked salmon parcels filled with fresh crab, tomato and saffron and then, perhaps, roast beef on potato rosti, wild mushrooms and shallot marmalade. Full of style – and the sound of the sea will hypnotise.

rooms	50: 48 twin/doubles, 2 suites.
price	£185-£270; singles £140-£170. Suite £260-£445.
meals	Lunch £13.50. Dinner, 3 courses, £30; and à la carte.
closed	6 January-6 February.
directions	From Jersey airport, B36 for St Brelade for 1.5 miles. Right at lights onto A13, for St Ouen's Bay, for 1 mile, then right into La Rue De La Sergente. Hotel signed at top of hill.

Patrick Burke

tel	01534 744101
fax	01534 744102
e-mail	info@theatlantichotel.com
web	www.theatlantichotel.com

map 3   entry 189

Eulah Country House

Mont Cochon, St Helier, Jersey JE2 3JA

Eulah is a rare and wonderful treat, designed for hedonists, perfectionists and stressed business people who still need to plug in. Sink in, soak up and let this beautifully restored Edwardian house take the strain. Not all the luxuries here – and there are many – are so engagingly self-mocking as the four-poster bath... cushions are placed wherever there's a generous sofa. Tables and chairs are chunky, wooden and attractive; the sitting room has unexpected beams. Bedrooms are enormous, each carpeted with a meadow of rich, plain pile. Colours are bold but elegant – swathes of material swoop up from behind headboards and over pillows to the ceiling. Few of us imagine having such vast and impressive beds at home; the bathroom fittings are the ones you dare not buy for yourself. It is sumptuous and plush. Long, lush views stretch across St Helier and St Aubin's Bay, and Penny runs the place with easy good humour. Whether you're in the sauna or the swimming pool, you may wonder if it's a home or a hotel – in spite of the luxury, we found it hard to tell the difference.

rooms	9: 6 doubles, 3 twin/doubles.
price	£150–£220.
meals	Light supper on request. Restaurants nearby.
closed	Never.
directions	From St Helier, A2 west, then right at lights on B27. Through next lights up Mont Cochon. Entrance 100 yds on right.

Penny Clarke

tel	01534 626626
fax	01534 626600
e-mail	eulah@jerseymail.co.uk
web	www.eulah.co.uk

La Sablonnerie

Little Sark, Via Guernsey, Sark GY9 0SD

If you tell Elizabeth which ferry you're arriving on, she'll send down her horse and carriage to meet you. "Small, sweet world of wave-encompassed wonder", wrote Swinburne of Sark. The tiny community of 500 people lives under a spell, governed feudally and sharing this magic island with horses, sheep, cattle, carpets of wild flowers and birds. There are wild cliff walks, thick woodland, sandy coves, wonderful deep rock pools, aquamarine seas. No cars, only bikes, horse and carriage and the odd tractor. In the hotel – a 400-year-old farmhouse – there is no TV, no radio, no trouser press... just a dreamy peace, kindness, starched cotton sheets, woollen blankets and food to die for. The Perrées still farm and, as a result, the hotel is almost self-sufficient; you also get home-baked bread and lobsters straight from the sea. Elizabeth is Sercquaise – her mother's family were part of the 1565 colonisation – and she knows her land well enough to lead you to the island's secrets.

rooms	22: 5 doubles, 6 twins, 6 family, 1 suite; 2 doubles, 2 twins, sharing 2 baths.
price	£95–£155. Half-board £59.50–£75.50 p.p.
meals	Dinner, 5 courses, £30.
closed	2nd Monday in October–Wednesday before Easter.
directions	Take ferry to Sark and ask!

Elizabeth Perrée
tel 01481 832061
fax 01481 832408

map 3   entry 191

Photography by Michael Busselle

WALES

"The church is near but the way is icy.
The tavern is far but I will walk carefully."
UKRANIAN PROVERB

The Big Sleep Hotel

Bute Terrace, Cardiff CF10 2FE

Cheap but chic and sure damn groovy, this novel and gutsy designer hotel is a perfect launch-pad from which to discover a regenerated Welsh capital. Retro 70s style and 90s minimalism blend to stunning effect inside a 10-storey former office block near Cardiff railway station. The building was converted to a hotel by a previous owner and then resurrected as The Big Sleep by two innovators with flair and a friend in the actor John Malkovich, who helped back the project. To keep costs down, Cosmo supplied the formica from his Bath-based factory – the first in Britain to bend the material – and Lulu sourced the fake 'teddy-bear' fur to make full-length curtains and to carpet the gorgeous penthouse suite. Swimming pool blues and stark white walls were inspired by 1950s Italian architect Gio Ponti. So far, only rooms on the ninth floor, and the two suites on the tenth, have had the treatment; the rest will follow. Most have spectacular city views, especially at night. Elsewhere, modular seating re-upholstered in white PVC, a colourful lobby, and deep red 60s wallpaper in the busy bar. Fun and great value.

rooms	81: 42 doubles, 30 twins, 7 family, 2 suites.
price	£45–£99.
meals	Continental breakfast only.
closed	Christmas Day & Boxing Day.
directions	M4, junc. 29, A48(M), signed Cardiff East. 3rd junc., A4232 to city centre. At 1st r'bout, 2nd exit, 1 mile past Lloyds TSB, left at lights on A4160. Right at 3rd set of lights, under bridge. Hotel on left.

Cosmo Fry & Lulu Anderson

tel	02920 636363
fax	02920 636364
e-mail	bookings@thebigsleephotel.com
web	www.thebigsleephotel.com

map 2   entry 192

Tŷ Mawr Country Hotel

Brechfa, Carmarthenshire SA32 7RA

Tŷ Mawr embraces all that is best about Wales, and John and Pearl fit perfectly, having returned to run a hotel in the valley where they met as teenagers. Full of kindness and chatty enthusiasm, they clearly love looking after you. Tŷ Mawr translates as 'big house' and this is a classic 15th-century Welsh building, with lots of exposed stone, low wooden beams, log fires and handsome sash windows. The list of guests who have stayed here over the years is impressive, and eclectic: a platoon of Dragoons during the 1843 Rebecca Riots, President Jimmy Carter on a fishing trip, Pavarotti and Shirley Bassey, separately... and Alexi Sayle; it was also a grammar school in the 1860s. Simple but attractive bedrooms have William Morris fabrics and wallpaper, claw-foot baths and handmade soap. The food is local and free-range from named sources. Dine *al fresco* in summer; the River Marlais runs through the lawned garden. Marlais was Dylan Thomas's middle name as his grandfather lived in the village. Big-hearted, open-minded, even the housekeeper joins in the fun, taking guests' pets for a walk.

rooms	6: 2 doubles, 1 twin, 1 family, 1 four-poster; 1 double, with private bath.
price	£82–£106; singles £55–£65. Half-board (min. 2 nights) £130 p.p.
meals	Sunday lunch £13.50. Packed lunch from £5. Dinner, 5 courses, £26.
closed	Never.
directions	M4 west onto A48, then B4310 exit, for National Botanic Gardens of Wales, north for 9 miles to Brechfa. In village centre.

John & Pearl Richardson

tel	01267 202332
fax	01267 202437
e-mail	info@tymawrhotel.co.uk
web	www.tymawrhotel.co.uk

Hurst House

East Marsh, Laugharne, Carmarthenshire SA33 4RS

Arriving at Hurst House is like falling off the end of the world onto a pillow of unadulterated style. This pocket of sophistication is miles from anywhere, isolated by windswept marshland that spreads endlessly in all directions; from a distance, the hotel looks half-crushed by the weight of the sky. The building is Georgian and older, with parquet floors, sash windows, stone fireplaces and exposed beams, but the interiors couldn't be more contemporary, with bold colours, chic furniture, seductive lighting, pristine bathrooms and Bang & Olufsen stereos and laptops connected to the internet in every bedroom; all carefully designed with you in mind. Matt and Poppy are young, friendly Londoners who believe in good food, generous service and great parties – there's no hint of stuffy pretension here. No need to worry about the neighbours either as they own 69 acres of marsh towards the coast. A pond created near the house is fantastic at night, lit by underwater fibre optics, and a spa is planned for derelict barns. Dion the chef is young, talented and changes the menu according to what's local and in season. Worth coming just for the brochure. Fabulous.

rooms	4 doubles.
price	£100.
meals	Lunch £11.95. Dinner £22.95; à la carte, about £26.
closed	Never.
directions	From St Clears, A4066 for Pendine, through villages of Laugharne & Broadway. 0.5 miles past 2nd village, left down track towards marshes, signed. Follow signs.

Matt Roberts & Poppy Roth

tel	01994 427417
fax	01994 427730
e-mail	info@hurst-house.co.uk
web	www.hurst-house.co.uk

map 2   entry 194

Conrah Country House

Chancery, Aberystwyth, Ceredigion SY23 4DF

This delightful Edwardian hotel is known throughout Wales for the warmth of its welcome, winning loads of awards over the years. It's also very much a family affair. Pat and John came here more than 20 years ago and in that time, their son Paul and his wife Sarah have grown into the business. Arrive down a leafy avenue that opens into a view north across fields towards Cader Idris and Snowdonia. Their ha-ha is the longest in Wales, designed to stop livestock ruining the lawn without interrupting the view; it's also your likely reaction to seeing someone walk off it by accident. The house was rebuilt in 1911 after a fire destroyed the original Georgian mansion. Rooms in the main house are traditionally floral, comfortable and have that view. For something really special, stay in one of the three terrific courtyard rooms; they're bold, beamed and full of style, with lots of space and low windows that give tantalising glimpses of the garden — it almost feels like a different hotel. Follow footpaths to the sea far enough to work up an appetite for excellent, award-winning food. Long may it continue.

rooms	14: 8 doubles, 5 twins, 1 single.
price	£110–£140; singles £75–£90. Half-board (min. 2 nights) £80–£100 p.p.
meals	Lunch from £3.75. Dinner, 2 courses, £24; 3 courses, £27.
closed	2 weeks at Christmas.
directions	From Aberystwyth, A487 south towards Cardigan for 3 miles. Hotel signed on right.

Pat & John Heading

tel	01970 617941
fax	01970 624546
e-mail	enquiries@conrah.co.uk
web	www.conrah.co.uk

Bodidris Hall

Llandegla, Wrexham, Denbighshire LL11 3AL

Avoiding the pheasants and sheep on the mile-long driveway is the first challenge; the second is to get every ounce of pleasure from this astonishing house. Bodidris is over 600 years old, built in local stone on a much older site, once slept in by Elizabeth I and still using the well that has supplied its water for all that time. Criminals wanted in Flintshire could step across the hall into Denbighshire – the place is awash with history. Huge beams run through inappropriate places, the stairs are uneven, all is delightfully unmodernised. A baronial bedroom might have an avocado corner bath but it matters not a jot. Come for an authentic slice of grand, old living with magnificent suits of armour, gargantuan fireplaces, stags' heads, mullion windows and walls, thick with ivy. Ceri and Ken run it with great affection, as if it were their own – she is immensely helpful. The food is as good and established as the house, the two acres of kitchen garden working hard to feed you. There are nine acres to play in, and a lake with swans and just nine bedrooms in the whole house. King Arthur's Labyrinth is close, as is Llangollen for the annual Eisteddfod. Splendid.

rooms	9: 5 doubles, 1 twin, 3 four-posters.
price	£99–£199; singles £75–£150.
meals	Lunch, 4 courses, £14.95. Dinner, 5 courses, £29.95.
closed	Never.
directions	From Wrexham, A525 towards Ruthin, then right at Crown Hotel on A5104 towards Chester. Hotel on left after 1 mile.

Ceri & Ken Roberts

tel	08707 292 292
fax	01978 790335
e-mail	ceri@bodidrishall.com
web	www.bodidrishall.com

map 6   entry 196

West Arms Hotel

Llanarmon Dyffryn Ceiriog, Denbighshire LL20 7LD

Come here, you who dream of a traditional inn in a gorgeous village where the road ends and the real country begins. The smell of fresh bread may greet you, perhaps the scent of fresh flowers, or a crackling fire. Hear the sound of the River Cleriog through the open front door; sit in the half-glow of the dimly-lit bar, warm and cosy. It's as a 16th-century inn should be, of flagstone, beam, and leaded window. Décor is simple, the layout all higgledy-piggledy, with old Welsh colours, traditional furniture, a few antiques and inglenook fireplace. Bedrooms are clean and modest, on different levels, some with oak beams and low ceilings; plainer ones at the back have pastoral views. The river runs through peaceful garden, with the rolling Berwyn Hills beyond for walks, wildlife and the Pistyll Rhaeder waterfall. Geoff and Gill are laid-back but dedicated, thoroughly at one with what they're doing. The chef is Welsh and superb – a local TV celebrity no less! – and backed by three French chefs. All manner of country pursuits can be arranged, from painting to shooting, and sheepdog trials are held in the village… so pour yourself a sherry and take your time to decide.

rooms	15: 2 doubles, 2 twins, 9 twin/doubles, 2 suites.
price	£95-£138; singles £52.50-£74.
meals	Bar lunch from £3.95. Packed lunch from £6. Dinner £26.75.
closed	Never.
directions	From Shrewsbury, A5 north to Chirk, then left at r'bout on B4500, signed Ceiriog Valley, for 11 miles to Llanarmon DC. Hotel in centre.

Geoff & Gill Leigh-Ford

tel	01691 600665
fax	01691 600622
e-mail	lford@www.thewestarms.co.uk
web	www.thewestarms.co.uk

Egerton Grey Country House Hotel

Porthkerry, Barry, Glamorgan CF62 3BZ

It is the wish of the management that all visitors should loll, loaf and laze in the lap of unaccustomed luxury for as long as they like... chin chin! Richard and his partner, Huw, encourage utter indolence with exuberant humour and panache in what is one of Britain's classic country-house hotels. Chandeliers sparkle, antiques gleam, curtains are swagged, beds floral, paintings original and the sense of deep-cushioned luxury completely intentional. Once a rectory, the building lies down a single track lane in 200 acres of country park. Look over seven acres of lawned terrace and gardens through a beautiful Victorian viaduct to the sea in the distance. A fine old horse-chestnut shades the croquet lawn, and a giant copper beech adds grace to the setting. All the bedrooms have great views, an eclectic mix of furniture, pristine bathrooms, even water bottles! The conservatory is Victorian – as are many of the roll-top baths – and Richard's Rolls Royce is ancient, too. Eat well in the panelled dining room; much of the food is home-grown, the rest is local. All this five minutes from Cardiff airport – without the planes, you'd never know. Leave your cares behind.

rooms	10: 5 doubles, 2 twins, 1 single, 1 four-poster, 1 suite.
price	£95–£130; singles from £75. Half-board (min. 2 nights) from £60 p.p.
meals	Lunch £13.50. Dinner, à la carte, about £25.
closed	Never.
directions	M4, junc. 33, follow signs to Cardiff airport, by-passing Barry. Left at small r'bout by airport, signed Porthkerry, then left after 500 yds down lane, signed.

Richard Morgan-Price & Huw Thomas

tel	01446 711666
fax	01446 711690
e-mail	info@egertongrey.co.uk
web	www.egertongrey.co.uk

map 2   entry 198

Plas Bodegroes

Pwllheli, Gwynedd LL53 5TH

Close to the end of the world and worth every single second it takes to get here. Chris and Gunna are inspirational, their home a temple of cool elegance, the food possibly the best in Wales. Fronted by an avenue of 200-year-old beech trees, this Georgian manor house is wrapped in climbing roses, wildly roaming wisteria and ferns. The veranda circles the house, as do the long French windows that lighten every room; open one up, grab a chair and sit out reading a book. Not a formal place — come to relax and be yourself. Bedrooms are wonderful, the courtyard rooms especially good; exposed wooden ceilings and a crisp clean style give the feel of a smart Scandinavian forest hideaway. Best of all is the dining room, almost a work of art in itself, cool and crisp with modern art and Venetian carnival masks on the walls — a great place to eat Chris's ambrosial food. If you can tear yourself away, explore the Llyn peninsula: sandy beaches, towering sea cliffs, country walks. Snowdon is also close. Gunna and Chris will direct you.

rooms	11: 7 doubles, 2 twins, 1 single, 1 four-poster.
price	£80–£130; singles £40–£80. Half-board from £65 p.p.
meals	Dinner £32.50. Sunday lunch £15.50.
closed	December–February & Monday.
directions	From Pwllheli, A497 towards Nefyn. House on left after 1 mile, signed.

Chris & Gunna Chown

tel	01758 612363
fax	01758 701247
e-mail	gunna@bodegroes.co.uk
web	www.bodegroes.co.uk

Llwyndû Farmhouse & Restaurant

Llanaber, Barmouth, Gwynedd LL42 1RR

It's a good mile down the steepish hill to the gracious sweep of Cardigan Bay, but it looks as though you could hurdle the wall and jump straight into it; an old stone wall frames the view perfectly. The beach is long and wide, a good place to walk, as are the Rhinog mountains which take to the skies behind. And walkers will love Llwyndû. It's warm and earthy, generously simple, with bold colours on ancient stone walls, spiral stone stairways that lead nowhere, a woodburner in the big inglenook and a likely priest's hole cupboard. Peter, a historian turned cook, has brought life to the simple, everyday story of the house and its past owners; you can read up on it. Old wills hang on the walls, the proof of fables. Bedrooms are split between the main house and the converted granary; there are two four-posters, beams, bold Peter-painted stone walls, good bathrooms and bunk beds for children. All this in four pretty acres, with great views up and down, cats, dogs and a horse that comes home for the holidays.

rooms	7: 2 doubles, 1 twin, 2 family, 2 four-posters.
price	£64–£74.
meals	Dinner £17.95–£21.95. Packed lunch £4–£5.
closed	Christmas Day & Boxing Day. Restaurant closed Sunday evening.
directions	From Barmouth A496 north. Through Llanaber. Farmhouse signed right where street lights & 40mph limit end.

Peter & Paula Thompson

tel	01341 280144
fax	01341 281236
e-mail	intouch@llwyndu-farmhouse.co.uk
web	www.llwyndu-farmhouse.co.uk

map 5   entry 200

Penmaenuchaf Hall

Penmaenpool, Dolgellau, Gwynedd LL40 1YB

A long, windy road leads to the hall and it's worth taking for the views over the Mawddach estuary. You can stand at the front of the house, on the Victorian stone balustrade, and gaze down on the tidal ebb and flow, or walk around to the back to blazing banks of rhododendrons, azaleas and camellias, and a rising forest behind. By the time you manage to pass through the front door, all is equally delightful. The house is pristine: rugs, wooden floors and oak panelling, flowers erupting from jugs and bowls, leather sofas and armchairs, open fires and seagrass matting, and, everywhere, those views. Upstairs, bedrooms – more views, of course – come in different shapes and sizes, the big being *huge*, the small being warm and cosy. One room up in the eaves has a fine *bergère* bed. In the dining room, stiff white napery and the best of modern British cooking. Fish in the hotel's 13 miles of river; back in the garden, they grow as much as they can. You'll warm to Mark's sense of humour, too. *Children over six welcome; pets by arrangement.*

rooms	14: 7 doubles, 5 twins, 1 family, 1 four-poster.
price	£116–£176; singles £75–£115.
meals	Lunch £3.50–£15.95. Dinner, 4 courses, £28.50; and à la carte. Afternoon tea from £4.95.
closed	10 days before Christmas.
directions	From Dolgellau, A493 west for about 1.5 miles. Entrance on left.

Mark Watson & Lorraine Fielding

tel	01341 422129
fax	01341 422787
e-mail	relax@penhall.co.uk
web	www.penhall.co.uk

The Bell at Skenfrith
Skenfrith, Monmouthshire NP7 8UH

Indulge all the senses at this swish gastro pub in an old fishing inn on the Welsh-English border. Follow remote country lanes to a blissful village setting, with a ruined Norman castle and a meandering river, crossed by an old humpback bridge. Lie back on a grassy riverbank outside and just take it all in. Inside is smartly done, but run with warmth – Janet treats staff like members of the family. Expect the best of everything: coffee comes from a proper cappuccino machine, food is mostly organic and the wine superb – William got the first issue of *Decanter* magazine for his 11th birthday and hasn't looked back. Bedrooms are luxurious, with piqué bed linen, Jura limestone, Farrow & Ball colours, home-made biscuits, fresh flowers and a hi-tech console by the bed which lets you listen to music in the bath. Fully refreshed, drink at a long bar, or flop in a big sofa next to a blazing fire. Eat in an elegant, formal dining room, with linen napkins and sparkling wine glasses, or at wooden tables in the bar, looking onto the garden terrace. Toast the occasion with perry, English 'champagne' and much underrated.

rooms	8: 3 doubles, 1 twin, 2 four-posters, 2 attic suites.
price	£85-£140; singles from £65.
meals	Bar lunch from £12. Packed lunch from £5. Cream tea £3.95. Dinner, à la carte, £27-£32.50.
closed	Mondays from November to Easter.
directions	From Monmouth, B4233 to Rockfield; B4347 for 5 miles; right on B4521, signed Ross-on-Wye. Skenfrith 1 mile. On right before bridge.

William & Janet Hutchings

tel	01600 750235
fax	01600 750525
e-mail	enquiries@thebellatskenfrith.com
web	www.skenfrith.com

map 2   entry 202

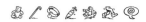

Lake Vyrnwy Hotel

Llanwddyn, Montgomeryshire SY10 0LY

Lake Vyrnwy lives in a wonderfully remote pocket of Wales, surrounded by pine forests and ancient grazing land. Both lake and hotel are man-made: the lake was completed in 1891 to provide Liverpool's water, taking two years to fill, and lying in a 24,000-acre catchment that continues to protect the water's purity today; the hotel was built shortly afterwards to allow civic dignitaries from the city to come and ogle at the dam, then the biggest in Europe – they also came to fish the 400,000 trout that were released into the water. The view *is* stupendous, the lake stretching five miles into the distance, home to rolling mists and dramatic bursts of sunshine. Walk, or cycle around it, canoe, sail or fish here – all can be arranged. Once inside, a sense of old style splendour envelopes. The Bisikers have done a wonderful job restoring the hotel back to its former glory, with wooden floors, a grand piano, heavy oak furniture, even a postbox in the entrance hall. Bedrooms are excellent and most have the lake view, as do the award-winning restaurant, the yellow drawing room, the library with leather armchairs and the terraced bar. A place to return to again and again.

rooms	35: 32 twin/doubles, 2 four-posters, 1 suite.
price	£120-£190; singles from £90. Half-board £77.50-£110 p.p.
meals	Bar meals from £8. Dinner £29.50.
closed	Never.
directions	A490 from Welshpool, then B4393 to Lake Vyrnwy. Brown signs from A5 at Shrewsbury as well.

The Bisiker Family

tel	01691 870692
fax	01691 870259
e-mail	res@lakevyrnwy.com
web	www.lakevyrnwy.com

Penally Abbey

Penally, Nr. Tenby, Pembrokeshire SA70 7PY

It's not often a hotel exceeds your expectations, but then there aren't many places like Penally. It's not a grand hotel and doesn't pretend to be. It just does well the simple things that make a stay memorable. Steve's gentle, unflappable manner suits front of house: chatting to guests one minute, taking orders and mixing a drink at a small bar the next – he makes it look so easy. There's an unhurried charm about the whole place; you won't feel rushed into doing anything. The building is a former 1790s abbey; there's also a ruined 13th-century church called St Diniel's, suggesting even earlier roots – and lit up at night. A beautiful garden looks across Carmarthen Bay. The beach is a 10-minute walk and great for pebble collectors – beautiful coastal walks lead from here. Bedrooms are all different: most in the main house have gorgeous four-posters and antiques, while those in the Tuscan-style coach house are more cottagey. Elleen cooks in a self-taught French style, much of it picked up in the kitchen of a French château many years back. The Tenby sea bass was exquisite.

rooms	12: 3 doubles, 1 twin, 8 four-posters.
price	£124–£144; singles £98. Half-board £90–£102 p.p.
meals	Dinner £28. Lunch by arrangement.
closed	Never.
directions	From Tenby, A4139 for Pembroke. Right into Penally after 1.5 miles. Hotel signed at village green. Train station 5 mins walk.

Steve & Elleen Warren

tel	01834 843033
fax	01834 844714
e-mail	info@penally-abbey.com
web	www.penally-abbey.com

map 1   entry 204

Twr-y-Felin

St David's, Pembrokeshire SA62 6QS

In this great, spiritual centre of Europe, lots of adrenaline is pumping for planet earth... and you're welcome to jump off a cliff and join in. Andy runs pulsating adventure holidays with a green slant from an old windmill that's been converted into a hotel. There's nothing preachy about his approach; he prefers to reverse widespread indifference to the environment by setting hearts racing: kayak, rock climb, sail, surf... even 'coasteer' with a wetsuit over cliff and rock — all overseen by qualified instructors. Pembrokeshire's rugged coastline and crashing surf is just as good to walk; or gaze out to sea past Ramsey Island from the top of the windmill. The hotel is carbon neutral, as is Alastair Sawday Publishing; it plants trees to offset the pollution it causes — you're charged a £1 tax for driving here! Andy is at the forefront of a local campaign to make St David's the first — and smallest — sustainable city in the world. Most of the food served is organic and locally produced. Bedrooms are clean with good linen and life downstairs is laid-back. Hands on, no frills, friendly and worth a modern day pilgrimage.

rooms	11: 2 twin/doubles, 1 single, 2 family; 2 doubles, 2 twins, 1 single, 1 family, sharing 4 showers.
price	£80–£90; singles £40–£45.
meals	Lunch £5–£9. Dinner £19.50.
closed	Never.
directions	From Haverfordwest, A487 to St David's. Entering city, 1st left after flagpoles, signed, then next left down lane. Entrance on right.

Andy Middleton

tel	01437 721678
fax	01437 721838
e-mail	stay@tyf.com
web	www.tyf.com

Three Main Street

Fishguard, Pembrokeshire SA65 9HG

A beautiful Georgian townhouse and restaurant with rooms, less than a minute's walk from Fishguard's busy market square. Marion and Inez have made quite a splash in Wales building a reputation for sublime food, served in style and with generosity. Rugs, stripped wooden floors, candles, hand-written menus and classical music or jazz all combine to give a warm and relaxed, slightly bohemian feel to the place. Big bedrooms have a hint of Art Deco and are homely with fresh flowers, rugs, sofas, good furniture, maybe a walnut bed. The whole place is extremely comfortable – superb value for money – but the pounding heart of Three Main Street is the kitchen whence comes exceptional food. Inez makes the pastries and puddings while Marion looks after the starters and main courses – maybe baked goat's cheese on toasted brioche, sea bass baked with garlic, chilled lemon and lime soufflé. Take to the nearby coastal path and walk off your sins amid the divine Welsh landscape. Day trips to Ireland are also possible; it's only an hour-and-a-half away by Sea Lynx.

rooms	3: 2 doubles, 1 twin.
price	£70–£80; singles £50.
meals	Dinner, 2 courses, £24; 3 courses, £30.
closed	February. Restaurant closed Sunday & Monday. Lunch served Easter–October only.
directions	Main Street runs off town square in town centre. All roads lead to it.

Inez Ford & Marion Evans

tel	01348 874275
fax	01348 874017

map 1   entry 206

Cnapan

East Street, Newport, Nr. Fishguard, Pembrokeshire SA42 0SY

The welcome here is immediate and wonderful – you'll feel like an old friend by the time you've walked through the front door! Locals love it here, too. Michael and Judith were on duty the Saturday afternoon we arrived, up to their eyeballs supervising a *cawl* lunch to raise money for the twinning committee, but they still made us feel our arrival was the best thing to have happened all day. Michael answered the door with a big, mischievous smile, while Judith immediately pulled her hands out of a mixing bowl in the kitchen, gave them a wipe and came over to shake our hands. Inside, bright rooms with traditional stone walls and lovely sea views have all you'll need to feel comfortable and cosseted: fresh flowers, comfy sofas and lots of books. Upstairs, past a photo album of family and friends that covers a whole wall, find homely bedrooms without a whisper of bad taste. Newport is a bustling town in the heart of Pembrokeshire National Park; walks to hill, moor, sea and cliff start from the door, with regular buses to bring you back to the best food around. *Self-catering cottage, sleeps 6, £270-£580 p.w.*

rooms	5: 1 double, 3 twins, 1 family, plus extra bath.
price	£62; singles £38.
meals	Lunch from £2.75. Dinner £20.
closed	Christmas, January & February. Restaurant closed Tuesday evening October to Easter.
directions	From Cardigan, A487 to Newport. 1st pink house on right.

John & Elund Lloyd,
Michael & Judith Cooper

tel	01239 820575
fax	01239 820878
e-mail	cnapan@online-holidays.net
web	www.online-holidays.net/cnapan

Gliffaes Country House Hotel

Crickhowell, Powys NP8 1RH

Gliffaes is matchless — a perfect place: grandly comfortable but as casual and warm as home. It's a house for all seasons — not even driving rain could mask its beauty. Stroll along the rhododendron-flanked drive and wander the 33 acres of stunning gardens and woodland, or just bask in the sun on the high, buttressed terrace as the River Usk cuts through the valley 150 feet below. In winter, curl up by fires burning in extravagantly ornate fireplaces — one looks like the Acropolis. Tea is a feast of scones and cakes laid out on a long table at one end of a sitting room of polished floors and panelled walls. The house could be a garden shed and you'd still love it — as long as the Suters remained at the helm, just as Susie's parents did before them. The clan has been welcoming guests for over 50 years — the fourth generation, aged seven and nine, are ready for some rope-learning, while the first generation, the "granny patrol", is still seen walking her dog; go and have a chat — she's amazing. Bedrooms are excellent, the cooking British with Mediterranean flavours and a hint of the orient, and fisherfolk can cast to their heart's content.

rooms	22: 3 doubles, 13 twin/doubles, 6 singles.
price	£69–£170; singles from £57.
meals	Light lunch from £3.50. Dinner £29.
closed	1st 2 weeks in January.
directions	From Crickhowell, A40 west for 2.5 miles. Entrance on left, signed. Hotel 1 mile up windy hill.

James & Susie Suter

tel	01874 730371
fax	01874 730463
e-mail	calls@gliffaeshotel.com
web	www.gliffaeshotel.com

map 2   entry 208

The Felin Fach Griffin

Felin Fach, Brecon, Powys LD3 0UB

Add a dash of London to a liberal dose of the Brecon Beacons and you have The Felin Fach Griffin. This bold venture mixes the buzz of a smart city bistro with the easy-going pace of good old country living, and it's proving very popular. Full of casual elegance, downstairs fans out from the bar into several eating and sitting areas, with stripped pine and old oak furniture. Make for three monster leather sofas around a raised hearth and settle in. Dine at a smartly-laid table, or opt for the rustic charm of the small backroom bar; the food has won rave reviews and there's usually a nice chatty atmosphere. Breakfast is served around one table in the morning room; make your own toast on an Aga, as you like it, or as it comes, depending on how engrossed you become in the newspapers provided. Bedrooms are done in a modern Scandinavian style, clean and simple, with a few designer touches: cylindrical bedside tables and a carved antique four-poster came from India. Charles and Huw host with aplomb. Both are young and ambitious, as are smiley staff who genuinely seem to be enjoying themselves. It's cool to relax here. *Dogs welcome by arrangement.*

rooms	7: 2 doubles, 2 twin/doubles, 3 four-posters.
price	£72.50–£82; singles from £47.50
meals	Lunch about £15. Dinner about £20.
closed	Christmas Day, New Year's Day & occasionally. Restaurant closed Monday lunchtime.
directions	From Brecon, A470 for Builth Wells to Felin Fach (4.5 miles). On left.

Charles Inkin & Huw Evans-Bevan

tel	01874 620111
fax	01874 620120
e-mail	enquiries@eatdrinksleep.ltd.uk
web	www.eatdrinksleep.ltd.uk

Three Cocks Hotel

Three Cocks, Brecon, Powys LD3 0SL

You don't have to walk through it: "the house just creaks on its own," says Michael of this 500-year-old coaching inn built around a tree. Michael and Marie-Jeanne are exceptionally friendly, bringing energy and experience from Belgium, where they ran a restaurant for 10 years. They obviously know their Belgian onions. Michael, who is English, but Belgian by marriage, produces incredible Belgian dishes – i.e. French without the portion control – in the stone-walled restaurant that's peppered with some fine old Dutch oils. The house is hugely welcoming with a bright red carpet, stone walls, a crackling fire, heavy rugs and lots of lovely Belgian beer. It's a very sociable place; the warm and simple bedrooms are TV-free, so people stay up late chatting in the limed-oak panelled drawing room downstairs. When you do make it to bed, you'll find beams, sloping floors, timbered walls, thick old eiderdowns and comfy beds. At breakfast, the feasting continues with home-baked bread that melts in the mouth.

rooms	7: 4 doubles, 2 twins; 1 twin with private bath.
price	£69; singles, £45-£69.
meals	Dinner, 4 courses, £28.
closed	December-14 February.
directions	On A438 Brecon-Hereford road. 27 miles from Hereford, 11 miles from Brecon, 4 miles from Hay-on-Wye.

Michael & Marie-Jeanne Winstone

tel	01497 847215
fax	01497 847339
web	www.threecockshotel.com

map 2   entry 210

Llangoed Hall

Llyswen, Brecon, Powys LD3 0YP

One of the most refined hotels in Britain, Llangoed is a fond tribute to the late Laura Ashley, doyenne of the stylish floral print. It was always her long-held dream to do up this Clough Williams-Ellis house; she used to drive past it often up until her sudden death in a fall. Sir Bernard saved it from certain demolition shortly afterwards and took on the project in her memory. As a result, this magnificent Edwardian manor house has risen like a phoenix. Sir Bernard has decorated with brand new wallpaper and fabric styles inspired by his wife's original designs. There's something of the Victorian collector in him, too, with corridors and rooms full of remarkable artefacts and curios from around the world — from amazing model railway memorabilia to extremely rare Whistler lithographs in the breakfast room, from old Penguin editions to original Roberts radios. Bedrooms are big and beautiful, some with lovely views. There's a maze big enough to get lost in and a private path to the River Wye for picnics on a small beach. Afternoon tea served on a silver tray is sheer indulgence. It's all done in house-party style and you're invited.

rooms	23: 20 twin/doubles, 3 suites.
price	£145–£320. Half-board (min. 2 nights) from £105 p.p.
meals	Lunch from £16.50. Afternoon tea £6–£12.50. Dinner from £37.50.
closed	Never.
directions	From Brecon, A470 for Builth Wells for about 6 miles, then left on A470 to Llyswen. Left in village at T-junc. Entrance 1.5 miles further on right.

Sir Bernard Ashley

tel	01874 754525
fax	01874 754545
web	www.llangoedhall.com

The Lake Country House

Llangammarch Wells, Powys LD4 4BS

Grand but not stuffy, and so cosseting, Lake House is the genuine article – a real country house. Afternoon tea is served in the drawing room where seven beautiful rugs warm a brightly polished wooden floor and five chandeliers hang from the ceiling. The hotel opened 100 years ago and the leather-bound fishing logs and visitor's books go back to 1894. A feel of the 1920s lingers. Fires come to life in front of your eyes, seemingly unaided by human hands, walking sticks wait at the door, grand pianos, antiques and grandfather clocks lie about the place and snooker balls clack in the distance. The same grandeur marks the bedrooms; most are suites: trompe l'œil wallpaper, rich fabrics, good lighting, stacks of antiques, crowns above the beds, a turndown service – the works. Jean-Pierre runs his home with gentle charm, happy to share his knowledge of this deeply rural slice of Wales. The grounds hold a lake to fish – you can hire rods – a nine-hole golf course, the River Ifron where kingfishers swoop, and acres of peace and quiet. Riding can also be arranged.

rooms	18: 8 twin/doubles, 10 suites.
price	£130-£250; singles £90-£145.
meals	Lunch, 3 courses, £18.50. Dinner £35.
closed	Never.
directions	From Builth Wells, A483 west for 7 miles to Garth. Signed from village.

Jean-Pierre Mifsud

tel	01591 620202
fax	01591 620457
e-mail	info@lakecountryhouse.co.uk
web	www.lakecountryhouse.co.uk

map 2   entry 212

Carlton House

Dolycoed Road, Llanwrtyd Wells, Powys LD5 4RA

A Welsh spa town — Wales's prettiest — with one of the most talented chefs in Britain? Mary Ann joined the cooking elite in 2002, winning a Michelin star; high time, said her legion of fans. They've been coming to this marvellously eccentric restaurant with rooms for years. Victorians flocked to Llanwrtyd Wells in the 1800s, drawn in the belief that the natural springs could cure everything from a troubled soul to a wart on the toe. The 1900 townhouse has a wonderful feeling of several black and white movies rolled into one as you walk up the gunmetal galleried staircase to rooms full of faded charm. The Gilchrists are old pro's, and great company. Alan, an ever engaging and unflappable host, orchestrates all in the ground-floor restaurant, full of blue and modern furniture and screened off by book shelves. Mary Ann is entirely self-taught and cooks with instinctive brilliance; she decides what to cook only hours before she puts on her apron. Their brasserie across the road is fun for a light meal, too. Pony-trekkers, cyclists and walkers fill the town in summer... Carlton suits all year.

rooms	6: 4 doubles, 2 twin/doubles.
price	£60–£80; singles £45. Half-board (min. 2 nights) from £49.50.
meals	Dinner £27–£37. Packed lunch £3.50.
closed	Last 2 weeks December (open for New Year).
directions	From Builth Wells, A483 to Llanwrtyd Wells. 1st right in town. House 50 yds on right.

Alan & Mary Ann Gilchrist

tel	01591 610248
fax	01591 610242
e-mail	info@carltonrestaurant.co.uk
web	www.carltonrestaurant.co.uk

Milebrook House Hotel

Milebrook, Knighton, Powys LD7 1LT

Your arrival at Milebrook is peculiarly comforting – all very English and understated, with no hidden surprises. The parquet floor in the hall smells of lavender floor wax, the clock ticks quietly, the flowers are fresh and Beryl is likely to come out of the kitchen in her apron to greet you. Fabrics are blended rather than matched; the furniture comfortable rather than remarkable; and the service is attentive and unobtrusive. Within the walls of the kitchen-garden cluck the chickens that produce the eggs for your breakfast. There too grow the flowers and the vegetables for your table – a table to reckon with, for their chef trained in France and is keen to win recognition. He mixes classic French with the best of English, ably assisted by that garden. There's wild terrain, too, devoted to a mature arboretum and a wildlife pond. Elsewhere, terracing, a gazebo and pergola with roses growing over obelisks, and still room for a croquet lawn. The River Teme runs along the bottom of the garden where you can fly-fish and the surrounding countryside belongs to an ever-decreasing portion of England that can still be called 'tranquil'. Come to rest completely.

rooms	10: 5 doubles, 4 twins, 1 family.
price	£86-£92; singles £56-£60. Half-board, 2 nights, £117-£126 p.p.
meals	Dinner £23.50; à la carte about £28.50.
closed	Restaurant closed Monday lunchtimes.
directions	From Ludlow, A49 north, then left at Bromfield on A4113 towards Knighton for 7 miles. Hotel on right.

Rodney & Beryl Marsden

tel	01547 528632
fax	01547 520509
e-mail	hotel@milebrook.kc3ltd.co.uk
web	www.milebrookhouse.co.uk

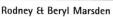

map 6   entry 214

Tŷ Siarad

Pontdolgoch, Nr. Cearsws, Powys SY17 5JE

A 17th-century drover's cottage full of delicious treasures, Tŷ Siarad, or 'The Talkhouse', is an exquisite find in the rolling wilderness of mid-Wales. After stints in Yorkshire, London and Cambridge, Melanie and Colin struck out west and the awards followed. The three bedrooms are rich and relaxing: Tirion, meaning 'gentle and happy', has a nautical feel, the bathroom decorated in blue Moustier tiles; Tybie, named after a Welsh saint, is for lovers, with a wonderful wrought iron bed and a mosaic bathroom of Sicilian sandstone; and Myfanwy feels ever so French, with restored oak frames and a hand-painted oval mirror in the bathroom. All have Quercus smellies, as favoured by Prince Charles, no less! The bar is full of memorabilia collected over the years and the dining room acts the part with proper tables and chairs, old prints and flowers. Colin is an exceptionally talented chef: try *sewen* – Pembrokeshire sea trout – or saltmarsh lamb, a favourite of foodies as the salt flavours the meat naturally. Breakfast is a treat, too, with fresh orange juice, duck eggs, wild mushrooms and local honey. Walk it off in beautiful scenery.

rooms	3 doubles.
price	£75–£95; singles £65. Half-board, Friday & Saturday, from £55 p.p.
meals	Dinner, à la carte, about £25.
closed	Christmas & New Year, 1 week in Spring & Autumn.
directions	From Newtown, A489 west, then right before level crossing on A470, for Cearsws & Dolgellau. Inn on left after 1 mile, under railway bridge.

Melanie & Colin Dawson

tel	01686 688919
fax	01686 689134
e-mail	info@talkhouse.co.uk
web	www.talkhouse.co.uk

Photography by Michael Busselle

SCOTLAND

"Here only the mountains shared our secrets."
JASON ELLIOT

Darroch Learg

Braemar Road, Ballater, Aberdeenshire AB35 5UX

The Royal Family escapes to the fir district of Deeside in summer; the Franks family stays all year welcoming those in search of genuine Scottish hospitality. They have been here 40 years and know how to run a good hotel; nothing is too much trouble. Darroch Learg is Gaelic for 'an oak copse on a sunny hillside' and this turreted 1888 granite building is in a raised position on the outskirts of the pretty village of Ballater. Views stretch across the Dee Valley to Lochnagar, snow-capped for much of the year. The main part of the hotel is a baronial Victorian manor house, with a twist of Scottish grandeur thrown in for good measure. Regency-style bedrooms are split between here and a next-door annexe: all are subtly different, with warm colours, local watercolours, fresh flowers, thick curtains to keep out the nip of winter and modern bathrooms with spoiling touches; most rooms have the view. An intimate conservatory-style dining room, with lamps at each table, draws in the view as well. Chef David Mutter's modern Scottish cooking has won various awards, supported by a good wine list. You'll feel good staying here.

rooms	17: 5 doubles, 9 twin/doubles, 1 single, 2 four-posters.
price	£126–£156; singles £63–£83. Half-board from £67–£92 p.p.
meals	Dinner £34. Sunday lunch £18.50.
closed	Christmas week & last 3 weeks in January.
directions	From Perth, A93 north to Ballater. Entering village, hotel 1st building on left above road.

Nigel & Fiona Franks

tel	01339 755443
fax	01339 755252
e-mail	nigel@darroch-learg.demon.co.uk

Minmore House

Glenlivet, Banffshire AB37 9DB

Driving up from Balmoral in the late afternoon sun, you could be forgiven for thinking the colour green was probably created here. The east of Scotland often plays second fiddle to its 'other half' in the west, but this lush cattle-grazing land is every inch as beautiful. Amid it all is Minmore, a great wee pad run with breezy good cheer by Victor and Lynne. They used to run a restaurant in South Africa and once cooked for Prince Philip; today, their food continues to wins rave reviews. Their kingdom stretches to 10 spotless bedrooms and a suite that Lynne describes as "very zoosh". Guests swap highland tales in a pretty sitting room or, best of all, in a carved wooden bar, half-panelled, with scarlet chairs, a resident Jack Russell, the odd trophy and 104 malts. The garden is a twitcher's paradise, with lapwing, curlew and a rare colony of oystercatchers. Free-range chickens wander about and those with an iron constitution may fancy the unheated swimming pool! Visit the famous Glenlivet distillery, or take bicycles deep into the Ladder Hills where buzzard, falcon and even eagles soar. An Indian head massage, or some reflexology unwinds, too.

rooms	10: 4 doubles, 3 twins, 2 singles, 1 suite.
price	£120; singles £55. Suite £180–£240. Half-board £90 p.p.
meals	Light lunch £12–£15. Full picnic £10. Dinner, 4 courses, £30.
closed	November & February.
directions	From Aviemore, A95 north to Bridge of Avon, then south on B9008 to Glenlivet. House at top of hill, 400 yds before distillery.

Victor & Lynne Janssen

tel	01807 590378
fax	01807 590472
e-mail	minmorehouse@ukonline.co.uk
web	www.minmorehousehotel.com

 map 13 entry 217

Royal Hotel

Tighnabruaich, Argyll & Bute PA21 2BE

In that never-ending search for a tourist-free destination, Tighnabruaich is near the top of our list, an end-of-the-road village, lost to the world and without great need of it. The Royal is its relaxed and informal hub. Yachtsmen tie up to the moorings and drop in for lunch, the shinty team pops down for a pint after a game, and fishermen land fresh mussels and lobster straight from the sea for Roger to cook. Roger and Bea — ex-pat Scots — returned from London with an eye to "buying something run-down so they could..." run it up? Which is exactly what they've done: stripped wooden floors and a roaring fire in the brasserie, tartan carpets and leather sofas in the restaurant. Claire, their daughter, has joined the team, and now cooks. Food is a big pull: masses of fresh seafood, and local venison, as stalked by Winston Churchill of Dunoon. Big views of the Kyles of Bute are getting bigger as conservatories are being added. Bedrooms are big and warm, homely and comfy, and most have sea views. Play tennis on a nearby tennis court where you can lose balls in the sea, or take a short ferry ride to Bute.

rooms	11: 9 doubles, 2 twins.
price	£94–£124; singles £74.50. Half-board from £65 p.p.
meals	Dinner, à la carte, about £30. Meals in brasserie from £10.
closed	Christmas.
directions	From Glasgow, A82 north, A83 west, A815 south, A886 south, A8003 south, then B8000 north into village. Hotel on seafront.

Roger & Bea McKie

tel	01700 811239
fax	01700 811300
e-mail	info@royalhotel.org.uk
web	www.royalhotel.org.uk

Ardanaiseig

Kilchrenan, By Taynuilt, Argyll & Bute PA35 1HE

It's enough to make you believe in fables: "All you need to stay in love," was how one guest described this seductive place. The pleasure of the journey to Ardanaiseig unfolds with lingering suspense: from the village of Kilchrenan, an even smaller single track road leads into a mighty landscape of loch and mountain. Wind through heath and ancient woodland, then down an avenue of beech trees, through a collection of rare and exotic rhododendron, to a baronial 1834 house right on the shores of Loch Awe. Celtic legend says the lake has magical properties after Bheithir, goddess of ageless beauty, accidentally let the well of eternal youth on neighbouring Ben Cruchan spill over. Guests enthuse about the light here – over breakfast, watch mists swirl over the soft silhouettes of islands out on the lake. The hotel is impeccable inside, full of the eclectic style of its art dealer owner. Bedrooms have lots of flair; Tervine is wonderfully over the top; others are more restrained. Enchanting.

rooms	16: 8 doubles, 8 twin/doubles.
price	£78-£250; singles £69-£155. Half-board (min. 3 nights) £59-£148 p.p.
meals	Light lunch from £2.75. Afternoon tea £2-£10. Dinner, 5 courses, £38.50.
closed	January-mid-February.
directions	From Glasgow, A82 then A85 to Taynuilt. Left for Kilchrenan on B845. Left in village at Kilchrenan pub down track for 3.9 miles. Hotel at end down drive.

Bernie Gray

tel	01866 833333
fax	01866 833222
e-mail	ardanaiseig@clara.net
web	www.ardanaiseig.com

map 9   entry 219

Lerags House

Lerags, By Oban, Argyll & Bute PA34 4SE

A rare touch of city chic on the beautiful west coast, Lerags is a stylish old building with a contemporary country-house feel. Charlie, a sail maker, and Bella, a cook, both in their late thirties and originally from Australia, came for six months, stayed for nine years, and now own their place by the sea; they absolutely love it here. Built in 1815, the house is large, with gardens that run down to tidal mud flats: watch the ebb and flow from the dining room. Cool interiors mix natural colours and light pine surfaces with pale olive sofas, fresh lilies, lots of straight lines and a deliberate lack of clutter. Charlie and Bella represent an emerging generation of hoteliers: more style, less formality, good prices, great service and exceptional food – guinea fowl in a gin and juniper sauce with crème fraîche and spring onion mash caught the eye. Don't think you have to be young to enjoy it either. At the end of the road – a brisk stroll of less than a mile – is a beach for uninterrupted walks, or a constitutional dip. Day trips to Mull, Crinan and Glencoe are all easy. There's Fingal the dog, too.

rooms	8: 4 doubles, 1 twin, 1 single, 2 suites.
price	£70; suites £90; singles from £33. Half-board £56-£77 p.p.
meals	Dinner, 4 courses, £28. Packed lunch £6.
closed	Christmas.
directions	From Oban, south on A816 for 2 miles, then right, signed Lerags for 2.5 miles. Hotel on left, signed.

Charlie & Bella Miller

tel	01631 563381
e-mail	stay@leragshouse.com
web	www.leragshouse.com

The Manor House

Gallanach Road, Oban, Argyll & Bute PA34 4LS

A 1780 dower house for the Dukes of Argyll – their cottage by the sea – built of local stone, high on the hill, with long views over Oban harbour to the Isle of Mull. A smart and proper place, not one to bow to the fads of fashion: sea views from the lawn, cherry trees in the courtyard garden, a fire roaring in the drawing room, a beautiful tiled floor in the entrance hall and an elegant bay window in the dining room that catches the eye. Compact bedrooms are pretty in blues, reds and greens, with fresh flowers, crisp linen sheets, radios, padded headboards and piles of towels in good bathrooms; those that look seaward have pairs of binoculars to scour the horizon. Downstairs, sample Loch Fyne kippers for breakfast, sea bass for lunch and, if you've room, duck in redcurrant sauce for supper; try their home-baking, too. Ferries leave for the islands from the bottom of the hill – see them depart from the hotel garden – while at the top, overlooking Oban, watch the day's close from McCaig's Folly; sunsets here are really special. *Children 12 years and over welcome.*

rooms	11: 8 doubles, 3 twins.
price	Half-board £60–£85 p.p.
meals	Lunch £7–£13.
	Dinner, 5 courses, £28.95.
closed	Christmas.
directions	In Oban, follow signs to ferry. Hotel on right 0.5 miles after ferry turn-off, signed.

Gabriella Wijker

tel	01631 562087
fax	01631 710378
e-mail	manorhouseoban@aol.com
web	www.manorhouseoban.com

map 9   entry 221

Barcaldine House

Barcaldine, Oban, Argyll & Bute PA37 1SG

House-party in true Scottish style at this baronial mansion just north of Oban. Barcaldine is a bastion of the Campbell clan: seven generations lived here, starting with Red Patrick who built the original house in 1709 to escape the confines of the family castle; clansmen across the Highlands were doing the same as devilish intrigue replaced full-scale war. The house is full of lived-in elegance; take afternoon tea in the splendid Wedgewood-style drawing room with white cameo reliefs, wooden floors and comfy sofas, or retire after dinner to the wood-panelled snooker room on the first floor and sit in worn leather armchairs under a fabulous vaulted ceiling, surrounded by antler trophies. Bedrooms are lovely: floral designs, the odd antique, fresh flowers, maybe a roll-top bath for long soaks after the day's exertions, maybe a friendly ghost – there are two according to legend: the Blue Lady and an unknown Highlander. Wendy looks after guests with helpful enthusiasm, while Gary cooks with pride; his scones are delicious. Walks start from the back of the house.

rooms	7: 4 doubles, 3 twins.
price	£70–£90.
meals	Dinner, à la carte, 4 courses £30. Packed lunch £5.
closed	Never.
directions	From Fort William, A82 to North Ballachulish, then A828 to Barcaldine. Entering village, house on left up drive, signed.

	Wendy Graham & Gary Smith
tel	01631 720219
fax	01631 720219
e-mail	barcaldine@breathe.co.uk
web	www.countrymansions.com

Ballachulish House

Ballachulish, Argyll & Bute PA39 4JX

For today's traveller, seeing this charming Scottish laird's house come into view after a long day's trek in the mountains must surely be as special as it was for clansmen of yore – only for different reasons! Once a refuge from hostile neighbours, now a sanctuary from the capricious elements of nature, Ballachulish appears part fortress, part country house, tucked at the foot of mighty Glencoe mountain, scene of the 1692 massacre of the recalcitrant MacDonald clan. Flop into a comfortable chair by an open fire and savour the warm glow of more peaceful endeavours. The McLaughlins have altered little of the house's 18th-century origins, retaining its elegant simplicity. Bedrooms have big sleigh beds, the odd combed plaster ceiling and nice touches like fresh fruit. Most have mountain views across a part-walled garden of herb beds, stone fountain, orchard and specimen trees; two at the front have loch views over a croquet lawn. Raise a smile and your glass to "Lang may your lum reek", inscribed on a tiled iron range in the dining room. The welcome is generous and the food wonderful; the range of Scottish cheeses is unsurpassed. *Children over 10 welcome.*

rooms	9: 4 doubles, 3 twins, 1 single, 1 suite.
price	£60–£140; singles £50–£60.
meals	Dinner, 5 courses, £30.
closed	Never.
directions	From Glasgow, A82, via Crianlarich and Glencoe, to Ballachulish, then A828 at r'bout, signed Oban. Under Ballachulish Bridge. Entrance 100 yds further on left, past golf course.

Marie & Michael McLaughlin

tel	01855 811266
fax	01855 811498
e-mail	mclaughlins@btconnect.com
web	www.ballachulishhouse.com

map 9   entry 223

Culzean Castle

The National Trust for Scotland, Maybole, Ayrshire KA19 8LE

Few places to stay in the world come close to Culzean, pronounced 'Cullane' — Scotland's sixth most popular tourist destination defies overstatement. Built into solid rock a couple of hundred feet above crashing waves, the castle is considered to be architect Robert Adam's final masterpiece. It was presented to the Scottish people in 1945 by the 5th Marquess of Ailsa and the Kennedy family. General Eisenhower was given use of the top floor during his lifetime — Scotland's thankyou for his contribution to the war effort. You stay on the same floor where every room is a delight; Ike's bed is always popular. The rest is awe-inspiring: hundreds of portraits, including one of Napoleon, the round drawing room that juts out over the sea, the central oval staircase with two galleries and 12 Corinthian columns, and the Armoury, with 713 flintlock pistols and 400 swords, which always reminds you to pay the bill. Tour the castle before the tourists invade at 11am, take a stirring cliff walk in 560 acres of idyllic coastal scenery, and dine together country-house style. All guaranteed to multiply your wildest dreams by the power of ten.

rooms	6: 1 double, 3 twin/doubles, 1 four-poster; 1 twin, with private bath.
price	£200-£400; singles from £140.
meals	Dinner, by arrangement, 4 courses with wine, £50.
closed	Never.
directions	From A77 in Maybole, A719 for 4 miles, signed.

Jonathan Cardale

tel	01655 884455
fax	01655 884503
e-mail	culzean@nts.org.uk
web	www.culzeancastle.net

Knockinaam Lodge

Portpatrick, Wigtownshire, Dumfries & Galloway DG9 9AD

The writer, John Buchan, knew of this 1869 shooting lodge and described it in *The Thirty-Nine Steps* as the house to which Hannay fled. It's still a good place to hide out, hunkered down with hills on three sides and the sea at the end of the vast lawn. In spring, the grounds transform as hundreds of thousands of bluebells appear. Sunsets can be awesome, too, with the Irish Sea streaked red. Knockinaam is as good as its setting, a supremely comfortable country house – a Michelin star in the dining room, breakfasts fit for kings, a wine list for the gods and 144 malts in the panelled bar. Everywhere you'll find crisp, uncluttered elegance. Big windows flood gracious rooms with light, an open fire burns in the panelled drawing room, and an antique Queen Anne sofa takes the strain. Bedrooms have big beds, the best fabrics, the best pillows and cushions piled high; two have sea views. Michael and Pauline are easy-going perfectionists who came over from Canada to make this peaceful land of Galloway their home; as Michael will tell you, the weather here is much better than you'd think – his daily log for 2001 reveals 130 days of summer sunshine.

rooms	10: 7 doubles, 2 twins, 1 single.
price	Half-board £90–£170 p.p.
meals	Bar lunch from £3.50. Lunch, 3 courses, £30. Dinner, 4 courses, included; non-residents £40.
closed	Never.
directions	From A77 or A75 follow signs for Portpatrick. 2 miles west of Lochans, left at smokehouse. Follow signs to Lodge for 3 miles.

**Michael Bricker &
Pauline Ashworth**

tel	01776 810471
fax	01776 810435
e-mail	reservations@knockinaamlodge.com

map 9   entry 225

Cavens Country House Hotel

Kirkbean, By Dumfries, Dumfries & Galloway DG2 8AA

Strength in adversity — *In Arduus Fortis* — runs Angus's family motto, and it's an appropriate one given the heroic effort that created this splendid country-house hotel. Tales of derring-do tackling grotty nylon, formica and Anaglypta so affected our inspector, he went back to work for them for a whole summer! It's hard to appreciate their labours now, surrounded by rich fabrics, gorgeous colours and elegant antiques, but it's wonderful to enjoy the fruits, especially next to an open fire in the lovely Green Room, with single malt in hand and a gorgeous view stretching across the Solway Firth. This 1752 house was built by Sir Richard Oswald, a wealthy tobacco importer, who owned the view from the window, and more. Jane and Angus plan to knock down a later extension and restore the original front door. Bedrooms are done in a classic country-house style with views over the six-acre garden and beyond; one has an arched ceiling. Angus has run hotels before but nothing on quite so cosy a scale. It gives him an opportunity to cook, something he loves; his food is very much Scottish with a French twist. You're in safe hands.

rooms	7: 5 doubles, 1 twin, 1 family.
price	£80–£110; singles from £65.
meals	Dinner, 4 courses, £25. Packed lunch.
closed	Never.
directions	From Dumfries, A710 to Kirkbean (12 miles). Hotel signed in village.

Jane & Angus Fordyce

tel	01387 880234
fax	01387 880467
e-mail	enquiries@cavens.com
web	www.cavens.com

Corsewall Lighthouse Hotel
Stranraer, Dumfries & Galloway DG9 0QG

When the road runs out, you've arrived at this working lighthouse, in operation since 1816. Tom, the retired keeper, still pops in to clean the glass and he'll stop for a chat about its history. It has a breathtaking position with views north, east, south and west, of Loch Ryan and the Rhinns of Galloway. Watch ferries passing as they cross the Irish Sea, and enjoy the rare pleasure of seeing a setting sun slip beneath the horizon. When gales blow up, the rain can be horizontal — invigorating stuff. It's not surprising to find a nautical theme running throughout the hotel, which lies at the foot of the actual tower: ships' bells, model lighthouses, the odd knot and pictures of boats. You can sleep in the main house, or in the old keeper's cottage, where a conservatory has been added, giving awesome views. Bedrooms are fairly compact, everything is ship-shape, with bathrobes, good linen, and a sofa where space allows. Thick stone walls and an open fire weatherproof the dining room; five-course feasts may include red Thai salmon, roast rack of Galloway lamb, and poached pear in a port wine. Delicious. Walks start from the door.

rooms	9: 1 double, 4 twin/doubles, 3 suites; 1 double, with private bath.
price	Half-board £70–£130 p.p.
meals	Dinner, 5 courses, included. Packed lunch from £5.
closed	Never.
directions	From Stranraer, A718 north through Kirkcolm, then follow signs to lighthouse.

Gordon Ward

tel	01776 853220
fax	01776 854231
e-mail	lighthousehotel@btopenworld.com
web	www.lighthousehotel.co.uk

map 9   entry 227

The Witchery by the Castle

Castlehill, Royal Mile, Edinburgh EH1 2NF

Ornately Gothic in style and grandly exuberant, this glorious restaurant with rooms should really be a theatre – it's a such magical and passionate setting. Described as "one of the seven wonders of the world", it might best suit a Jacobean drama – there are enough drapes and alcoves to conceal a medium-sized cast of conspirators and lovers. The Witchery is the inspiration of James Thomson. He has trawled the flea-markets of Europe to fill two 16th-century tenements next to the gates of Edinburgh Castle with sumptuous architectural bric-a-brac, from the medieval to the quasi-Byzantine; the spiral staircase, the candles, the stone floors, the tapestries, even the shadows delight. The six suites are incredible: the Inner Sanctum has one of Queen Victoria's chairs, the pillars in the Old Rectory came from London's Trocadero theatre, and the red, black and gold Vestry has a fabulous trompe l'œil draped and swagged bathroom. A bottle of champagne is included, as is a continental breakfast in bed – the home-made pastries are superb. The three restaurants excel – one fills a rooftop – and if you can drag yourself away, Edinburgh's not bad either.

rooms	6 suites.
price	From £195.
meals	Lunch £9.95.
	Dinner, à la carte, about £30.
closed	Christmas Day & Boxing Day.
directions	Find Edinburgh Castle. Witchery 20 yds from main castle gate.

	Mark Rowley
tel	0131 225 5613
fax	0131 220 4392
e-mail	mail@thewitchery.com
web	www.thewitchery.com

The Inn at Lathones

Lathones, St Andrews, Fife KY9 1JE

Once upon a time in the Kingdom of Fife, two people fell in love, married and lived happily ever after in this old inn; beer flowed, food was plentiful, customers burst into song, even a dwarf highwayman occasionally dropped in after 'work'. Legend says when the landlady died in 1736, the wedding stone above the fireplace in the lounge cracked, so strong was their love. Today, she and her horse haunt the wonderful Stables, the oldest part of the inn, with its garlands of hops and bottle-green ceiling — but in the friendliest way. Lathones could charm the most cantankerous ghost: superb food, the draw of an open fire, leather sofas to sink into, and a warm, Scottish welcome. Walk into the bar to find bottles of grappa and eau-de-vie asking to be sampled, while Marc Guibert's menu is mouth-watering: try local grilled sea bass followed by a clootie dumpling served with fresh strawberry. Comfortable, traditional-style bedrooms are split between a coach house and an old blacksmith's house either side of the inn. Historic St Andrews and the East Neuk of Fife fishing villages are close.

rooms	14: 12 twin/doubles, 2 singles.
price	£120–£160; singles £65–£85.
meals	Lunch £9.50.
	Dinner, à la carte, from £20.
	Packed lunch from £5.
closed	2 weeks in January.
directions	From Kirkcaldy, or St Andrews, A915 to Largoward. Inn 1 mile north on roadside.

Nick White

tel	01334 840494
fax	01334 840694
e-mail	lathones@theinn.co.uk
web	www.theinn.co.uk

map 10   entry 229

Summer Isles

Achiltibuie, By Ullapool, Ross-shire, Highland IV26 2YG

Geraldine's description of The Summer Isles as a "roof in a lovely location" is a wonderful understatement. This old fishing inn may be unremarkable from the outside, but the laid-back house-party feel is irresistible. The hotel has been in Mark's family since 1969. They took over the reins a few years back, having opted out of London life… friends have been beating a path to their door ever since. Both are natural hosts, with a deep affection for this beautifully remote part of the west coast of Scotland – the land rises from sea, sand dunes and rock pools to towering peaks, and all at the front door. Geraldine loves to paint when she gets the time; her interior design isn't bad, either: dried grasses shoot out of terracotta pots, beach pebbles spill across windowsills and colourful blobs of art leap from white walls. Bedrooms range from gorgeous suites with sea views to quirky log cabins; nothing disappoints. Chris Firth Bernard's cooking should woo you, too – he retained his Michelin star again in 2002. Easily one of the best places to stay in Scotland. *Children over 6 welcome. Sea trout fishing on Loch Oscaig June-September.*

rooms	13: 9 doubles, 4 suites.
price	£104–£220; singles £95–£150.
meals	Light lunch from £4. Dinner, 5 courses, £40.
closed	Mid-October-Easter.
directions	From Ullapool, A835 north for Unapool for about 9 miles, then left on single track road, to Achiltibuie. Follow signs to village. Hotel on left, sea on right.

	Mark & Geraldine Irvine
tel	01854 622282
fax	01854 622251
e-mail	summerisleshotel@aol.com
web	www.summerisleshotel.co.uk

Pool House Hotel

Poolewe, Wester Ross, Highland IV22 2LD

Fabulous ostentation is not a quality usually associated with Scotland but in a small corner of the Highlands, one hotel has taken luxury to a sublime level. We liked what we saw the first time we visited the Pool House on the shores of Loch Ewe. Since then, the Harrisons have courageously converted 14 rooms into four sumptuous suites with sea views, and a sumptuous single. The result is awe-inspiring. The Diadem suite is based on a Titanic theme – Margaret is related to the ship's captain. The room's brass light fittings were made with the same moulds used on the Titanic and the Edwardian bath, with its original shower column, was made in 1912, the year the fated liner set sail. Elsewhere, beautiful French furniture, a Regency clock, Art Deco beds – truly impressive stuff. It's also the greenest hotel in Scotland, with worm farms making liquid compost and waterless lavatories – as used by NASA – scooping the coveted Loo of the Year award. Everyone here is lovely and the food's top notch – some things never change. You may see a sea eagle, or the Aurora Borealis.

rooms	5: 1 single, 4 suites.
price	£250-£350; single £90. Half-board £125 p.p.
meals	Lunch £14. Dinner, 4 courses, £25-£35.
closed	January-February.
directions	Poolewe on A832 north of Gairloch & south of Laide. Hotel on Loch Ewe.

	Peter, Margaret, Mhairi & Elizabeth Harrison
tel	01445 781272
fax	01445 781403
e-mail	enquiries@poolhousehotel.com
web	www.poolhousehotel.com

map 12   entry 231

The Old Mill Highland Lodge

Talladale, Loch Maree, Ross-shire IV22 2HL

Chris and Jo are a remarkable pair providing the sort of effortless hospitality that few hotels can match. Old Mill isn't plush, but it doesn't pretend to be. It's about delightful home comforts, relaxing company and extremely good nosh. We sent along two self-confessed foodies who can be highly critical. They found Chris's food fresh, flavoursome and imaginative. Praise indeed! Jo, a keen photographer, is good on detail, remembering everyone's Christian names. Both are great travellers and the comfy living room is full of travel books – novels, too, and photo albums charting the fortunes of this 1840 horse-driven mill since a rebuild in the 70s. The best bedroom is upstairs; those downstairs are pet-friendly. The Honeysuckle room is gorgeous, with a big spoiling duvet, giant pillows and garden views – watch the tame pine marten being fed, and fall asleep to the sound of burns hurrying through two acres of garden to Loch Maree, regarded as one of, if not *the* best loch in Scotland. It's wider than most, with islands in the middle and Caledonian pine forests at the foot of Beinn Eighe, so bring your walking boots. Great value.

rooms	6: 2 doubles, 3 twins; 1 double, with private bath.
price	Half-board £70 p.p.
meals	Dinner included. Packed lunch £4.
closed	20 October–15 March.
directions	Hotel on A832, 10 miles north of Kinlochewe & 10 miles south of Gairloch, signed.

Chris & Jo Powell

tel   01445 760271

Tigh an Eilean

Shieldaig, Loch Torridon, Highland IV54 8XN

Tigh an Eilean is the holy grail of the west coast; when you arrive you realise it's what you've been looking for all these years. A perfect place in every respect, from its position by the sea in this very pretty village, to the magnificence of the Torridon mountains that rise all around; this area is one of the wonderlands of the world, an undisputed heavyweight champion of natural beauty. And Sheildaig itself is an exceptionally friendly village with a strong sense of community, the hub of which is the pub – like the shop, it is owned by the hotel – where locals come to sing their songs, play their fiddles, drink their whisky, and talk. Most surprising of all is the hotel. Christopher and Cathryn, two ex-London lawyers, now run an immaculate bolt hole, a faultless place, airy and stylish, with tartan cushions on window seats, sensational views, home-made shortbread, and bedrooms that elate. No TVs, no telephones, but kind, gentle staff who chat and advise. Relax in sitting rooms with plump sofas, an honesty bar and an open fire. Eat in the smart restaurant, or try the pub – fewer frills but lots of fun. Exceptional.

rooms	11: 4 doubles, 4 twins, 3 singles.
price	£110; singles £49.50. Half-board from £74 p.p.
meals	Bar meals from £5. Dinner in restaurant £27.
closed	November-March.
directions	On loch front in centre of Shieldaig.

Christopher & Cathryn Field

tel	01520 755251
fax	01520 755321
e-mail	tighaneileanhotel@shieldaig.fsnet.co.uk

map 12　entry 233

Applecross Inn

Shore Street, Applecross, Wester Ross IV54 8LR

No Highland fling would be quite complete without a visit to this simple little inn looking across the sands of Applecross; they extend about half a mile at low tide, and views go on for miles, to Rassay, then Skye beyond. Weather permitting, arrive by Bealach-Na-Ba, the highest mountain pass in Britain. The view at the top is magical, a 50-mile sweep of Hebridean heaven, of sea and mountain, of island and sky. Down at the inn, Judith continues to win rave reviews for her rooms and for her food. More renovation and redecoration will bring bright and breezy blues and yellows to the walls, and bathrooms to every room; all are great value. And so to the food: expect the freshest seafood, scooped from the water out front and cooked simply. The inn has become a magnet for foodies, a place of pilgrimage for those in search of dressed crab, squat lobster, queen scallops, or half a pint of fat prawns. Eat outside in good weather, but the down-to-earth bar is just as good; locals and visitors mix easily. As one guest wrote: "To be Applecrossed; a rare and wonderful experience." Don't miss it.

rooms	7: 1 double, 2 twins, 2 singles, 2 family.
price	£60–£70; singles £30.
meals	Bar meals from £5. Packed lunch £5. Dinner about £20.
closed	New Year's Day.
directions	From Loch Carron, A896 north for 5 miles, then left over Bealach-Na-Ba pass for 11 miles to village. Inn on left. Use alternative route via Kenmore when snow closes pass.

	Judith Fish
tel	01520 744262
fax	01520 744400

Glenelg Inn

Glenelg, By Kyle of Lochalsh, Highland IV40 8JR

Why drive when you can skim across the water in a motor boat? Catch Christopher going your way and he may give you a lift. As for his inn — just perfect. Bedrooms have Colefax & Fowler fabrics, bowls of fruit, great views — splash out on the suite and get an *enormous* room, beautifully decorated, with breakfast in bed gazing over the sea to Skye. A new cottage suite with its own garden has been recently added — privacy for couples, ideal for a family of four. There's also the restaurant and sitting room; the latter more country house drawing room, with leather sofas, an open fire and oil paintings. The epicentre of this lively place is the panelled bar, full of fishermen, farmers and sailors: low beams, open fires, and in one corner, a pile of old fish boxes to sit on (it might sound awful, but they're perfect). Try excellent bar meals — steamed mussels, wild salmon, venison — and listen to music: pipers, fiddlers and folk musicians all pass by. In summer, sit in the garden with its awesome views. The tiny Kylerhea ferry nearby will take you to Skye and back. Wonderful.

rooms	7: 2 doubles, 2 twins, 1 family, 1 suite. Cottage also available.
price	Half-board £79–£99 p.p.
meals	Bar lunch from £8. Dinner, 4 courses, £29.
closed	Never.
directions	West off A87 at Sheil Bridge. Keep left into village and inn on right. The Kylerhea ferry from Skye is a beautiful alternative.

Christopher Main

tel	01599 522273
fax	01599 522283
e-mail	christophermain@glenelg-inn.com
web	www.glenelg-inn.com

map 12   entry 235

Doune

Knoydart, Mallaig, Inverness-shire PH41 4PL

Ever imagined taking a boat from a tiny Scottish fishing village and landing in paradise? Doune might persuade you if you haven't. The boat collects you at Mallaig, then crosses Loch Nevis, with the mighty mountains of Knoydart rising to the east... and lands in a sacred place, with no roads, a friendly community and a glorious view of Skye and the Cullins across the Sound of Sleat. Straining an ear confirms your first thought – the only sounds you can hear are natural: water lapping, the call of a bird, a whistling wind... and the whoops of joy of other guests as the combination of solitude, beauty, comfort and hospitality triggers an overpowering happiness in all. Hike and see no one all day, dive and find your own supper, or stroll over to Inverie and the pub – a couple of hours' walk. For at least one day, though, we recommend you do absolutely nothing. Food is exceptional – maybe something from the sea in front, or from the hills behind – and the kindest people look after you. Lodge bedrooms, by the way, are perfect: wood, windows and cathedral roofs. Hard to find better value anywhere in Britain.

rooms	3: 2 doubles, 1 twin, all with extra bedding. Lodge sleeps 12.
price	Half-board £51 p.p; singles £60. Full-board, 7 days, £306 p.p.
meals	Dinner & packed lunch included.
closed	October-Easter.
directions	Park in Mallaig and the boat will collect you at an agreed time.

Liz & Andy Tibbetts

tel	01687 462667
fax	01687 462667
e-mail	liz@doune-marine.co.uk
web	www.doune-marine.co.uk

Kilcamb Lodge
Strontian, Highland PH36 4HY

You'll find water at the end of Kilcamb's garden — Loch Sunart leads to Mull, Coll, Tiree... America. The position is breathtaking, with Glas Bheinn in the distance, rising from the loch shore. Walk down to the water's edge along paths that wind through a sea of bluebells in spring. It's a wonderful spot to be shipwrecked. Ian and Jenny chose the place because it reminded them of New Zealand; they spent three years there after Ian decided he needed a change from teaching folk to fly helicopters in Lincolnshire. It's not the first time they've upped and left on a sabbatical: 10 years ago, they built a boat and sailed their four children to the Mediterranean. In good weather, a boat will take you out, too, to catch langoustine, lobster and crab; obliging chefs will then cook your catch for supper. The house is exquisite: small, relaxed and welcoming, with smart carpets, open fires and comfy sofas. Bedrooms have fresh flowers, lovely fabrics and big, spoiling bath towels — you'll find curtains drawn and beds turned down when you turn in after dinner. Ardnamurchan, Scotland's most westerly point, lies at the end of the road — further west than Land's End, they say. *Cots and highchairs available.*

rooms	11: 4 doubles, 7 twin/doubles.
price	£70–£145.
meals	Lunch from £6. Dinner, 2 courses, £23.50; 4 courses, £32.50.
closed	Never.
directions	From Fort William, A82 south for 10 miles to Corran ferry, then A861 to Strontian. Hotel west of village on left, signed. From Fort William, via A830 & A861 takes an hour longer.

Ian & Jenny Grant

tel	01967 402257
fax	01967 402041
e-mail	enquiries@kilcamblodge.com
web	www.kilcamblodge.com

map 9   entry 237

Old Pines Restaurant with Rooms

Spean Bridge, By Fort William, Highland PH34 4EG

Old Pines is a must for anyone in search of that appealing combination of relaxed informality and seriously good food. Sukie and Bill do things effortlessly, be it marshalling one of their children off to bed while greeting a guest, or sitting down in the garden for a chat while chopping herbs from their organic garden. In between, Sukie somehow finds time to prove her fast-growing reputation as one of Scotland's top chefs, cooking up truly ambrosial food that's eaten communally in the stone-flagged, chalet-style dining room. Bill readily shares his enthusiasm for local scenery, wildlife, history, culture and wine; nothing at Old Pines is too much trouble. Pretty rooms, comfortable sofas, log fires and loads of books await inside, while plants and flowers frame Ben Nevis in the conservatory. Kids can eat and play with the Barbers' brood: a fenced garden with trampoline and a playroom with pool and table tennis provide ample distraction. Bedrooms are chalet-style with stripped pine walls and duvets, all perfect, but it's the Barbers who really make this place so special: kind, generous, fun and thoroughly down-to-earth. Don't miss it.

rooms	8: 2 family, 2 twins, 2 doubles, 1 single; 1 single, with private bath.
price	Half-board from £80 p.p.
meals	Dinner, 5 courses, plus afternoon tea included; non-residents £22–£32.
closed	Mid-January–mid-February. Restaurant closed Monday.
directions	On A82, 1 mile north of Spean Bridge left just after Commando Memorial onto B8004 to Gairlochy. Old Pines 300 yds on right.

Bill & Sukie Barber

tel	01397 712324
fax	01397 712433
e-mail	specialplaces@oldpines.co.uk
web	www.oldpines.co.uk

The Cross

Tweed Mill Brae, Kingussie, Highland PH21 1TC

It may not be deep countryside, but this is a special destination in its own right. Unwind on a beautiful terrace, surrounded by copper beech, hazel, willow, alder, and sycamore; the trees enfold you in peace and quiet. They bring wildlife, too: dippers, heron, otters, red squirrel – even roe deer. Inside, whitewashed stone walls meet cool, contemporary design, with plush red carpets, old wooden beams, an open-plan feel and modern art scattered pleasingly about the place. Upstairs, clean lines and light rooms have a Scandinavian feel, with skylights in eaved walls. Bedrooms have the same smart, minimalist feel with halogen lights and excellent beds. Rooms on one side have the river right below them; one has a small balcony. At the heart of The Cross is the restaurant – one of the best in Scotland. Ruth's exceptional food has won stacks of awards – the wine list is outstanding too – so climb that mountain in the afternoon and have no guilt at supper. Not a place to be hurried. *Children over eight welcome.*

rooms	9: 7 doubles, 2 twins.
price	Half-board £95–£115 p.p.
meals	Continental breakfast only. Dinner, 5 courses, included.
closed	December–February. Restaurant closed Tuesday.
directions	At the only traffic lights in Kingussie, right up hill (if coming from north), and signed left.

Tony & Ruth Hadley

tel	01540 661166
fax	01540 661080
e-mail	relax@thecross.co.uk
web	www.thecross.co.uk

map 13 entry 239

The Dower House

Highfield, Muir of Ord, Highland IV6 7XN

Neither a restaurant, nor a hotel, this historic house in the cottage-*orné* style happily defies attempts to label it. It's a must for anyone who enjoys good food in an intimate country-house setting but that only partly does it justice; maybe better to compare it to the small, reliable and quite adorable Mini that Robyn somehow coaxed into transporting several of the larger artefacts up here. Mena describes Robyn's eclectic brand of no-frills cooking as "gutsy and colourful", which could just as well describe the chef himself, a broad presence dressed in bold Mediterranean colours; his enthusiasm and eye for the extraordinary fill the house, as much as your plate. Impeccable rooms are full of surprises: a working pianola, a magnificent Victorian half-tester and trompe l'œil of wisteria curling up one of the bathrooms – what better way to work up an appetite than a lazy soak. Dinner starts in a graceful dining room, with a piano at one end, and finishes with home-made truffles and coffee by an open fire in the cosy sitting room. You may wonder what you've done to deserve all this... a gem of a place.

rooms	5: 2 doubles, 2 twin/doubles, 1 suite. Self-catering lodge for 6.
price	£110–£130; singles £65–£85. Suite £150.
meals	Dinner £35.
closed	Never.
directions	A9 north of Inverness to Tore r'bout, then left on A832 for Muir of Ord. In village, A862, for Dingwall. Entrance 1 mile on left.

Robyn & Mena Aitchison

tel	01463 870090
fax	01463 870090
e-mail	stay@thedowerhouse.co.uk
web	www.thedowerhouse.co.uk

Glenmorangie, The Highland Home at Cadboll

Fearn, By Tain, Ross-shire IV20 1XP

Glenmorangie – glen of tranquillity – and so it is; this is heaven. Owned by the eponymous distillery, this 1700s farmhouse of thick walls and immaculate interiors stands in glorious country, with a tree-lined path down to the beach; you may see your supper landed by fishermen, or search for driftwood instead. A perfect place, a real find, with levels of service to surpass most others, where staff are attentive, yet unobtrusive, and where the comforts seem unending. Bedrooms are exceptional: decanters of whisky, *fleur de lys* wallpaper, tartan blankets and country views. Rooms flood with light, there are bathrobes and piles of towels, the best linen and blankets. Downstairs, the portrait of the Sheriff of Cromarty hangs on the wall, a fire crackles between plump sofas in the drawing room, and views of the garden – apple-blossom white, cherry-blossom pink – draw you out. Here you find a half-acre walled garden, both beautiful and productive, with much for your plate. Fields all around, absolute peace, delicious food, golf at Royal Dornoch, Tain and Brora. We've hardly scratched the surface. Exceptional.

rooms	9: 6 twin/doubles, 3 cottage suites.
price	Half-board £110–£185 p.p.
meals	Light lunch from £5. Dinner, 4 courses, included; non-residents £38.50.
closed	Never.
directions	A9 north from Inverness for 33 miles to Nigg r'bout. Right on B9175, for Nigg, over r'way crossing for 1.5 miles, then left, following signs to house.

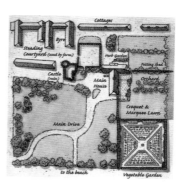

Helen McKenzie-Smith

tel	01862 871671
fax	01862 871625
e-mail	relax@glenmorangieplc.co.uk
web	www.glenmorangie.com

map 13　entry 241

2 Quail Restaurant

Castle Street, Dornoch, Sutherland IV25 3SN

One of the best restaurants in Scotland and in one of the few places in the Highlands that can be truly described as 'pretty'. Officially a county town in the Royal Burgh of Dornoch – granted by King Charles I in 1628 – it's really a village. The stone used in the buildings has a hint of the Cotswolds and this small and stylish restaurant is right in the middle of it all, a short stroll from the Cathedral. Michael and Kerensa look after you impeccably, with contrasting styles: he does calm chef in control of superb ingredients, she does dynamite front of house, sizzling with energy and enthusiasm. Both keep you smiling. Eat in one of two dining rooms; beautiful Buchanan tartan carpets, russet tablecloths and shelves of books worth reading suggest the warmth of autumn, of leaves just turning. Upstairs, three pleasant bedrooms have a mixture of authentic Victorian and Edwardian furniture; all feels welcoming and comfortable. Settle in and dream about the meal to come as the smell of the stockpot wafts up the stairs. *Children eight and over welcome.*

rooms	3: 1 double; 1 twin; 1 twin/double, with private bath.
price	£70-£90.
meals	Dinner, 4 courses, £32.50; booking essential.
closed	Christmas & 2 weeks in February/March.
directions	From Inverness, A9 north for 44 miles, then right on A949, for Dornoch. Restaurant on left before Cathedral.

	Michael & Kerensa Carr
tel	01862 811811
e-mail	stay@2quail.com
web	www.2quail.com

Argyll Hotel

Isle of Iona PA76 6SJ

When the boat stops at six o'clock in the morning, The Argyll is a good spot to be marooned. Walk over to the west coast, about a mile away, for awesome sunsets – there's nothing between you and America. Daniel and Claire, a young and gentle couple, have preserved the old, cosy island feel, adding their own sweet touches, too. Rooms are spot-on and full of simple, homely comforts: piles of old paperbacks, armchairs, comfy beds and boiling hot water bursting from bathroom taps – you won't think you're being deprived of a thing. Sitting rooms have open fires, there's a pretty conservatory and the dining room has a lovely old-fashioned feel. Food is wholesome, home-cooked and mostly organic, with seasonal vegetables from the garden. Outside, Iona is magical, a mystical dreamscape, home to a hermit's cave, the Abbey and sandy beaches; St Columba landed on one of them, bringing Christianity to Scotland in 563 AD. Mark, maintenance man, friend and sailor, will take you under sail to Fingal's Cave, seal colonies and dolphins. A perfect place for those who want solitude to be fun.

rooms	16: 5 doubles, 2 twins, 1 family, 6 singles, 1 suite; 1 double, with private bath.
price	£44–£104; singles £39–£48. Half-board from £55 p.p.
meals	Dinner, à la carte, about £20. Light lunch & cream tea.
closed	November–March.
directions	Oban ferry to Craignure on Mull, then west to Fionnphort for Iona ferry. Cars not allowed on Iona but can be left safely at Fionnphort.

Claire Bachellerie
& Daniel Morgan

tel	01681 700334
fax	01681 700510
e-mail	reception@argyllhoteliona.co.uk
web	www.argyllhoteliona.co.uk

map 11   entry 243

Highland Cottage

Breadalbane Street, Tobermory, Isle of Mull PA75 6PD

A double first for Highland Cottage; this is clearly the loveliest place to stay in Tobermory, and the tastiest place to eat. Expect to be plied with treats from the kitchen: gallons of fresh orange juice served in crystal glasses, piping-hot coffee and the full cooked works. On one table, guests spoke glowingly of supper the night before: haddock risotto, saddle of venison, hot raspberries and ice cream – Highland Cottage is emerging as one of the jewels of Scottish cooking. Elsewhere, nothing disappoints. Bedrooms are exceptional: regal fabrics, crushed-velvet cushions, silk bedspreads, tartan tiles in fine bathrooms, Cadell prints, huge porcelain lamps, a French sleigh bed, even the odd sea view. In the sitting room, Tobermory light floods in, CDs wait to be played, pot-boilers wait to be read: try *Kidnapped* – it's set on the island. If you can tear yourselves away, head to Iona, Fingal's Cave, or just wander around Tobermory, the prettiest town in the Western Isles, with its Highland games, art festivals, yachting regattas, and the daily to and fro of islanders stocking up on supplies. Marvellous.

rooms	6: 2 doubles, 2 twins, 2 four-posters.
price	£95–£115; singles from £72.50.
meals	Dinner, 4 courses, £28.50.
closed	Mid-October–mid-November, & Christmas. Restricted opening January & February.
directions	From Oban ferry, A848 to Tobermory. Across stone bridge at mini-r'bout, then immediate right into Breadalbane St. On right opposite fire station.

David & Jo Currie

tel	01688 302030
e-mail	davidandjo@highlandcottage.co.uk
web	www.highlandcottage.co.uk

Calgary Hotel & Dovecote Restaurant

Calgary, Nr. Dervaig, Isle of Mull PA75 6QW

On a good day, Calgary feels like the Mediterranean — you could be in Italy or France; not that you'll complain on the bad days as the Isle of Mull is beautiful whatever the weather. Matthew and Julia have let their world evolve naturally, doing their own thing with brilliant *joie de vivre*: tea shop, restaurant, art gallery, the occasional free-range child, a very relaxed atmosphere and lots of commitment. Matthew has renovated the entire place himself with simple, rustic-style elegance. The fabulous restaurant has brick arches, whitewashed walls, polished wood floors and huge wooden chairs that could pass for Balinese thrones; he makes them in his workshop. In the courtyard, wrought iron tables and terracotta pots are scattered around a fountain and the gallery has fine local art and ceramics, all of which you can buy. Bedrooms fit the mood perfectly: pretty fabrics, whitewashed walls, comfy beds — nothing disappoints. Walk down to Calgary beach for wonderful sunsets; a woodland sculpture walk is also on the way. Truly inspiring and not to be missed.

rooms	9: 4 doubles, 2 twins, 1 single, 2 family.
price	£66–£80; singles from £33–£40.
meals	Lunch from £5. Dinner about £20.
closed	December-February. Open weekends November & March.
directions	From Dervaig, B8073 west for 5.5 miles. House signed right before Calgary Bay.

Julia & Matthew Reade

tel	01688 400256
fax	01688 400256
e-mail	calgary.farmhouse@virgin.net
web	www.calgary.co.uk

map 11   entry 245

Tiroran House

Isle of Mull PA69 6ES

The drive to Tiroran takes you through some of the wildest and most spectacular scenery in Scotland. There's a magical sense of time almost ticking backwards on the Isle of Mull – perhaps it's the single track roads that connect most of the island, or maybe it's the rolling mists that stroke the heathland landscape in shrouds of pink, orange, and purple; the alchemy of light here can be astounding. Tiroran lies on the north shore of Loch Scridain, an arm of sea that separates the Ross of Mull from nearby Ben More, the only munro on the island. A stirring burn tumbles past the house through an enchanting garden and down to the sea; it's the dreamiest of walks. Colin and Jane used to run a bigger hotel on the mainland but they wanted something smaller, more intimate. Sit under the shade of a grape vine in the conservatory, or relax in one of two lounges, with log fires and nautical prints. Jane is an excellent cook, so meals are a special occasion, and Colin, ever helpful, is full of suggestions. Bedrooms are all different and most have garden views; binoculars are provided to spot grazing deer.

rooms	6: 3 twins, 3 doubles.
price	£104-£110; singles £55-£70.
meals	Dinner from £26.
closed	November-March.
directions	From Craignure or Fishnish car ferries, A849 for Bunessan & Iona car ferry, right on B8035 for Gruline for 4 miles. Left at converted church. House 1 mile further.

	Colin & Jane Tindal
tel	01681 705232
fax	01681 705240
e-mail	colin@tiroran.freeserve.co.uk
web	www.tiroran.com

Stein Inn

Stein, Waternish, Isle of Skye IV55 8GA

White cottages bob by the quay in this remote, tiny fishing village, the setting for Skye's oldest inn. Angus stocks 80 single malts, thirst-quenching ales and seasoned opinion behind the bar of this rough-hewn, fire-warmed hostelry. Stand under blackened joists and talk about anything with this affable rogue spirit. In good weather, sit out by the shore of the sea loch: across the water, the headland rises dramatically; to the north, a few low-slung islands lie scattered. Lose yourself with a pint watching locals potter about in their boats against a setting sun. With the sea being so close, the food is really good, too: from your window, watch the catch landed, hauled from the sea to your plate, impossibly fresh. If cosiness comes from contrast and setting, then the clean, closely-eaved, blue-carpeted and pine-panelled rooms above the bar are perfect. There are moorings for yachts — sailors can ring ahead to have provisions waiting — but far wiser to spoil yourselves with a couple of nights on land.

rooms	5: 2 doubles, 2 family, 1 single.
price	£49-£62; singles £24.50-£29.50.
meals	Bar lunch from £4.50. Dinner about £13.
closed	Christmas Eve & New Year's Day.
directions	From Isle of Skye bridge, A850 to Portree. Follow sign to Uig for 4 miles, left on A850 for 14 miles. Hard right turn to Waternish on B886. Stein is 3.5 miles along loch side.

Angus & Teresa McGhie

tel	01470 592362
fax	01470 592362
e-mail	angus.teresa@steininn.co.uk
web	www.steininn.co.uk

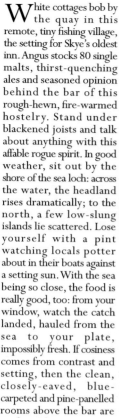

map 11　entry 247

Viewfield House

Portree, Isle of Skye IV51 9EU

A former factor's house with a genuinely relaxed country-house feel, Viewfield blends grandeur with odd touches of humour brilliantly. A family friend once placed notes by various of the house's belongings, detailing their history, all of which were fictional; one survives today. It's a fine ancestral seat, built in 1790, with huge windows in the sitting room, roaring fires, piles of wood, rugs on stripped wooden floors and 100-year-old wallpaper in the dining room. At seven-thirty each evening a gong summons guests to dinner – Hugh and Linda take it in turns to cook. Meals are either taken communally around an enormous central table, or individually to one side; most who opt for the latter the first night, choose the former the second. Each night Hugh wears a kilt displaying the family tartan, while Linda, a Californian, remains delightfully unfazed by the splendour of the surroundings: ancestors on the walls – their portraits, that is – and beautiful period furniture. Bedrooms are exquisite: luxurious beds, pretty fabrics, crisp cotton linen… even polished stair rods on the way up. Outside, climb through woods to Fingal's Seat for 360° views, or swim in a loch.

rooms	12: 4 doubles, 5 twins, 1 single; 1 double, 1 single, sharing bath & shower.
price	£80–£90; singles £35–£60. Half-board £55–£67.50 p.p.
meals	Packed lunch £4. Dinner, 4 courses, £20.
closed	Mid–October–mid–April.
directions	A87 onto Skye to Portree. On outskirts of town, opp. BP garage.

Hugh & Linda Macdonald

tel	01478 612217
fax	01478 613517
e-mail	info@viewfieldhouse.com
web	www.viewfieldhouse.com

Hotel Eilean Iarmain

Isleornsay, Sleat, Isle of Skye IV43 8QR

For those seeking a Gaelic bolt hole, this bastion of all things Hebridean is a must. Kind, local staff – some speak gentle Gaelic – welcome you in a hall of tartan. This is the end of the road – only the Sound of Sleat lies ahead where local fisherman land their catch at the small jetty. The hotel is a dreamy cross between a shooting lodge and a gentleman's club. Hessian cloth hangs on the walls and fires burn gently under the gaze of a trophy. Bedrooms are just right, country-house in style, with the odd half-tester. Across the way, fabulous suites in the old stables have an indulgent feel: bright, airy, full of pretty fabrics and sea views. Sir Iain is keenly involved in the regeneration of Skye's woodland by helping to reinstate old oakwoods. Next door, there's an art gallery and an award-winning whisky company, while across a small stretch of water is Robert Louis Stevenson's lighthouse. Back in the bar, the occasional ceilidh breaks loose and fiddles fly. Scottish to the core.

rooms	15: 5 doubles, 6 twins, 1 half-tester, 4 suites.
price	£100-£160; singles from £80; suite £180-£200.
meals	Bar meals from £7. Dinner, 4 courses, £31.
closed	Never.
directions	A87 over Skye Bridge (toll £5.50), then left after 7 miles onto A851, signed Armdale. Hotel on left after 8 miles, signed.

Sir Iain & Lady Lucilla Noble

tel	01471 833332
fax	01471 833275
e-mail	hotel@eilean-iarmain.co.uk
web	www.eileaniarmain.co.uk

map 11   entry 249

The Pines

Woodside Avenue, Grantown-on-Spey, Moray PH26 3RJ

Michael and Gwen have created a retreat from the Highland elements full of soothing colours, exceptional art and sumptuous good taste. The house was also a hotel in the 30s; an advert in a guide book from the time says it had "all modern amenities, including electricity". This guide book is glad to report the wiring was brought up to date, along with the rest of the house, when the Stewarts arrived in 1998. The granite masonry may look a bit stark but walk through the door and all is luxuriously welcoming, with two Cavalier King Charles spaniels eager to greet you. Gwen, a former teacher, cooks, and Michael, a former accountant, is the affable host with a passion for art. His first purchase at the age of 17 was a landscape painted on the back of a chocolate box – he never made that mistake again! The jewels of his collection are paintings by David Foggie, some of family members – the painter taught his great uncle. The whole house, including the bedrooms, is full of originals. The pretty garden leads to woods; keep going and you'll reach the River Spey for long hikes, fishing and the odd whisky distillery. A wonderful port of call.

rooms	8: 4 doubles, 3 twin/doubles, 1 single.
price	£66-£90; singles from £38. Half-board £55-£70 p.p.
meals	Dinner, 4 courses, £25. Packed lunch.
closed	November-February.
directions	A95 north to Grantown-on-Spey. Right at 1st set of traffic lights onto A939 for Tomintoul, then 1st right into Woodside Ave. House 500 yds on left.

Michael & Gwen Stewart

tel	01479 872092
fax	01479 872092
e-mail	info@thepinesgrantown.co.uk
web	www.thepinesgrantown.co.uk

Woodwick House

Evie, Orkney KW17 2PQ

Poet George MacKay Brown's inscription in the garden of this quiet haven reads, "Drink here voyager, you are about to embark on the salt sound towards Eynhallow and the Kirk of Magnus". Trees are in short supply on Orkney but Woodwick sits in a wild sycamore wood fed by a burn that tumbles down to a small bay overlooking the Island of Gairsay; walk through wild flowers and hanging lichen, to the sound of rushing water and babbling crows – magical. Woodwick promotes "care, creativity and conservation", so come here to think, free of distraction. The house is nothing fancy, just clean and homely, friendly and peaceful. Built in 1912, it stands on the site of a larger building destroyed during the Jacobite rebellion; all that remains is a remarkable 'doocot', a perfect space for quiet contemplation. There's a wisteria-filled conservatory, a candlelit dining room (food is organic where possible), two sitting rooms, an open fire, a piano, books and lots of old films you've been meaning to see for ages. A nearby ferry takes you to some of the smaller islands, while the Italian Chapel and numerous ancient sites are an absolute must. *Cots available. Pets £7 for duration of stay.*

rooms	8: 2 doubles, 2 twins; 2 doubles, 1 twin, 1 single, all with basins, sharing 1 bath.
price	£56–£84; singles £32–£50.
meals	Dinner £24. Lunch & packed lunch by arrangement.
closed	Never.
directions	From Kirkwall or Stromness, A965 to Finstown, then A966, signed Evie. Right after 7 miles, just past Tingwall ferry turning, then left down track to house.

	Ann Herdman
tel	01856 751330
fax	01856 751383
e-mail	mail@woodwickhouse.co.uk
web	www.woodwickhouse.co.uk

 map 13   entry 251

Killiecrankie Hotel

Pass of Killiecrankie, By Pitlochry, Perth & Kinross PH16 5LG

You're well-positioned here for all things highland: the games at Braemar, fishing, walking, castles, golf... and whisky, about which Tim, once a big shaker in the wine trade, knows a thing or two. He and Maillie have come north of the border to cook great food, to serve good wines and to provide the sort of comfortable indulgence that caps a hard day's pleasure with rod, club or map. Food is top of the list, with an ever-changing menu of fresh, local produce, reasonably priced wine by the glass to complement each course, and a vegetarian menu that could convert the most ardent carnivore... for an evening at least; meat is available, too. Much is home-grown, thanks to a dedicated effort to bring the kitchen garden back to life: soft fruits, potatoes, asparagus, leeks, mangetout... and there are more edible plans for the future. Inside, a revamp is on the cards as well, though the place is lovely already. Bedrooms are a good size, cosy and warm, with lashings of hot water and views down the Garry Valley. There's a small bar, a snug sitting room, with books and games, and an RSPB sanctuary near the house that's home to buzzards.

rooms	8: 2 doubles, 4 twin/doubles, 2 singles.
price	Half-board £79–£99 p.p.
meals	Lunch from £2.95. Dinner, 4 courses, included; non-residents £35.
closed	January–mid-February.
directions	A9 north of Pitlochry, then B8079, signed Killiecrankie. Straight ahead for 2 miles. Hotel on right, signed.

Tim & Maillie Waters

tel	01796 473220
fax	01796 472451
e-mail	enquiries@killiecrankiehotel.co.uk
web	www.killiecrankiehotel.co.uk

Loch Tummel Inn

Strathtummel, By Pitlochry, Perth & Kinross PH16 5RP

Listen to Michael. "When you get here, you can stop travelling...People need to be still and remember what their childhood senses are for – just look, listen, smell and let it all seep in." These wise sentiments sum up the simple, honest pleasures in store at this lovely old coaching inn on a remote stretch of road overlooking Loch Tummel. Michael is in his element here; he and his wife Liz moved up from Sussex nine years ago. He's very much the consummate host orchestrating proceedings from behind the bar, and a firm believer in preserving the art of conversation; there's no piped music, your mobile phone won't work, and televisions are only provided on request. Idiosyncratic bedrooms have earthy, rustic charm, with checked bedspreads, china and good bathrooms; soak in a bath of soft hill water in one room next to a log fire and gaze at snow-capped mountains. There's also a sweet *bothy* room, with an open fire, where guests can retreat for some privacy. Breakfast is served in a converted hayloft with loch views, while the bar serves good local food, including salmon smoked on the premises. Perthshire in autumn is stunning.

rooms	6: 3 doubles, 1 family; 1 double, 1 single, both with private bath.
price	£70–£90; singles £45–£60.
meals	Bar lunch from £2.95. Dinner from £11.
closed	Winter.
directions	From Perth, A9 north, then turn off after Pitlochry, signed Killicrankie. Left over Garry Bridge onto B8019. Inn 8 miles on right.

Liz & Michael Marsden

tel	01882 634272
fax	01882 634272

map 9   entry 253

The Four Seasons Hotel

St Fillans, Perth & Kinross PH6 2NF

This is a great position with forest rising immediately behind and Loch Earn stretching out seven miles distant. It all comes into play; ski, sail, canoe or fish on the loch – even learn to fly on it; or simply take to the hills for fabulous walks. The hotel has simple chalets on the lower slopes and each has long views, through pine trees, across water. Andrew is a great traveller, a Scot born 'down south' who has come home, and his love and enthusiasm for this heavenly spot are contagious. He has refurbished the interior completely, bringing bright colours to the walls, a gentle elegance to the rooms, superb food to the tables and a relaxed spirit to the whole place. Sit out on the small terrace underneath cherry trees for evening drinks and stare out across the loch or stay in front of the fire with a warming malt – The Four Seasons is well-named. Bedrooms in the house are excellent: smart, with plush carpets, huge beds and those at the front have loch views. Fish successfully and they'll cook your catch for supper. A super place.

rooms	18: 7 doubles, 5 twins; 6 family chalets for 4.
price	£70–£98; singles from £35. Half-board from £56 p.p.
meals	Bar meals from £8. Dinner, 4 courses, £28.
closed	January & February.
directions	St Fillans on A85 at eastern tip of Loch Earn, 12 miles west of Creiff, 25 miles north of Stirling.

Andrew Low

tel	01764 685333
fax	01764 685444
e-mail	info@thefourseasonshotel.co.uk
web	www.thefourseasonshotel.co.uk

Creagan House

Strathyre, Callander, Perth & Kinross FK18 8ND

We search high and low for places like Creagan; it brings to life all the ingredients that make a place special. Run with huge skill and passion by Gordon and Cherry, it is decorated not by numbers, nor by fashion, but by enthusiasm, evolving slowly and naturally. The welcome is second to none and the food magnificent — local Scottish produce, carefully sourced and cooked with great flair by Gordon. Expect some nice surprises, too, such as a small treatise entitled *The Iconography of the Creagan Toast Rack*; worth reading while waiting for eggs and bacon at a long slab of polished oak in the baronial dining room. A small bar is stocked with 45 malt whiskies, with a guide to help choose; one of its ceiling beams was 'acquired' from the Oban railway line. No airs and graces, just the sort of attention you get in small, owner-run places. Bedrooms in the eaves have Sanderson wallpaper, old furniture and no TVs. "You don't come to Creagan to watch a box," says Cherry. Bag a munro instead — walking sticks at the door will help you up Ben Shean.

rooms	5: 4 doubles, 1 twin.
price	£95; singles £57.50.
meals	Dinner £24.75.
closed	February.
directions	From Stirling, A84 north through Callander to Strathyre. Hotel 0.25 miles north of village on right.

Gordon & Cherry Gunn

tel	01877 384638
fax	01877 384319
e-mail	eatandstay@creaganhouse.co.uk
web	www.creaganhouse.co.uk

map 9   entry 255

Monachyle Mhor

Balquhidder, Lochearnhead, Perth & Kinross FK19 8PQ

The position here is fabulous, with Loch Voil at the bottom of the hill, mountains rising all around you, and cars that pass at the rate of one an hour; the road ends two miles up the track. Monachyle is a great place to be, far prettier than it first seems, with a rambling old farmhouse feel spruced up into a funky factory of fun: bold colours, good food, dynamic people… though don't let the pictures put you off; while Tom cooks brilliantly, his photography leaves much to be desired! Everything you see has evolved more by chance than design. They started here as farmers – and still are – then began doing B&B, and now, somehow, have a hotel. Various members of the family are involved, the place is extremely relaxed, but standards are kept extremely high – a perfect combination. The old, tiny, panelled bar with its cosy wood fire is a great spot for a pint. Bedrooms are split between the house, barns and coach house. All are excellent: country-cosy, fairly big, with splashes of colour. Locals fill the place at weekends… you even pass Rob Roy's grave on the way in.

rooms	10: 5 doubles, 2 twins, 3 suites.
price	£85–£140; singles from £55.
meals	Dinner £32.50.
	Sunday lunch £19.50.
closed	January & February.
directions	M9, junc. 10, A84, then left at Kings House Hotel, following signs to Balquhidder. Continue along Loch Voil. Hotel on right up drive, signed.

Rob, Jean, Tom & Angela Lewis

tel	01877 384622
fax	01877 384305
e-mail	info@monachylemhor.com
web	www.monachylemhor.com

Churches

Albert Road, Eyemouth, Berwickshire TD14 5DB

As an introduction to hospitality north of the border, this fabulous restaurant with rooms is anything but traditional and we applaud it for that. Sure, Scotland wouldn't be Scotland without its tartan and thistles but it's always a pleasure to celebrate anywhere that's trying to be a little different. Marcus and Rosalind are a young couple doing just that. He's the exceptional chef, trained at some of the best places in London, America and France, and she brings a lawyer's nous to managing front of house. As for location, it couldn't be better: an old manse, overlooking the pretty harbour at Eyemouth – the name alone should be enough to tempt you. The place looks good and you'll eat well. Watch the catch unloaded, then eat it later: mussel and saffron soup, smoked salmon with sweet chilli prawns, baked halibut on basil *linguini* with a

velvet crab bisque – Marcus is at the peak of his powers and his team of chefs. Inside, the hotel has a classy, modern feel, with lots of stylish black and white, wooden floors, wrought iron beds, the odd luxurious four-poster... there's even a moongate in the garden.

rooms	6: 3 doubles, 1 twin, 1 family, 1 four-poster.
price	£80–£110; singles £60–£80.
meals	Continental breakfast included; full Scottish £4.95. Dinner, à la carte, £24.
closed	Never.
directions	From Berwick, A1 north for 7 miles, then right, signed Eyemouth. Follow brown signs to hotel.

Marcus Lamb & Rosalind Dryden

tel	01890 750401
fax	01890 750747
e-mail	info@churcheshotel.co.uk
web	www.churcheshotel.co.uk

map 10   entry 257

Scarista House

Isle of Harris, Western Isles HS3 3HX

In a book where views count, Scarista takes the oatcake. The landscape here is nothing short of magnificent. The beach? Two or three miles of pure white sand, hidden from the rest of the world, and you'll probably be the only person on it. Then there's the gentle curve of the crescent bay, ridges running down to a turquoise sea and sunsets to astound you. One of the most beautiful places I have ever visited – anywhere in the world. When Patricia and Tim took over it was the fulfilment of a dream. They have been coming to the island for many years – they can guide you to its secrets – and are absolutely committed to their life here. Their house – an old manse – is a perfect island retreat: shuttered windows, peat fires, rugs on bare oak floors, whitewashed walls. Bedrooms are just right, with old oak beds, mahogany dressers, maybe a writing desk facing out to sea. Food is delicious; Tim and Patricia cook brilliantly. Kind island staff may speak in Gaelic, books wait to be read. There's golf – the view from the first tee is surely the best in the game. Worth every moment it takes to get here.

rooms	5: 3 doubles, 2 twins.
price	£130; singles from £75.
meals	Packed lunch £5.50. Dinner, 4 courses, £35.
closed	Occasionally in winter.
directions	From Tarbert, A859, signed Rodel. Scarista is 15 miles on left, after golf course.

Patricia & Tim Martin

tel	01859 550238
fax	01859 550277
e-mail	timandpatricia@scaristahouse.com
web	www.scaristahouse.com

WHAT'S IN THE BACK OF THE BOOK ...

ANNUAL EVENTS 2003

January 1	London Parade — floats & marching bands leave Parliament Square at noon: 020 8566 8586; www.londonparade.co.uk
January 10-12	Saturnalia Beer Festival, Llanwrtyd Wells, Powys: 01591 610666
January 10-26	London International Mime Festival, The South Bank 020 7637 566; www.mimefest.co.uk
January 25	Burn's Night — celebration of Scottish poet
February 6-9	Cheltenham Folk Festival: 01242 227979
March 1-9	Bath Literature Festival: 01225 463362; www.bathlitfest.org.uk
Shrove Tuesday, March 4	Purbeck Marblers & Stonecutters Day, Corfe Castle, Dorset — football game through village; lesh@corfe-castle.demon.co.uk
March 7-9	Folk 'n' Ale Weekend, Llanwrtyd Wells, Powys: 01591 610666
March 11-13	Cheltenham Gold Cup — national-hunt horseracing festival: 01242 226226; www.cheltenham.co.uk
April 3-5	Grand National, Aintree, Liverpool — national-hunt horseracing: www.aintree.co.uk
April 10-13	British Juggling Convention, Brighton: www.bjc2002.co.uk
April 11-12	Scottish Grand National, Ayr — horseracing: 01292 264179; www.ayr-racecourse.co.uk
April 13	London Marathon: 020 7620 4117; www.london-marathon.co.uk
Good Friday, April 18	Marbles Championship, Tinsley Green, nr. Crawley, Sussex www.marblemuseum.org
Easter Saturday, April 19	Oxford & Cambridge University Boat Race; www.theboatrace.org Nutters Dance, Bacup, Lancashire: 01706 870119
Easter Monday, April 21	Hare Pie Scramble and Bottle Kicking, Hallaton, Leicestershire: 0116 265 7310
April 25-28	Mull Music Festival, Isle of Mull: 01688 302009
April 30-May 3	Minehead Hobby Horse, Somerset — pagan festival: 01643 702624
May-July	Glyndebourne Opera Festival, East Sussex: 01273 813813; www.glyndebourne.com
May 5, May Day	Padstow Obby Oss, Cornwall — pagan festival: 01872 322900 Magdalen College, Oxford — choir sings at dawn: 01865 726871
May 1-5	Cheltenham Jazz Festival: 01242 227979
May 8	Helston Furry Dance, Cornwall — pagan festival: 01872 322900
May 12	May Fayre and Puppet Festival, St Paul's Church, Covent Garden, London: 020 7375 0441
May 16-June 1	Bath International Music Festival: 01225 463362; www.bathmusicfest.org.uk
May 20-23	Chelsea Flower Show, Royal Hospital, London: 020 7834 4333; www.rhs.org.uk
May 23-27	Orkney Folk Festival, Stromness: 01856 850773
May 23-26	Llanelli Festival of Walks, Carmarthenshire: 01554 776505

ANNUAL EVENTS 2003

Spring Bank Holiday Monday	Cheese Rolling, Brockworth, Gloucestershire: 01452 421188; www.cheese-rolling.co.uk
May 23-June 1	Hay-on-Wye Literature Festival, Herefordshire www.hayfestival.co.uk
May 30	Cotswold Olimpicks, Chipping Campden, Gloucestershire – rustic sports festival & torchlight procession: 01386 841206; www.chippingcampden.co.uk
June	World Nettle Eating Championships, Dorset
Early June	Fleadh, Finsbury Park, North London – Irish music festival: 020 8963 0940; www.meanfiddler.com
June 7	Man Versus Horse, Llanwrtyd Wells, Powys – runners vs horse riders over 23 miles: 01591 610666
June 6-22	Aldeburgh Festival, Suffolk – classical music: 01728 687110; www.aldeburgh.co.uk
June 6/7	The Derby, Epsom, Surrey – flat horseracing: 01372 470047; www.epsomderby.co.uk
June 20-23	Royal Highland Show, Edinburgh – agricultural display: 0131 335 6200; www.rhass.org.uk
June-mid-August	Royal Academy Summer Exhibition, London – everyman art: 020 7300 8000; www.royalacademy.org.uk
June 6-12	Appleby Horse Fair, Appleby-in-Westmorland, Cumbria: 01452 421188
June 17-20	Royal Ascot, Berkshire – flat racing: 01344 622211; www.ascot-authority.co.uk
June 20-25	St Magnus Festival, Orkney – classical music: 01856 871445; www.orkneyislands.com
June 21	Kithill Midsummer's Night Bonfire, Bodmin Moor, Cornwall: 01872 322900
June 21-23	Round Mull Yacht Race, Isle of Mull: 01631 569100
June 23-July 6	Wimbledon Lawn Tennis Championships; www.wimbledon.org
June 28	World Worm-Charming Championships, Willaston, Cheshire: 01270 663957
June 28-30	Glastonbury Festival, Somerset: www.glastonburyfestivals.co.uk
June 29-30	Scottish Traditional Boat Festival, Portsoy – old boats, ceilidhs: 01261 84295; www.thebpl.co.uk/boatfest
July-early September	The Proms, Royal Albert Hall, London: 020 75898212; www.royalalberthall.com
July	Whitstable Oyster Festival
July 2-6	Henley Royal Regatta, Oxfordshire; www.hrr.co.uk
July 5-6	Game Fair, Scone Palace, Perth: 01620 850577; www.scottishfair.com
July 5-14	Frome Festival – arts, theatre, music: 01373 455690

ANNUAL EVENTS 2003

July 4-20	Cheltenham International Festival of Music: 01242 227979
July 8-13	Llangollen International Musical Eisteddfod, North Wales: 01978 861501; www.international-eisteddfod.co.uk
July 11-13	Swanage Jazz Festival, Dorset: 01929 425371
July 24	Tobermory Highland Games, Isle of Mull: 01688 302270
July 25-28	Cambridge Folk Festival: www.cam-folkfest.co.uk.
July 26-28	Womad Rivermead, Reading – world and dance music: 01225 744494; www.womad.org
August	Battle of the Flowers, Jersey
August 1-8	Sidmouth International Festival, Devon – folk music, arts; www.mrscasey.co.uk/sidmouth
August 8-12	Bristol Balloon Fiesta, Ashton Park; www.bristolfiesta.co.uk
August 9-10	Brecon Jazz Festival Powys; www.breconjazz.co.uk
August 10-30	Edinburgh Festival – comedy, theatre, film; www.eif.co.uk
August 16-24	Victorian Week, Llandrindod Wells, Powys: 01597 822600
August 23-25	Notting Hill Carnival, London – Caribbean festival www.nottinghillcarnival.org.uk
	Cartmel Races, Cumbria – horseracing: 0151 5232600
August 25	World Bog Snorkelling Championships, Llanwrtyd Wells, Powys: 01591 610666
September 14	Leuchars Air Show, nr. St Andrews, Scotland: 01334 839000; www.airshow.co.uk
September 18-20	Ayr Gold Cup – horseracing: 01292 264179; www.ayr-racecourse.co.uk
September 21	World Gurning Championships, Egremont, Cumbria: 01946 821554
October 10-12	Tour of Mull Rally, Isle of Mull – rally driving: 01254 826564
November 2	London to Brighton Veteran Car Run: 01753 681736
November 5	Guy Fawkes Night
November 13	Biggest Liar in the World, Bridge Inn, Wasdale, Cumbria: 019467 26221
December 31	Scotland – Hogmanay
	Piccadilly Circus, London
	Tar Barrels Parade, Allendale, Northumberland
	Mari Llwyd Torch Lit Walk, Llanwrtyd Wells, Powys: 01591 610236

WHAT'S IN A NAME?

British place names	...have evolved over many centuries of invasion, conquest, trade and settlement by different races and cultures. Here are a few examples:
Aberystwyth	Place at the mouth of the River Ystwyth, 'the winding river'. From the Welsh *aber*, 'river mouth'.
Barnard Castle	Named after the 12th-century castle of landowner Bernard Balliol.
Bideford	Bieda's ford. Bieda is an Old English man's name.
Birmingham	The Beormings' village. Beorma is an Old English man's name, and the Beormings were his people. *Ham* is Old English for 'village'.
Brecon	Brychan's kingdom, after 5th-century King Brychan.
Brighton	Brihthelm's village. Brihthelm is an Old English name. Abbreviated from Brighthelmstone to Brighton in the 18th century.
Bristol	After Brycgstow, Old English for 'bridge' and 'meeting place'.
Bury St Edmunds	Fortified village owned by St Edmund's Abbey. St Edmund, the King of East Anglia, was buried here after he was captured and killed in 870 fighting the Danes.
Buxton	First called Buckestanes, Old English for 'rocking stones'.
Cambridge	Bridge over the River Cam. Cam is a corruption of the Celtic river name Granta, 'the marshy river'.
Cardiff	Roman day fort. From the Welsh *caer*, meaning 'fort' and *dydd* meaning 'day'.
Cheltenham	The enclosure at the hill. From the Old English hill name Celte.
Chipping Norton	From the Old English *ceping* and *north-tun* 'the northerly farm',
Cirencester	The Roman fort at Corinium, the Celtic name of the city.
Clitheroe	The place at the rocky promontory. Old English *clyder-hoe*.
Dingwall	Meadow where a Thing, a Scandinavian council meeting, assembles. From the Old Norse *vollr*, 'a meadow'.
Dolgellau	Meadow of booths, probably herdsmen's huts. From the Welsh *dol*, 'river meadow', and *cell*, 'a booth, a cell'.
Dover	Place at the waters. From the Celtic *dobra*, 'water'.
Edinburgh	The fort of Eidyn, originally Eidyn Gaer in Welsh. From the name Eidyn, and *caer*, a 'fort'. Then translated into Gaelic, Dun Eideann, and then into Old Englsih and its present form, Edinburgh.
Evesham	Eof's meadow by a stream. From Eof, an Old English man's name.
Exeter	The Roman town of Isca, the Celtic name for the River Exe, meaning 'the water'.
Fishguard	The fish pound. From the Scandinavian *fiski-garthr*.
Grantown-on-Spey	Named after the politician Sir James Grant, who founded the town.
Harwich	The army camp. From the Old English *herewic*.
Henley-on-Thames	Place at the high glade. From the Old English *hean-lea*.

WHAT'S IN A NAME?

Honiton	Huna's estate. Huna is an Old English name, and *tun* means 'estate'.
Hove	Place at a shelter. From the Old English *hufe*, 'a hovel'.
Keswick	The cheese farm. From the Old English *cese-wic*.
Knutsford	Knut's ford. Knut is an Old Danish name.
Llangollen	The church of St Collen. From the Welsh *llan*, 'church'.
London	The Romans called it Londinium, the Latin form of a Celtic name Londonion, of unknown meaning.
Looe	Settlement at a pool. From the Cornish *lo*, 'pool, inlet of water'.
Ludlow	Place at the hill by the noisy rapid. From Old English *hlude*, 'the loud one', and *hlaw*, 'hill'.
Lymington	Estate at Limen. From the Old English *tun*, 'estate', and a Celtic name meaning a place 'at the elms'.
Manchester	From the Celtic *mamucium*, 'at the breast-like hill'.
Margate	Place at the gate leading to the sea. From the Old English *mere*, meaning 'sea or lake'.
Matlock	From the Old English *maethel*, 'meeting place', and *ac,* 'oak'.
Okehampton	Village on the River Okement, the Celtic for 'the swift river'.
Penrith	From the Welsh *pen*, 'chief', and the Old Welsh *rit*, 'ford'.
Penzance	Place at the holy headland. From the Cornish *pen*, 'cape', and *sans*, 'holy'.
Pitlochry	The allotment at the stony place. From the Pictish Celtic *pit* 'a portion, share', and the Gaelic *cloichreach*, 'stony ground'.
Ross-on-Wye	From the Welsh *rhos*, 'moor' or 'heath'.
St Davids	Place at the church of St David. The Welsh name Tyddewi means 'the house of David'.
Salisbury	The fortified town called Searo. From the Old English *bur*, 'fort, town', and the Romano-British town name Sorviodunum.
Skipton	Place at a sheep farm. From the Old English *scip-tun*.
Stroud	From the Old English *strod*, 'marshy land with brushwood'.
Taunton	The estate on the River Tone, 'the roaring river'.
Tenby	The little fort. From the Welsh *dinbych*.
Whitstable	The pillar of the councillors. From the Old English *witan*, 'council wise men', and *stapol*, 'pillar'.
Winchester	The Roman fort called Venta, the Celtic for 'market town'. Chester comes from *ceaster*, the Old English for fort.
Windemere	Vinnand's Lake. From Vinnandr, an Old Norse name, and the Old English *mere*, 'lake'.
Wareham	From the Old English *waer*, 'weir', and *ham*, 'village'.
York	Eburos's place. Eburacum in Celtic. From Eburos, man's name, and *acum*, 'an estate belonging to'.

WHAT IS ALASTAIR SAWDAY PUBLISHING?

A dozen or more of us work in two converted barns on a farm near Bristol, close enough to the city for a bicycle ride and far enough for a silence broken only by horses and the occasional passage of a tractor. Some editors work in the countries they write about, e.g. France; others work from the UK but are based outside the office. We enjoy each other's company, celebrate every event possible, and work in an easy-going but committed environment.

These books owe their style and mood to Alastair's miscellaneous career and his interest in the community and the environment

These books owe their style and mood to Alastair's miscellaneous career and his interest in the community and the environment. He has taught overseas, worked with refugees, run development projects abroad, founded a travel company and several environmental organisations. There has been a slightly mad streak evident throughout, not least in his driving of a waste-paper-collection lorry for a year, the manning of stalls at jumble sales and the pursuit of causes long before they were considered sane.

Back to the travel company: trying to take his clients to eat and sleep in places that were not owned by corporations and assorted bandits he found dozens of very special places in France – farms, châteaux etc – a list that grew into the first book, French Bed and Breakfast. It was a celebration of 'real' places to stay and the remarkable people who run them.

The publishing company grew from that first and rather whimsical French book. It started as a mild crusade, and there it stays – full of 'attitude', and the more appealing for it. For we still celebrate the unusual, the beautiful, the individual. We are passionate about rejecting the banal, the ugly, the pompous and the indifferent and we are passionate too about 'real' food. Alastair is a trustee of the Soil Association and keen to promote organic growing and consuming by owners and visitors.

It is a source of deep pleasure to us to know that there are many thousands of people who share our views. We are by no means alone in trumpeting the virtues of resisting the destruction and uniformity of so much of our culture – and the cultures of other nations, too.

We run a company in which people and values matter. We love to hear of new friendships between those in the book and those using it, and to know that there are many people – among them farmers – who have been enabled to pursue their decent lives thanks to the extra income the book brings them.

ALASTAIR SAWDAY'S

**British Hotels, Inns &
Other Places**
Edition 4   £12.99

British Bed & Breakfast
Edition 7   £14.99

Paris Hotels
Edition 3   £8.95

**French Hotels, Inns &
Other Places**
Edition 2   £11.95

French Holiday Homes
Edition 1   £11.99

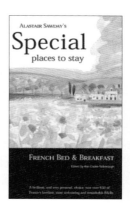

French Bed & Breakfast
Edition 7   £14.99

www.speciapla

Garden Bed & Breakfast
Edition 1   £10.95

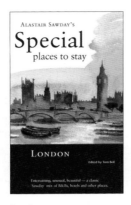

London
Edition 1   £9.99

Ireland
Edition 3   £10.95

Spain
Edition 4   £11.95

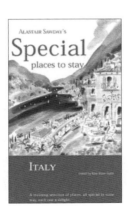

Italy
Edition 2   £11.95

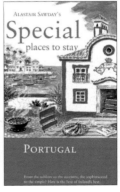

Portugal
Edition 1   £8.95

Britain

France

Ireland

Italy

Portugal

Spain...

all in one place!

On the unfathomable and often unnavigable sea of internet accommodation pages, those who have discovered **www.specialplacestostay.com** have found it to be an island of reliability. Not only will you find a database full of honest, trustworthy, up-to-date information about Special Places to Stay across Europe, but also:

- Links to the web sites of well over a thousand places from the series

- Colourful, clickable, interactive maps to help you find the right place

- The facility to make most bookings by e-mail –
  even if you don't have e-mail yourself

- Online purchasing of our books, securely and cheaply

- Regular, exclusive special offers on titles from the series

- The latest news about future editions, new titles and new places

The site is constantly evolving and is frequently updated. We've revised our maps, adding more useful and interesting links, providing news, updates and special features that won't appear anywhere else but in our window on the world wide web.

Just as with our printed guides, your feedback counts, so when you've surfed all this and you still want more, let us know – this site has been planted with room to grow.

Russell Wilkinson, Web Producer
website@specialplacestostay.com

If you'd like to receive news and updates about our books by e-mail, send a message to newsletter@specialplacestostay.com

THE LITTLE EARTH BOOK

The Little Earth Book

'Only dead fish float with the current;
live fish swim against it.'

Over 30,000 copies sold.

A fascinating read. The earth is now desperately vulnerable; so are we. Original, stimulating short essays about what is going wrong with our planet, and about the greatest challenge of our century: how to save the Earth for us all. It is succinct, yet intellectually credible, well-referenced, wry yet deadly serious.

Researched and written by a Bristol architect, James Bruges, The Little Earth Book is a clarion call to action, a stimulating collection of short essays on today's most important environmental concerns, from global warming and poisoned food to unfettered economic growth, Third World debt, genes and 'superbugs'. Undogmatic but sure-footed, the style is light, explaining complex issues with easy language, illustrations and cartoons. Ideas are developed chapter by chapter, yet each one stands alone. It is an easy browse.

The Little Earth Book provides hope, with new ideas and examples of people swimming against the current, for bold ideas that work in practice. It is a book as important as it is original. Learn about the issues and join the most important debate of this century.

Did you know.....

- If everyone adopted the Western lifestyle we would need five earths to support us?
- In 50 years the US has — with intensive pesticide use — doubled the amount of crops lost to pests?
- Environmental disasters have already created more than 80 MILLION refugees?

www.littleearth.co.uk

And now The Little Food Book! Same style, same purpose: it blows the lid off the food 'industry' — in a concise, entertaining way. Written by Craig Sams, Chairman of the Soil Association, it is pithy, deeply informative and an important contribution to the great food debate.

REPORT FORM

Comments on existing entries and new discoveries

If you have any comments on entries in this guide, please let us have them. If you have a favourite house, hotel, inn or other new discovery, not just in Britain, please let us know about it.

Book title: _____

Entry no: _____

New recommendation: _____

Country: _____

Name of property: _____

Address: _____

_____

_____

Postcode: _____

Tel: _____

Date of stay: _____

Comments: _____

_____

_____

From: _____

Address: _____

_____

_____

Postcode: _____

Tel: _____

Please send the completed form to:

Alastair Sawday Publishing,
The Home Farm Stables, Barrow Gurney, Bristol BS48 3RW,
or go to www.specialplacestostay.com and click on 'contact'.

BH4   Thank you.

ORDER FORM UK

All these Special Places to Stay books are available in major bookshops or you may order them direct.
Post and packaging are FREE.

		Price	No. copies
French Bed & Breakfast	Edition 7	£14.99	
French Hotels, Inns and other places	Edition 2	£11.99	
French Holiday Homes	Edition 1	£11.99	
Paris Hotels	Edition 3	£ 8.95	
British Bed & Breakfast	Edition 7	£14.99	
British Hotels, Inns and other places	Edition 4	£12.99	
Garden Bed & Breakfast	Edition 1	£10.95	
London	Edition 1	£ 9.99	
Ireland	Edition 3	£10.95	
Spain	Edition 4	£11.95	
Portugal	Edition 1	£ 8.95	
Italy	Edition 2	£11.95	
The Little Earth Book	Edition 2	£ 5.99	
Please make cheques payable to Alastair Sawday Publishing	Total £		

Please send cheques to: Alastair Sawday Publishing,
The Home Farm Stables, Barrow Gurney, Bristol BS48 3RW.
For credit card orders call 01275 464891 or order directly
from our website www.specialplacestostay.com

Title   First name

Surname

Address

Postcode

Tel

If you do not wish to receive mail from other
like-minded companies, please tick here ☐

If you would prefer not to receive information about
special offers on our books, please tick here ☐

BH4

ORDER FORM USA

All these books are available at your local bookstore, or you may order direct. Allow two to three weeks for delivery.

			Price	No. copies
Portugal		Edition 1	$14.95	
Spain		Edition 4	$19.95	
Ireland		Edition 3	$17.95	
Paris Hotels		Edition 3	$14.95	
Garden Bed & Breakfast		Edition 1	$17.95	
French Bed & Breakfast		Edition 8	$19.95	
French Hotels, Inns and other places		Edition 2	$19.95	
British Bed & Breakfast		Edition 7	$19.95	
London		Edition 1	$12.95	
Italy		Edition 2	$17.95	
French Holiday Homes		Edition 1	$17.95	
		Total $		

Shipping in the continental USA: $3.95 for one book, $4.95 for two books, $5.95 for three or more books. Outside continental USA, call (800) 243-0495 for prices. For delivery to AK, CA, CO, CT, FL, GA, IL, IN, KS, MI, MN, MO, NE, NM, NC, OK, SC, TN, TX, VA, and WA, please add appropriate sales tax.

Please make checks payable to: **Total $**
The Globe Pequot Press

To order by phone with MasterCard or Visa: (800) 243-0495, 9am to 5pm EST; by fax: (800) 820-2329, 24 hours; through our web site: www.globe-pequot.com; or by mail: The Globe Pequot Press, P.O. Box 480, Guilford, CT 06437

Date

Name

Address

Town

State

Zip code

Tel

Fax

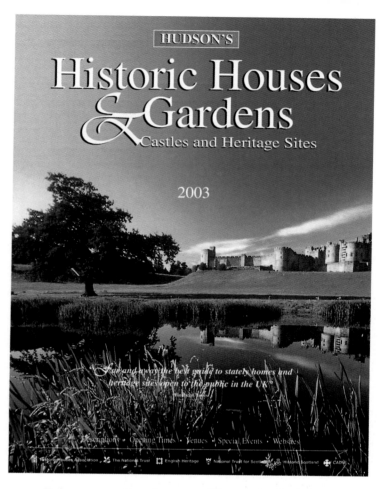

Discover the best-selling, definitive annual heritage guide to Britain's castles, stately homes and gardens open to the public.

600 pages featuring 2000 properties with
more than 1500 colour photographs.
An invaluable reference source <u>and</u> a good read.

QUICK REFERENCE INDICES

Good value

These places offer a double or twin room based on two people sharing for under £80 per night. Check when booking.

England

Bath & N. E. Somerset • 1 • 2 • 3 • Berkshire • 5 • Brighton • 7 • 10 • Cheshire • 13 • Cleveland • 14 • Cornwall • 15 • 16 • 17 • 18 • 20 • 26 • 27 • 28 • 29 • 30 • Cumbria • 33 • 35 • 36 • 39 • 40 • 41 • 43 • 45 • Devon • 50 • 51 • 52 • 53 • 57 • 59 • 63 • 64 • 66 • Dorset • 69 • 71 • 73 • 74 • 76 • Essex • 79 • Gloucestershire • 82 • 83 • 84 • 88 • 89 • 92 • 93 • 94 • Herefordshire • 102 • Kent • 109 • 110 • London • 114 • Manchester • 119 • Norfolk • 124 • 125 • Northumberland • 129 • Oxfordshire • 130 • Shropshire • 142 • 143 • Somerset • 144 • 149 • 150 • 153 • Suffolk • 155 • 158 • 159 • Sussex • 162 • 165 • Warwickshire • 167 • Wiltshire • 168 • 169 • 170 • Yorkshire • 174 • 175 • 182 • 185 •

Wales

Cardiff • 192 • Gwynedd • 199 • 200 • Pembrokeshire • 205 • 206 • 207 • Powys • 208 • 209 • 210 • 213 • 215 •

Scotland

Argyll & Bute • 219 • 220 • 221 • 222 • 223 • Dumfries & Galloway • 226 • 227 • Highland • 232 • 234 • 235 • 236 • 237 • 238 • 242 • Isle of Iona • 243 • Isle of Mull • 245 • Isle of Skye • 247 • 248 • Moray • 250 • Orkney • 251 • Perth & Kinross • 252 • 253 • 254 • Scottish Borders • 257 •

Wheelchair friendly

If you need places which are wheelchair-friendly, contact these places.

England

Birmingham • 6 • Brighton • 9 • Bristol • 11 • Cambridgeshire • 12 • Cornwall • 27 • Cumbria • 39 • Devon • 67 • Dorset • 69 • 75 • Essex • 79 • Gloucestershire • 81 • 84 • 95 • Hampshire • 97 • Herefordshire • 100 • Manchester • 120 • Norfolk • 124 • Northamptonshire • 127 • Oxfordshire • 135 • 138 • Sussex • 160 • Yorkshire • 176 • 178

Wales

Carmarthenshire • 193 • Powys • 214 •

Scotland

Ayrshire • 224 • Dumfries & Galloway • 227 • Highland • 238 • 240 • Isle of Mull • 244 • Isle of Skye • 248 • Perth & Kinross • 252 •

QUICK REFERENCE INDICES

Limited mobility

Need a ground-floor bedroom and bathroom?

England

Bath & N. E. Somerset • 1 • 2 • 4 • Berkshire • 5 • Cornwall • 18 • Cumbria • 31 • 34 • 35 • 38 • 43 • 44 • Derbyshire • 47 • Devon • 54 • 57 • 60 • Dorset • 76 • Durham • 77 • 78 • Gloucestershire • 80 • 85 • 90 • 91 • 96 • Hampshire • 98 • 99 • Herefordshire • 103 • Kent • 106 • Norfolk • 126 • Northumberland • 129 • Oxfordshire • 131 • 132 • 133 • 134 • 139 • 140 • Shropshire • 141 • Somerset • 144 • 148 • Suffolk • 155 • 157 • 158 • Sussex • 161 • 162 • Worcestershire • 172 • Yorkshire • 174 • 177 • 179 • 180 • 181 • 182 • 183 •

Channel Islands

Sark • 191 •

Wales

Ceredigion • 195 • Denbighshire • 197 • Monmouthshire • 202 • Pembrokeshire • 206 • Powys • 211 • 212 •

Scotand

Aberdeenshire • 216 • Argyll & Bute • 219 • Highland • 235 • 239 • Isle of Mull • 245 • 246 • Moray • 250 • Orkney • 251 • Perth & Kinross • 253 • 254 • 255 • 256 • Scottish Borders • 257 • Western Isles • 258 •

Organic & home-grown produce

These owners use mostly organic ingredients, chemical-free, home-grown or locally-grown produce. Entry number 103 has been certified as totally organic by the Soil Association.

England

Bath & N E Somerset • 4 • Berkshire • 5 • Brighton • 7 • 8 • 9 • Cheshire • 13 • Cornwall • 16 • 17 • 27 • 28 • Cumbria • 32 • 35 • 37 • 38 • 39 • 41 • 42 • 46 • Devon • 49 • 52 • 54 • 56 • 57 • 58 • 59 • 60 • 64 • 67 • 69 • 71 • 74 • 76 • Durham • 78 • Gloucestershire • 81 • 82 • 83 • 85 • 90 • 91 • 93 • 95 • 96 • Hampshire • 99 • Herefordshire • 101 • 103 • Isle of Wight • 104 • Kent • 108 • 109 • Norfolk • 121 • 122 • 123 • 125 • Northamptonshire • 127 • Oxfordshire • 135 • 136 • Shropshire • 141 • 143 • Somerset • 144 • 145 • 146 • 147 • 149 • 150 • Suffolk • 155 • 158 • Sussex • 162 • 163 • 164 • Wiltshire • 169 • Yorkshire • 174 • 175 • 178 • 180 • 186 • 187 •

QUICK REFERENCE INDICES

Restaurant with rooms

These places are licensed restaurants that also have accommodation.

QUICK REFERENCE INDICES

Tennis

There's a tennis court in the grounds of these places.

England

Cumbria • 44 • Derbyshire • 48 • Devon • 50 • 51 • 59 • 62 •
65 • Dorset • 75 • Isle of Wight • 104 • Kent • 107 • 108 •
Oxfordshire • 140 • Somerset • 148 • Suffolk • 159 • Sussex •
160 • 164 • Worcestershire • 172 • Yorkshire • 178 •

Channel Islands

Jersey • 189 •

Wales

Glamorgan • 198 • Montgomeryshire • 203 • Pembrokeshire •
207 • Powys • 208 • 211 • 212 •

Scotland

Aberdeenshire • 217 • Argyll & Bute • 218 • 219 •

Swimming
pool

These are places with a swimming pool in the grounds.

England

Cornwall • 22 • 24 • Devon • 50 • 59 • Durham • 78 • Isle of
Wight • 104 • Somerset • 148 • 152 • Sussex • 160 •
Worcestershire • 172 •

Channel Islands

Jersey • 189 • 190 •

Wales

Ceredigion • 195 • Pembrokeshire • 204 •

INDEX – PROPERTY NAME

INDEX – PROPERTY NAME

INDEX – PROPERTY NAME

INDEX – PROPERTY NAME

INDEX – PLACE NAME

INDEX – PLACE NAME

INDEX – PLACE NAME

EXCHANGE RATE TABLE

£ Sterling	US $	Euro €
1	1.57	1.56
5	7.83	7.80
7	10.96	10.91
10	15.66	15.59
15	23.48	23.39
17	26.61	26.51
20	31.31	31.18
25	39.14	38.98
30	46.97	46.77
35	54.79	54.57
40	62.62	62.37
45	70.45	70.16
50	78.28	77.96
70	109.58	109.04
90	140.90	140.20

August 2002

A photography PS – You may have noticed that none of the photographs of our hotels display signs such as the AA's. This is thanks to the wonders of technology – we remove them because they are usually ugly and because we are reluctant to feature other people's advertising. We hope you think that is reasonable. Few of our places carry such signs and otherwise, we only 'remove' objects that are temporary, such as parked cars.

EXPLANATION OF SYMBOLS

Treat each one as a guide rather than a statement of fact and check important points when booking.

Children are positively welcomed, with no age restrictions, but cots, high chairs etc are not necessarily available.

Full and approved wheelchair facilities for at least one bedroom and bathroom and access to all ground-floor common areas.

Ground-floor bedrooms for people of limited mobility.

No smoking anywhere in the house.

Pets are welcome but may have to sleep in an outbuilding or your car. Check when booking.

Payment by cash or cheques only.

Vegetarians catered for with advance warning.
All hosts can cater for vegetarians at breakfast.

Most, but not necessarily all, ingredients are organically grown, home-grown or locally grown.

Owners use only certified organic produce.

Working farm.

You can borrow or hire bikes.

Good hiking nearby.

Swimming pool on the premises.

Tennis.

Internet connections available.